RESIDENCE OF PROF. W. S. CLARK

MOUNT PLEASANT INSTITUTE
FOR BOYS
H. C. NASH, A. M., PRINCIPAL

AMHERST COLLEGE.

RESIDENCE OF J. W.

ERST, MASS.

THE

HIDDEN LIFE

OF

Emily Dickinson

JOHN EVANGELIST WALSH

SIMON AND SCHUSTER
NEW YORK

Copyright © 1971 by John Evangelist Walsh

Published by Simon and Schuster
Rockefeller Center, 630 Fifth Avenue
New York, New York 10020

Second printing

SBN 671–20815–2

Library of Congress Catalog Card Number: 73–133101
Designed by Edith Fowler
Manufactured in the United States of America
by American Book–Stratford Press, Inc., New York, N.Y.

Dickinson poems still in copyright are quoted by permission of the publishers and the Trustees of Amherst College from Thomas Johnson, The Poems of Emily Dickinson, Cambridge, Mass.: The Belknap Press of Harvard University Press, copyright © 1951, 1955 by the President and Fellows of Harvard College. Dickinson letters still in copyright are quoted by permission of the publishers from Thomas Johnson, The Letters of Emily Dickinson, Cambridge, Mass.: Harvard University Press, copyright © 1958 by the President and Fellows of Harvard College. I am also grateful to the Harvard University Press for its permission to regularize the Dickinson punctuation and use of capitals.

My gratitude also goes to the following for permission to quote copyright sources and other controlled materials: Yale University Press for Jay Leyda, The Years and Hours of Emily Dickinson; the Houghton Mifflin Co. for M. D. Bianchi, The Life and Letters of Emily Dickinson and Emily Dickinson Face to Face; Harper and Row for M. T. Bingham, Ancestors' Brocades and Emily Dickinson: A Revelation; the University of Massachusetts Press for The Lyman Letters; the President and Fellows of Harvard College for access to the Dickinson-Bianchi papers at Houghton Library; the Trustees of Amherst College for access to the Dickinson-Bingham papers at Amherst College.

Dedicated to the memory
of my mother
ANN WALSH
1891–1969

Look for me in the nurseries of Heaven

Contents

Prologue: EMILY'S HOUSE   17
—*a bedroom and an old white dress*

1. A LADY WHOM THE PEOPLE CALL THE MYTH   23
    —*a discovery and a surprising denouement*

2. NOBODY KNOWS THIS LITTLE ROSE   54
    —*a sketch of an unremarkable young lady*

3. AND SHATTER ME WITH DAWN   87
    —*how inspiration finally came to Emily*

4. GET GABRIEL TO TELL IT   110
    —*when Emily reached for a crown*

5. MY VERSE, DOES IT BREATHE?   139
    —*how despair brought down the curtain*

6. THUNDER IN THE ROOM   170
    —*in which Emily's great love is unmasked*

Contents

7. GREAT STREETS OF SILENCE   203
    —a not-quite surrender to the shadows

8. BASKING IN BETHLEHEM   231
    —a light shines in the darkness

    Notes and Sources   247

    Index   277

    Picture section follows page 96

Note

If care were not taken in the matter of sources, the narrative, shaped as it is from a thousand facts and interpretations of facts, would tend to disappear under a plague of reference notes. Happily, as well as being undesirable for the story I have to tell, such extensive apparatus is not necessary. The sources from which I drew my information are all primary and these are not voluminous; a full bibliography is in the Notes. Authorities for the more important statements of fact, when they require no commentary, are footnoted throughout the text. Other facts and quotations whose locution is not so given are in every case easily traceable, from the context, to one of the volumes listed under Main Sources. Further identification of sources will be found in the Notes, where I have also added some random thoughts that may be of interest.

To think reasonably upon any question has never been allowed by me as a sufficient ground for writing upon it, unless I believed myself able to offer some considerable novelty. Generally I claim (not arrogantly, but with firmness) the merit of rectification applied to absolute errors, or to injudicious limitations of the truth.

—De Quincey

THE

HIDDEN LIFE

OF

EMILY DICKINSON

Prologue:

EMILY'S HOUSE

THE EARLY DARKNESS of a Massachusetts winter, sifting in over the surrounding hills, had already enveloped the town of Amherst when I arrived at the stone steps leading up a slight rise to the Emily Dickinson house. The prickly bulk of tall, untrimmed hedges ranged along the entire 250-foot frontage of the Main Street property, parting at the steps momentarily to allow entrance. Under a single bulb, the large front door, back about five yards from the hedges and flanked by the four squat pillars of a diminutive porch, glowed starkly white. Above it the two-story brick structure loomed into a rustling mass of evergreen trees. Unquestionably, night was the proper setting in which to encounter the dwelling where America's best-known female poet had, for many years before her death in 1886, immured herself.

Admitted by a young woman, I entered a wide, high-ceilinged central hall that ran straight through to the rear of the house, where another door opened on to the backyard and where a carpeted stairway, set flush against the right wall, gave access to the upper floor. The young woman was a student boarding with Mr. and Mrs. Mudge, the faculty couple who with their three young children occupied the house. The Mudges were out but would be back later; in the meantime I was free to look round.

Off the hall to the left were two large parlors which were open to the public, though they were also employed along with most of the other rooms as the family's living quarters. Only Emily's bedroom, upstairs, had been entirely exempted from use. Now a miniature museum, it contained, as I was told, a few pieces of Emily's furniture, as well as one of the poet's famous white dresses, mounted on a clothes dummy. Her exclusive use of white dresses during the years of her seclusion was undoubtedly the most widely known and intriguing fact of her personal life and visitors were invariably pleased to see and touch one of the originals. I was looking forward to the experience myself, though I hardly expected the dress to yield any specially useful information about the woman who had worn it.

The two parlors, I saw, really formed one large room, stretching like the hall itself from the front of the house to the rear. At its middle were token wall extensions which once must have accommodated hanging curtains or folding doors. Tall windows opening on a side terrace and a couple of marble mantelpieces added just a touch of elegance. Each parlor section was about fifteen feet square, and while the total effect could not quite be called stately, as a whole it possessed a pleasantly spacious atmosphere. The furniture, a comfortable collection of old and new, was largely the property of the Mudges.

Built in 1813 by Emily's grandfather, the house was supposedly the first brick dwelling in Amherst. In its day it must have been particularly imposing; it is still marvelously well preserved, not altered greatly from the basic structural arrangement it had at Emily's birth in 1830. Five years before my visit Amherst College had acquired it from the Parke family, old-time Amherst residents, and it had been designated a national landmark. The price given by the college, $55,000, was nearly ten times what Emily's father had paid for it more than a century before. At that, it was a bargain, since Emily's skyrocketing reputation has already made it one of the most famous literary homes in the country. A few more years may even see it rivaling the Brontë parsonage in Haworth for its drawing power.

There was talk at first about turning the building into a poetry center, while some thought it would be better served as a haven for a poet-in-residence. When at last the decision was made to employ it as a simple faculty home—with the proviso that it would be open to visitors weekday afternoons—there was no rush of candidates for the privilege of living under Emily's roof. The attractions of a nominal rent, with the large expenses of upkeep and heating paid for by the College, had to be balanced against an insistent doorbell, an unpredictable parade of strangers and loss of a certain amount of privacy. There were no takers until the Mudges decided it might be something for their children to remember.

On the second floor the hallway was repeated, bedrooms standing to either side. Emily's sanctum was at the front, on the right, overlooking Main Street. A small brass plaque on the door identified it and announced that it had been set up in memory of her niece Martha. The furniture of the room, which was identical in size with the parlor section beneath it, was sparse. A narrow iron bed with tall railings at head and foot stood near a window; a side table, a bureau and an old Franklin stove were ranged round the walls. In a corner lay the ancient wooden cradle that had held Emily as a baby, by another window stood the small, square table on which she had written many of her poems. There were a number of pictures on the walls, and covering the floor was a faded, mat-type rug. In all, there were four good-sized windows, two looking south and two west. It was apparent the room even on sunless days would have been reasonably bright and cheerful.

Now, however, unused for so many years, it had a cold and uncomfortable feeling and it was difficult to imagine Emily living in it. Mrs. Mudge, who had been given charge of setting the room up, had nevertheless made a commendable effort to offer an interesting experience to visitors. The pictures were either Emily's own or copies of those she is known to have had. The stove was acquired because she was remembered to have used one like it. The bed, probably her own, was placed against the wall near one of the south windows because that was the only position that accorded with Emily's poetic description of the scene that always greeted her on waking: a distant hill, a steeple with a weathervane, and a chimney. The hill, Mount Norwottock, is obscured now by a new house across the street, but the chimney and the steeple—the sole remnant of the old college church—are still there. The poem in which Emily notes these things, I recalled, implies that they would have been visible as a group to her just-opening eyes, but even to my upright angle of vision that didn't seem possible. I lay down on the bed and found that only the chimney would have presented itself immediately. She had to sit up and crane a little to see the rest.

The white dress was nowhere in evidence, but after a few moments I discovered it hanging rather forlornly in the otherwise empty closet. Struck by a sudden thought that had never occurred to me before in all my studies of this strange woman, I found myself smiling. What must this closet, so bare now, have looked like when it held hanger after hanger of white dresses, a long rack weighed down with that glittering apparel? For some twenty years she had worn only white, with an occasional blue shawl—how many such dresses would she have needed to carry it off?

This particular dress was a simple summer affair of thin cotton, with pleating round the bottom from knee to hem. Holding it up to the young woman who had accompanied me upstairs, I saw that it had been made for a plumper person than the little woman usually described as delicate and frail. Later I found that measurements had been taken from it and it had even been fitted on a local woman. From this it has been concluded that Emily stood about five feet tall, or five-one, with a thirty-five inch bust and a waist measuring, in her last years at least, nearly thirty one inches. This slight corpulence of her maturity was probably a side effect of the illness to which she succumbed: Bright's disease frequently tends to put on weight through retention of water. The joking nickname she applied to herself in one of her last letters—"Jumbo"—had some unsuspected relevance, after all.

The third floor, an attic in Emily's day, now contains two finished rooms, both unexpectedly large under the sloping roof, as well as a third, unfinished chamber. Negotiating a cramped, twisting staircase leading to the cupola, I came up into a square, wooden enclosure furnished with shelf-benches on either side. About five feet square and eight or nine feet in height, its narrow windows gave a fine, sweeping view of the countryside to the east. In the other direction the sloping land was blocked by the crowding treetops. Emily, supposedly, had spent a good deal of time writing in this isolated elevation, especially, as might be suspected, in summertime, but I could not recall that she had made any actual reference to the place, either in poems or letters.

Downstairs again, I found that Mrs. Mudge had returned. How about life here, I inquired, what was it like with people such as myself constantly banging on her door? At first, she replied, all went well. The stream of visitors didn't create too great a strain on her busy household even when they began to show up three or four days a week, frequently interrupted suppers and occasionally wandered in unannounced. But the attempt to mesh family life with the accommodation of literary pilgrims gradually took its toll, and when she went upstairs one evening to be startled by a middle-aged woman standing mute and radiant-eyed in Emily's room, she petitioned for relief. Now tours are conducted regularly every Tuesday afternoon under the auspices of the Amherst Women's Club, though visitors at odd times are not always turned away.

At the door as I was leaving I remembered something I had wanted to ask. Why was Emily's dress kept in the closet and not on display as I had anticipated? Accessible to public view, it seemed to me, it would provide a fine dramatic focus for the room, otherwise somewhat tame. With a laugh Mrs. Mudge answered that until recently it had indeed been on permanent display, neatly fitted on the dummy. But her youngest boy, forgetting his mother's firm admonition that the room was off limits, had sneaked in unobserved one night and was enjoying his transgression until the white dress in the corner began to give off low moaning sounds. He stood his ground for a few seconds, a very few, and when the dress started to move slowly in his direction he was out of the room in a flash, down the stairs and into his mother's arms. Upstairs, on the floor behind the dummy, sat his older brother striving mightily to suppress his mirth. Since that incident the dress had seemed too spooky standing there in the corner. For the present at least it will remain in the closet.

Emily would have enjoyed that little drama, I thought as I descended the stone steps. It was her own story in perfect miniature. Now in her grave for more than eight decades, her life and work mercilessly probed for half a century, she has remained securely hidden behind the everlasting image of those white dresses, still able to startle and perplex anyone who draws too near, and it is easy to imagine her, wherever she is, laughing in quiet delight at the spectacle.

· 1 ·

A LADY WHOM THE PEOPLE

CALL THE MYTH

W HILE SHE WAS aware that a move from Washington, D.C., to quiet Amherst College in Massachusetts would enhance her young husband's career, Mabel Todd could not help feeling grieved by her departure from the sophisticated life she had known in the capital. At the age of twenty-four, Mabel was already a formidably talented as well as highly attractive young woman who felt instinctively that she would require a broader stage. A trained pianist, a painter of delicacy and finesse, she was also an amateur singer of ability, but her most cherished ambition touched none of these: more than anything else she wanted to write. She possessed, in addition, a compelling vivacity, which she took an intense pleasure in exercising, and an immense capacity for work. For such distinction, existence as a faculty wife in rural Massachusetts, where the spirit of a faded Puritanism still lingered, hardly promised even adequate breathing room. It was, then, with some understandable foreboding, but with no hint of the curious part she was to play in the unveiling of a major literary discovery, that she arrived with her husband and baby daughter in the town of Amherst in August 1881.

Her husband, David Peck Todd, had himself graduated from Amherst only six years before, and in that short time had gained a reputation as one of the country's leading astronomers. Recalled by the college to take charge of its new observatory, he felt no regret at leaving the glitter of Washington. A dedicated scientist, his daughter later described him, rather coldly to be sure, as being "more interested in his stars and telescopes than in the society of human beings." That scholarly preoccupation, acting on his vivacious young wife, may possibly have played a role in what followed, but having been the means of bringing Mabel to Amherst, his part in the narrative largely ceases. Through the events of the next eight years he is present but only occasionally seen or heard.

By the middle of September the Todds were settled in a gaunt old wooden house on a hill at the north end of town, from where they could overlook the elongated, tree-studded Common, and the sprawling college buildings at its further end. They soon began to receive welcoming calls from the faculty members, and at first Mabel felt only a renewed sinking of heart. The professors were mostly elderly men of sober exterior, and their wives, as she noted somberly, were "estimable ladies of quiet tastes dressing in dark colors, having their supper at six o'clock, not playing cards, nor dancing." Uneasy beneath this benevolent scrutiny, Mabel felt somehow that her visitors did not quite approve of her, and she could not always repress a pert response. When one matriarch, looking round at the numerous oversize windows in the large house, remarked that shades would create a big expense for the young couple, Mabel replied with satisfaction that she was going to dispense with them altogether. She would use silk curtains, she said, enjoying the look of doubt on the lady's face, in place of the drab shades that hooded nearly all the windows in Amherst. These callers, of course, were unfailingly courteous and not really unfriendly, as Mabel had to admit, but still she thought yearningly of the freer, more up-to-date ways of Washington, and in a letter to her mother she sighed, "I feel as if I were living in a novel." She was to repeat that thought very shortly, with better justification, when she found that even rustic Amherst had its peculiar attractions.

Toward the end of the month the Todds received a visit from the college treasurer, Austin Dickinson, and his wife Sue. Mabel, immediately sensing a difference, was delighted with them both. Mr. Dickinson—tall and slender, as she described him, with blue eyes, strong features, long sideburns and a booming voice— she considered to be remarkable looking and very dignified, but "a little odd." His wife, an India shawl draped casually on her shoulders, had a mature, dark beauty and expressed herself with a winning grace and elegance. Sue Dickinson, Mabel wrote her parents back in Washington, was "the most of a real society person here, and her presence filled the room . . . she is said to give extremely elegant little entertainments and musicales." The two families, it turned out, were near neighbors: the Dickinson house fronted on Main Street, only a short walk down the hill from the Todd place. A few days later the Todds returned the visit, and Mabel was again happily reporting to her parents that Sue's easy charm and sincerity had quite captivated her and, what obviously meant more to the young woman, "she understands me completely."

At the first of Sue's entertainments, a get-together for old and new members of the faculty, Mabel made the acquaintance of still another Dickinson: this was Lavinia, one of Austin's two unmarried sisters. As with Sue and Austin, Vinnie also made a decided impression on Mabel, especially by virtue of a nimble tongue that frequently let loose some arresting or colorful remark. Vinnie did not live with her brother, Mabel learned, but resided in an adjacent house, situated fifty yards or so to the east of Austin's place, a fine old red brick structure topped by an imposing square tower. This house, too, fronted on Main Street but stood rather closer to the road, looming behind its tall hedge with a mingled air of austerity and stateliness. With Vinnie there lived her seventy-seven-year-old mother, who was paralyzed and had been confined to bed for years, and another sister, Emily, aged fifty. These Dickinsons all seemed to be deliciously different and when Vinnie, after hearing her entertain Sue's guests, invited Mabel to sing for her ailing mother sometime soon, she eagerly accepted.

Not much had been said about Emily, who had not appeared at the party, but Mabel's curiosity was aroused and she soon found neighbors more than willing to talk. The picture she shortly put together for her parents was an intriguing one. "I must tell you about the *character* of Amherst, it is a lady whom the people call the *Myth*," she reported with undisguised glee. "She is a sister of Mr. Dickinson, and seems to be the climax of all the family oddity. She has not been outside of her own house in fifteen years, except once to see a new church, when she crept out at night, and viewed it by moonlight." Visitors to the house never encountered this wraith, she went on, but she had been occasionally glimpsed at her window lowering candy on a string into the clutch of laughing children. "She dresses wholly in white, and her mind is said to be perfectly wonderful. She writes finely." Mentioning the invitation she had received, Mabel passed on what some of her informants had been saying: "People tell me that the *Myth* will hear every note—she will be near, but unseen." The reason for this strange behavior—eccentric to say the least—was a mystery, though there was no lack of theories in the town, all of which began with a broken heart. "Isn't that like a book?"

For the imaginative Mrs. Todd this was an unexpected touch, much better in its way than anything Washington society had to offer. With Sue Dickinson's approbation softening some of the anticipated gloom of life in the hinterlands, she was feeling more at ease and few things now appeared so potentially rewarding as a personal friendship with Austin's shy sister. Vinnie's invitation seemed to promise the possibility of an early meeting, she felt; at least she would be inside the house and Emily just might materialize to offer her gratitude for the music that cheered her mother. But that invitation had been left rather vague and as the months passed no offer more definite was forthcoming.

The friendship with the other Dickinsons, meanwhile, continued to grow and there was much visiting between the two families. Sue's three children—Ned, twenty years old, Martha, five years younger, and little Gilbert, six—all made themselves at home in the Todd parlor, while Austin's house became for Mabel a "haven of pleasure." When she could do it without seeming intrusive, she talked with Sue about Emily and one day Sue unexpectedly brought out some of her sister-in-law's poems and read them to her. They were not quite what Mabel had envisioned as the musings of a secluded spinster, in fact were, like the woman herself, downright strange, yet they seemed "full of power."

Despite this quick intimacy with Austin's family it was the spring of 1882, about six months after Mabel's arrival, before any sign of recognition came from the silent resident of the other house. A surprise gift of flowers from Emily—hyacinth, heliotrope, and fittingly enough an "odd" yellow blossom that Mabel could not identify—came to her door. A little note that accompanied the box also seemed odd to Mabel. Written in pencil on a small slip of paper, it asked: "Will Brother and Sister's dear friend accept my tardy devotion? I have been unable to seek my flowers, having harmed my foot. Please accept them now, with the retarded fervor quickened by delay." Delighted, Mabel promptly dispatched a note of thanks, taking time to paint a small flower on her notepaper. But if she thought that Emily was getting ready to receive her in the flesh, she soon found herself mistaken. The spring drifted by without further contact and the Todds spent the summer with Mabel's parents in Washington.

In the fall, Mabel was finally permitted her first peek inside the red brick mansion. While she was at Sue's house for dinner early in September, Austin suggested a walk: they might drop in on his sister, he said, and perhaps Mabel could play something. A few moments later she found herself standing in the wide central hall of the other house, around her the soft glow of oil lamps throwing a diffused light over the dark brown woodwork and the patterned wallpaper. Vinnie greeted her warmly, recounting the praises Austin's children had been heaping on her, but there was no sign of Emily. Sometime later, at a square piano in a corner of the rear parlor, surrounded by old mahogany furniture, Mabel played a few numbers and sang, wondering as she did whether Emily had stolen down to hover listening in the hall outside, as the neighbors had predicted she would. "It was odd to think," she wrote later in her journal, "as my voice rang out through the big silent house, that Miss Emily in her weird white dress was outside in the shadow hearing every word, and the mother, bedridden for years, was listening upstairs." No sound came from the darkness, but when the recital was finished, Mabel's unspoken question received an answer. Maggie, the Irish servant, entered the parlor carrying a silver tray; on it was a glass of sherry and a folded sheet of paper. Sipping the wine, Mabel read:

> Elysium is as far as to
> The very nearest room,
> If in that room a friend await
> Felicity or doom.
>
> What fortitude the soul contains
> That it can so endure
> The accent of a coming foot,
> The opening of a door!

Immensely pleased with the poem, which she thought must have been written as she sang, but disappointed at her failure to catch sight of the white-clad figure, Mabel took her departure, with Vinnie expressing the hope that she would be able to come back often. A few days later Mabel recorded, with truly disarming objectivity, the impression she had made, especially on Vinnie: "She took me by the hand in the shyest, quaintest way, and said she saw plainly that she would have to yield to the same fascination that had enthralled her family." When on the following morning more flowers arrived from Emily, it probably seemed no more than reasonable to suppose that, in time, the recluse herself must surrender to that fascination. "I know I shall yet see her," Mabel told her journal firmly.

The spell cast over her by that first visit remained vivid for weeks as the elusive figure in the red brick house—who had now become "rare, mysterious Emily"—rose compellingly in her imagination. She began to fill her journal with tidbits gathered with care from among the villagers, supplying as well some of her own wishful thinking. Emily was "in many respects a genius . . . has her hair arranged as was the fashion fifteen years ago when she went into retirement . . . has frequently sent me flowers and poems, and we have a very pleasant friendship in that way." The flowers and poems could hardly be called frequent, and the friendship was rather tenuous, but after a year as Emily's neighbor Mabel had begun to experience an unaccustomed frustration; her words expressed not what had already taken place but only what she was determined would happen. Continued speculation about the reasons for Emily's mode of life were inevitable, and further gleanings on the topic were duly set down:

She is very brilliant and strong, but became disgusted with society and declared she would leave it when quite young. It is hinted that Dr. Holland loved her very much and she him, but that her father who was a stern old New England lawyer and politician saw nothing particularly promising or rewarding in the shy, half-educated boy, and would not listen to her marrying him. Of that I am of course not sure, but it might be so, for I know Dr. Holland has always been an intimate friend of the family. I have heard a great deal about Mr. Samuel Bowles who was the intimate friend of both Mr. and Mrs. [Austin] Dickinson. How they did love him!

Thus Mabel, joining in one of the favorite pastimes of Amherst's older residents, had finally come up with a name, possibly two. As she soon discovered, Dr. Holland and Sam Bowles were only the first of the many candidates that village gossip could supply for the honor of having blighted the susceptible Emily's heart.

After her initial triumph, growing impatient when another invitation failed to reach her, Mabel decided on a more personal approach. Emily loved flowers, she knew, in fact spent a great deal of time in her own little conservatory. Now painting flowers was one of the things that Mabel did supremely well; perhaps a large plaque offering one of her amazingly accurate renditions might be just the thing to catch the recluse off guard. The painting—an Indian pipe, Emily's favorite bloom, on a black panel —was done and sent off late in September while Mabel was on another trip to Washington. It succeeded in producing an unexpectedly prompt and effusive reply that "fairly thrilled" the young woman, her first real letter from Emily. Though brief, it was satisfyingly odd: "That without suspecting it you should send me the preferred flower of life, seems almost supernatural," ran the exciting note, "and the sweet glee that I felt at meeting it, I could confide to none. I still cherish the clutch with which I bore it from the ground when a wondering child . . . To duplicate the vision is almost more amazing, for God's unique capacity is almost too surprising to surprise . . ." It had taken a solid year but Emily, it appeared, was at last beginning to notice. When a second note, this time with another poem, arrived in Washington from "my—I may call her—dear friend," Mabel began happily to anticipate the meeting that seemed almost certain to follow her return to Amherst.

And it might have happened. Mrs. Todd just might have succeeded in becoming one of the very few persons who were allowed to see and talk with Emily Dickinson in the rigid isolation of her last years. But, while she never ceased trying, and was never able to rid herself of her obsession, she never did. The rush of unforeseeable events, as well as a tactical blunder of Mabel's own, unfortunately dissipated the promise obtained by the Indian pipe.

In November 1882, old Mrs. Dickinson, who had been ailing badly for the previous few weeks, died suddenly. This was not a tragic occurrence, and none of the Dickinsons took it as such; neither was the funeral, attended by the Todds and many of the townspeople, an occasion of great sorrow; it expressed the general sense that Mrs. Dickinson had been released from a dreary existence. For Mabel, however, the main excuse for her going to the house—to lighten the poor woman's days with music—was gone. And very shortly thereafter she found herself faced with a thoroughly unpleasant situation that for a time effectively halted her siege of Emily.

Sue Dickinson, it developed, was jealous. Nor was she without adequate reason for her feeling. Mrs. Todd had not been in Amherst very long before Austin began responding with interest to her sprightly charm. After a short acquaintance of some seven or eight months, he had delivered himself of a few injudicious remarks, innocent enough, no doubt, but too apt to carry excessive meaning. These quickly found their way into Mabel's journal along with a casual but revealing observation of her own. "Dear Mr. Dickinson—Ned's father—is so very fond of me," she wrote candidly. "It was one of the proudest moments of my life when he told me that I had more ideas that were congenial to him than any other person he ever met. For I most extravagantly admire him. He is in almost every particular my ideal man." When Professor Todd left Amherst, in the closing months of the year, at the head of a government party bound for California to record a transit of Venus, Austin was afforded more ample opportunity to sample Mabel's congenial ideas. The Dickinsons were expected to look after their youthful neighbor and Austin performed the task conscientiously. "He is delicate beyond expression," Mabel exclaimed, "tender and watchful and caretaking."

What appealed strongly to her, she said, was the poetic sensitivity she was just able to divine behind the bluff manner and the stiffish bearing. Some of her extravagant admiration must have made itself known to Austin for he was soon talking to her as he seldom talked to anyone—confiding that the tension between what he appeared to be and what he actually was had always given an excruciating wrench to his life. During a carriage ride to a nearby park with Mabel one day, he said he would like nothing better than to be buried where the sound of crickets could constantly surround him, leading his companion to solemnly declare him "a true, if silent, poet." The situation was, of course, all too human and familiar, but it was also more than usually unfortunate. In time it would become an important element in the biography of Emily herself, and repercussions from it would create the most chaotic and generally confused situation ever connected with the life and work of a major literary figure.

It was early the following year that Sue at last decided she had had quite enough of her fifty-three-year-old husband seeking consolation from a married neighbor half his age. Leaving no room for doubt as to her view of the friendship, she summoned the young woman to a meeting. Disappointingly, the only echo of what must have been an interesting confrontation is a brief notation by Mabel. "We had a long conversation," she jotted coolly and succinctly, "which was conducted with fairness (in general) on both sides. Since then things have been better." Things were not better for long, however, for within a month another "misunderstanding" took place between the two and Mabel at last awoke to the fact that Sue Dickinson's resentment ran deep. She was forced to the reluctant admission that "the old cordial, frank relations I am afraid can never be resumed." For a brief time Sue tried to go even further, insisting on a complete severance between the Todds and Dickinsons, and she failed only because Austin would not hear of it. Contact between the two families continued, though with much less visiting and drastically reduced caretaking on Austin's part.

The Todds by this time, in any case, were fairly launched in Amherst society and were no longer dependent on the Dickinsons for cordiality. Mabel was a principal singer in the important Congregational Church choir, was prodding the town's leading wives to form a women's club, was acting as a chaperon at college affairs, and was preparing to give music and painting lessons. When an amateur dramatic group decided to mount an ambitious production of a popular play, *The Fair Barbarian*, Mabel predictably was given the lead, and even her husband relinquished his telescope long enough to play a part.

Inevitably, rumors of the joust with Sue were soon filtering among this wider circle of friends, but Mabel was relieved to find that she had unexpected allies. One unidentified lady brushed off the whole affair as just one more instance of what she called Sue's propensity for fussing. Another of the more welcome results of the distasteful interlude was the comforting reaction of Vinnie. It now appeared that Austin's sister had her own obscure reasons for dislike of Sue and was not at all hesitant about stating the fact. While Mabel was away on holiday in the fall, a letter arrived from Vinnie assuring her that "all your friends are anxious to have you return, and I *know* there is no change of feeling toward you, save one house, and there I never hear your name and am never there! I hope you will come back determined to be superior to any indifference." Earlier, in April, soon after Sue's opening thrust, Vinnie had given some indication that she sympathized with Mrs. Todd's predicament, but this letter was unequivocal. The Dickinson sisters-in-law, it was clear, despite the appearance of family solidarity and the snug impression conveyed by the comradely closeness of the houses, were a good deal less than friendly. What Emily's attitude toward all this might be, Mabel could only guess. Once during the year, in May, Emily had sent some flowers, but a visit to the house in June had resulted only in some pleasant conversation with Vinnie. Emily had remained out of sight.

At this point, when it still perhaps seemed that Emily might yield, there occurred the most devastating of the events that put an end to any real hope for a meeting. Sue's eight-year-old son, Gilbert, a precociously intelligent and charming boy who had managed even at that early age to captivate everyone, fell ill of typhoid fever and in October he died. It was a sudden illness and both Dickinson houses were prostrated by the loss. Austin himself was sick for a while and began "looking like death," as Vinnie apprehensively observed. Sue was so pitifully struck that she could not bring herself to accompany the funeral to the cemetery, a reaction probably compounded by fears for her older son, Ned, who had lately shown signs of a severe epilepsy. Of the two women in the other house, it was Emily who broke down. She took to her bed, with no clearly defined sickness, where she was to spend the remainder of the year.

She was never to be entirely well again, in fact, and it was her physical incapacity that set the final barrier to Mabel's hopes. The following June, while she was in the kitchen helping Maggie with the baking, she collapsed to the floor without warning. As Mabel heard the story, it was noon when she fainted, and she did not open her eyes till dark. Convalescing through the summer, she seemed to be recovering her strength when a second attack took place: alone in the house on a Sunday, she blacked out and lay unconscious on the parlor floor for two hours before Vinnie returned home to find her.

Through this period of strain and difficulty, and for the next year or so, Mabel's visits to the house were infrequent, and in her conscientious recording of those that did take place, Emily goes unmentioned, though judging from later statements, she must now and then have taken up her station on the other side of the parlor wall. There were, for example, conversations carried on, somewhat awkwardly no doubt, "between the brightly lighted drawing room where I was received and the dusky hall outside."

No details of these talks are offered, however, an unusual omission for Mabel Todd. She became very familiar, she says, with the muted and rather breathless voice that drifted in from the darkened hallway, "its vaguely surprised note dominant," as it offered thanks for an hour or so of piano and singing. On one occasion, late in 1884, when Mr. and Mrs. Loomis, Mabel's parents, were visiting in Amherst, they were all entertained by Vinnie, but Emily, though somewhat stronger, kept to her room. Even the singing, joined in by Mrs. Loomis, could not draw her downstairs. Still, she was moved enough to send after them when they departed an appropriately involuted explanation of her seeming rudeness: "The Apostle's inimitable apology for loving whom he saw not, is perhaps monition to us, who are tempted to the same turpitude."

In 1885 the Todds departed for a summer in Europe and, ironically, it was this separation that at last brought some fuller notice from Emily, actually her longest letter since her joyous response to the Indian pipe painting. The letter, received in England, began by choosing to ignore the fact that there could be some reasonable doubt about the friendship between Mrs. Todd and Austin's wife, and Mabel must have wondered why she had again become "Brother and Sister's friend," but the idea that Emily had reached across the Atlantic to her was sufficient recompense. "I saw the American flag last night in the shutting West, and felt for every exile," Emily wrote, and then went on sentence after sentence in the same evanescent tone of impersonal observation, but supplying no word of affairs back in Amherst. "Touch Shakespeare for me," she requested and closed by signing herself "America." The itinerary of the Todd trip is not available but after that note it is perhaps safe to assume that Mabel visited Stratford. Pleased by this lengthy if fleeting notice she certainly was, but it would be interesting to know if, besides the letter's oddity, Mabel had begun to recognize the intensely ingrown mind of its writer, the preoccupied and self-contemplating personality it revealed. About such things she says nothing.

Emily's final illness, warily suspected as such by her family at the time it began, laid its hard grip on her early in 1886. Confined to bed a good deal of the time, she showed little improvement through the spring and Austin was in attendance on her for some part of every day. The trouble had been diagnosed as Bright's disease, with the condition alarmingly advanced. Mabel's concern when she heard the news was genuine: it had been almost five years since she had first become aware of the tantalizing presence in the red brick house, the poems and the white dresses, and she had developed a real if unreciprocated attachment for the woman she had never met. She had even begun to feel, it would appear, a kind of proprietorship. Once, at a dinner for faculty wives, one of the women had produced some gnomic verses sent her by Emily, had read them out in a manner less than serious and had then invited interpretations. Mabel had recoiled in anger from what seemed like desecration. "I was moved to wrath," she wrote in her diary that night, "and could hardly forbear a biting response. But I kept silent." The particular poem is not identified but it may have been a five-line verse Emily sent about this time to the wife of a local pastor with a basket of mayflowers:

> There are two Mays
> And then a Must
> And after that a Shall.
> How infinite the compromise
> That indicates I will!

That there might be some legitimate puzzling over such words never occurred to Mabel, nor that Emily herself might have smiled inwardly when she set them down. In Mrs. Todd's view by now, reverent and subdued tones were the only fitting tribute, a reaction that undoubtedly involved something of her own literary aspirations. She had already begun to publish short stories and articles and in her diary she confesses "a perfect passion all the time to write."

Early in April there was unexpectedly encouraging news about Emily's health; she had improved somewhat and had been allowed by her doctor to leave her bed and roam a little in her room, an hour at a time. At this, Mabel, not quite ready to admit defeat, seems to have employed one last stratagem. Accompanied by her seven-year-old daughter, Millicent, she strolled down the hill to the Dickinson grounds and "sauntered about in the sun." Millicent was turned loose and she busied herself with running through the nearby barn, jumping in the hay and in general upsetting the peace of the horses and hens, "a red-letter afternoon for her." And a noisy one, too, it would seem. But if Mabel had hoped to attract Emily to the window, thinking to elicit an invitation thereby, or if she merely wanted to set eyes, however briefly, on that elusive face, it didn't work. All the windows of the Dickinson house were shut, the blinds down and the curtains drawn. That was Mabel's final gesture. A month later Emily was dead.

The end, which was more or less expected, came with a lingering stealth that seemed only the fitting final inch of Emily's long withdrawal. On the morning of May 13 she went into a deep coma. The doctor was hastily called, but his ministrations had no effect and she continued unconscious through the day and into the night. The following noon Mabel hurried over to inquire and was told that Emily still had not awakened; she returned twice more that day to find the situation unchanged, and then spent the evening at Austin's house. The morning of the 15th found Emily sunk even deeper in oblivion and breathing with great difficulty. Mabel dropped by early and when she looked in again about five learned with dismay that all hope had been given up. She left reluctantly to attend choir practice and it was almost nine when she returned. Entering the somber house she could see that it was all over. Emily, she was told, had died just before six.

The funeral, held on the 19th, was attended by dignitaries from the college as well as by many relatives and neighbors. Few of those present were permitted to view the body, and Mabel for some inexplicable reason was not among the favored ones though her desire must have been plainly apparent. The library in which the small white casket reposed was shut off from the mourners, only now and then would Vinnie usher some longtime friend inside the doors. One of those to whom this privilege was extended, as Mabel heard with interest, was Thomas Wentworth Higginson, eminent in literary circles, who had come all the way from Cambridge to be present and to read, at the simple service held in the afternoon, Emily Brontë's well-known poem, *No Coward Soul Is Mine.*

The funeral also provided Mabel, and the rest of Amherst, with the crowning touch of Emily's eccentricity. As she had instructed Vinnie some time before, a hearse was dispensed with. Her body was taken from the house by the back door, the coffin being borne by honorary pallbearers from the library, through the central hall, to the rear yard. Here it was lifted to a flower-draped wooden bier on the sturdy shoulders of six Irish workmen, all of whom, as Mabel could not help noting, Emily had seen and talked with to the last. From the yard the coffin was carried across the sun-drenched fields, the mourners straggling behind, until the procession emerged on Triangle Street, where it turned north for a short distance and then entered a footpath leading to the cemetery. The grave, beside that of Emily's mother, father and grandfather, was lined with green boughs and as the gleaming casket was lowered, masses of flowers were heaped over it.

Mabel recorded nothing of her feelings at the graveside, but if she felt that her five-year vigil had ended in total frustration she would soon discover that her involvement with the enigma of Amherst was only beginning. For the rest of her life she would be haunted by the image of a woman she had never even glimpsed, and after her own death her daughter, Millicent, would continue to live under the same spell. Emily herself, with eerie if accidental foresight, had already predicted the shape of events to come in a note sent to Mabel on some unknown occasion, perhaps only shortly before the end. "The parting of those that never met," she had inquired archly, "shall it be delusion, or rather, an unfolding snare whose fruitage is later?" A snare and a delusion: appropriate terms for the singular drama that now began.

• •

The melancholy task of gathering up her sister's belongings was started by Lavinia Dickinson a few days after the funeral. Emily's bedroom had always been regarded by the family as her inviolable retreat; though the two sisters had been close, Vinnie had never taken much part in Emily's intellectual pursuits and had no real idea of what she might find. Bundles of old letters, received over many years, were soon turned up and these she proceeded to burn in accordance with Emily's wishes. The destruction of personal correspondence after a death was almost a ritual at that period in New England, and it was duly carried out by Vinnie, supposedly unaware that the papers she dropped into the flames contained answers to many facets of what was to become a celebrated literary puzzle. About a week later, while emptying a bureau, she came upon an unfamiliar box, locked and carrying no identification. When this was opened it was found to contain sheafs of letter paper, folded and threaded at the spine, and filled with writing. It was obvious at a glance that the writing was poetry.

Somewhat to Vinnie's surprise the box yielded fully sixty little booklets or packets into which, as initial examination revealed, there had been copied some seven hundred brief poems. Vinnie, of course, was aware that her sister had written a great deal of poetry, and the two had frequently shared the reading of it. But as she admitted later she had no idea that Emily had produced so much or had preserved her work so carefully. Her surprise grew, over the next few months, as she unearthed additional packets from further unspecified hiding places, as well as envelopes crammed with loose sheets and scraps of paper on which had been set down further poems, some of them no more than four or five lines and many in an obviously unfinished state. The existence of this hoard had never been revealed to anyone and no orders had been left for their destruction, thus their fate was entirely in Vinnie's hands.

No poet herself, and despite the studied strangeness of the verses, to her mind all the poems appeared to be perfectly wonderful. Soon, she conceived a fierce determination to have them published. Austin was later to say that Vinnie "had no comprehension of her sister, yet believed her a shining genius." From other evidence that estimate appears to be true enough, yet he may have put his finger on an equally salient factor when he wryly commented that in publishing the poems Vinnie hoped to share in her sister's fame. In any case, whether she did it for her sister, herself, or for both, with comprehension or without, it was only Vinnie in the beginning who insisted that the poems were worthy of the world's attention.

The first steps she took toward that end were recalled over forty years later by Mabel Todd, at a time when Emily had already achieved a high rank. Soon after Emily's death, Mabel claimed,* "her sister Lavinia came to me, as usual in late evening, actually trembling with excitement. She told me she had discovered a veritable treasure—quantities of Emily's poems which she had no instructions to destroy . . . these poems, she told me, must be printed at once. Would I send them to some 'printer' and how quickly could they appear?" Mabel's reply to this eager entreaty was that no competent judge would attempt to read the verses in Emily's often difficult handwriting, that they would all have to be copied out and then submitted to a publisher for evaluation. The process, she thought, would take a year at least. Vinnie, in despair at the prospect of such a delay, Mabel said, could only urge pathetically, "But they are Emily's poems!"

Earnestly requested to assume full responsibility, Mabel, as she recalled the scene in *Harper's,* was hesitant. Just to copy the

* *Harper's Magazine,* March 1930.

poems, she estimated after a closer look at the bundle of manuscript, even if the task were pursued four hours a day, would take two or three years. There was hardly enough time in a day to take care of her own interests and ambitions, and she had also begun to help her husband with his important astronomical writing. Too, despite the undeniable authority and grace of a good deal of the verse, she confessed to having some doubts that any publisher would be able to overlook what appeared to be glaring faults, especially in matters of rhyme and grammar. No, she concluded regretfully, someone else would have to be found. But Vinnie "was unalterably determined that mine should be the hand that should help Emily set sail," and she was continually begging Mabel to begin the copying. At length when Vinnie appeared at the Todd house one midnight and "almost went on her knees," Mabel in pity relented. She would put aside her own work and start the very next day, would copy as speedily as possible and try to interest a publisher.

Anxious to supply a permanent record of her part in the discovery of a major poet, in her article Mabel asserted that she and Emily had been intimate friends and that their relationship had from the first "progressed radiantly in enlarging affection." During their musical interludes, she admitted, Emily had not actually entered the room, but she could not quite bring herself to confess that she had never once laid eyes on her reticent auditor. At these meetings, she said, Emily had "generally remained" in the hall outside, leaving the reader to wonder what that "generally" was meant to convey. Emily had dressed always in white, she said, and described the poet as "an interrogative spot of light in the half dark hall," cleverly managing, without saying so, to give the impression that while Emily had lurked in the shadows she had still presented herself dimly to view.

At the time she published the *Harper's* article, all the other principals in Emily's belated literary debut were long since dead. Mabel alone remained, an embittered woman of seventy-four, striving to forget the incredible incident that had terminated her connection with that unique unveiling, an incident to which she never openly alluded. The version of the story which she supplied was the one she wanted desperately to believe. Ironically, the truth makes it much easier to sympathize with the blighted feelings that prompted the distortions.

It was to Sue Dickinson that Vinnie first took the poems, in high excitement, about a month after Emily's death. Sue had enjoyed a long intimacy with her dead sister-in-law and had received many poems from her own hands, but still she was surprised at the total that had been uncovered. Better able than Vinnie to appreciate Emily's accomplishment, her first enthusiasm was soon tempered by uncertainty, a reaction shared by Austin. She recognized the often extraordinary flashes of insight, could sense the brilliance in the abrupt swell of language, but like everyone else she was troubled by the serious lack of form. She did submit a few poems to magazines, and when they were returned, her doubts about commercial publication were redoubled. In addition, it seems, she could not escape the notion that such exploitation would be a cruel invasion of the privacy of one who had all her life shrunk from notice. "I sometimes shudder," she admitted after the poems had at last been released, "when I think of the world reading her thoughts minted in deep heart-broken convictions." In this mood of vacillation, with Vinnie's plaintive pleas for accompaniment, two years passed before Sue could make up her mind what to do. Finally she decided that she would not publish the poems but would issue them privately. A large selection from the best of the verse supplemented by passages from the more unusual of Emily's letters would make a fitting repository for that scintillating if erratic mind and personality. Thus she felt she could shield the poems while allowing them an immortality as unobtrusive as Emily's life had been. She was unprepared to find, in September 1890, that the decision had passed from her hands, and that the poems were about to be issued by a well-known Boston publisher.

In *The Christian Union,* a paper widely circulated in New

England, Sue read an article written by Thomas Wentworth Higginson containing fourteen of the poems along with an announcement that a small volume was about to be published "by her sister and friends, with some misgiving, and almost a sense of questionable publicity." This poetry, Higginson stated (with his own sure sense of publicity) was the lifework of a recluse who "lived literally indoors by choice for many years, and within the limits of her father's estate for many more—who shrank even from the tranquil society of a New England college town." Such personal detail Sue found even more distressing than the fact that the impending publication had been kept a secret from her. But her irritation at this was as nothing before the stricken sense of betrayal she felt on finding, a few days later, that the forthcoming volume had been edited not only by Higginson but by Mabel Todd as well.

It is quite probable that Vinnie did actually inform Mabel, soon after Emily's death, of the finding of the poems; she excitedly shared her discovery with more than one close neighbor.* Mabel was not at that time, however, invited to take charge or help in the attempt to find a publisher. Only later, and very likely at her own request, was she allowed a part in the excitement, when she was set to deciphering the more fugitive pencil scrawls on the loose scraps. Her first such efforts were desultory, and she was away from Amherst for nearly half of 1887, when she accompanied her husband on another trip, this time to Japan. It was not until the fall of the following year that she was requested by Vinnie—who had become disgusted with Sue's procrastination—to assume the work and her assignment was merely to prepare readable manuscripts for Higginson. Mabel, in her eagerness, sympathy and cultivation, was a logical choice, but she did not at first think of herself as being a "co-editor." Only gradually did she become involved to the point where she deserved and could expect recognition. The unsuspecting Vinnie,

* *Smith Alumnae Quarterly,* Winter 1954.

anxious to preserve at least the remnants of peace between the two Dickinson houses, certainly never contemplated seeing the name of Mabel Loomis Todd spread on the title page of her sister's poems.

By the fall of 1888 Mabel was steadily at work, dealing competently with the not inconsiderable complexities of the manuscripts. The handwriting, once she was familiar with it, presented no real problem, but the queer punctuation—an indiscriminate sprinkling of dashes, with commas and periods dropped in sparingly and almost at random—had to be regularized, with care taken not to interfere with the meaning. The unorthodox grammar, the anarchistic rhyme, and the unpredictable verbal twists all required a high degree of literary sensitivity to evaluate, and it quickly became evident to Mabel that her function was not one of simple mechanical reproduction but of actual editing. And when she at last presented Higginson with neat copies of some seven hundred poems, that busy gentleman, in dismay at the heap of manuscript, asked if she could save him effort by classifying them according to her notion of their quality.

The copying, reading and selection, and the hunt for a publisher, were all successfully completed by the summer of 1889; it was at this point that Vinnie sensed danger in the wind. "I dare say you are aware," she queried Higginson, "our co-worker is to be 'sub-rosa' for reasons you may understand," and she was amazed to find that Higginson considered the condition foolish and would not agree to suppress Mabel's name. To Mabel, when she heard of Vinnie's surreptitious interference, this was "treachery beyond my imagining." It was also a warning signal, but one which Mrs. Todd failed to heed.

With the names of Higginson and Mabel Todd prominently displayed on the title page, the poems of Emily Dickinson reached the public in November 1890. A short preface by Higginson introduced the unknown writer, in which he again skilfully emphasized Emily's paradoxical seclusion, saying that "she habitually concealed her mind like her person, from all but a very few friends," and except for those friends, "was as invisible to the world as if she dwelt in a nunnery." Once a year during her father's lifetime, he explained, she had come forth into the full light on the occasion of the annual college reception held at the Dickinson house. Arrayed in immaculate white, she would descend from the upper floor, act the smiling and gracious hostess for a while, in no way betraying uneasiness, and the next day would have disappeared once more from the life of the town.

The influence of Higginson's fame, as well as the provocative personality he so subtly outlined, coupled with the crystalline shimmer of the poems themselves, secured the book a rare reception. Reviewers contorted themselves to express their appreciation of what was generally referred to as her flawed genius, while the public bought up printing after printing, and a second volume was speedily prepared. This appeared about a year after the first, and excitement and sales continued, leading Higginson to capture the feelings of all concerned when he exulted, "I feel as if we had climbed to a cloud, pulled it away, and revealed a new star behind it." He could hardly have guessed that in displacing the cloud that obscured Emily's star, they had also uncovered an earthly bitterness that had long brooded behind the doors of both Dickinson houses and which now began its slow, malicious spread.

The first open breach occurred when excitement over the new poet was at its height. Sue had submitted to the New York *Independent* a few of the many poems Emily had personally sent her, two being accepted. When she became aware of this, Vinnie immediately bristled with talk of lawyers: Emily's poems were hers alone to dispose of, she insisted (correctly as it turned out) and she wouldn't hesitate to take Sue to court to prove her point. She probably had also heard of Sue's plans for a separate volume of her own, and such presumption would have seemed to her appalling. She did go so far as to write a Boston attorney, but by this time Sue had become convinced she had no legal claim to Emily's work and had yielded. Vinnie's anger continued to boil, however, and a few weeks later she gave vent to her feelings in a calculated act of destruction.

Finding in one of the packets an effusive poem Emily had written to Sue many years before, at about the time of her marriage to Austin, Vinnie decided to get rid of it. She was prevented from simply tearing it up by the fact that the folded sheet of letter paper on which it appeared contained five other brief poems, and these she wanted to retain. The six stanzas of Sue's verse occupied the second page and half of the third; the first page contained two short verses and there was another at the bottom of the third page. On the last page, the back of the folded sheet, there were two more. Thus hemmed in it might have seemed that either Sue's poem must escape or else all must be sacrificed, but the dilemma was neatly solved. Pulling the entire four pages from the packet, Vinnie trimmed off the inside edges in order to obliterate the thread holes, carefully ripped a small strip off the top edge of both sheets to make re-orientation difficult, then tore both sheets in half. This left the five poems intact while separating Sue's poem into three scraps, and she completed the destruction by heavily overscoring the offending lines in ink. The name "Sue" itself was blotted out with particularly vehement strokes of the pen. The mutilation done, the four resultant fragments were then distributed among the legitimate scraps that Emily herself had bundled together. The operation was coolly performed, the first sign of the controlled vindictiveness of which Vinnie was capable.

With the warm reception accorded the poems, Mabel Todd began to enjoy the kind of life she had yearned for, and on a more exalted level than she could probably have anticipated. As one of the principal proprietors of the newest American poet, her perfect passion for literature was given heady scope. Editing and selecting poems for the future volumes that were certain to follow, she also began gathering information for articles and, hopefully, lectures about Emily, and she kept careful scrapbooks of all the reviews and commentary she could find. A collection of

Emily's letters also was talked of, and Mabel made plans for such a volume with the encouragement of both Vinnie and the publisher. This was a development which, more than any other, indicated the extent to which rumors about the poet's personal life had influenced the reception of her poems: a new writer's correspondence does not often find its way into print so early. It was also this same public curiosity, widespread in New England particularly, that enabled Mabel Todd to extend the range of her activities.

She was eventually to become a highly effective and much-traveled speaker on a variety of topics. Her entry into the field began when she spoke to an audience of sixty in the Springfield Women's Club, delivering a sketch of Emily's life, work and personality. A month later she appeared before two hundred at the Boston Alumnae Club, where she explained that Emily Dickinson had really been a very normal person, if perhaps overly sensitive and somewhat timid. "Those ideas," one paper summed up her talk, "that made of Miss Dickinson a woman eccentrically dressed, an invalid, an irreverent woman, or the victim of a love tragedy, were explained away, and she was shown to have a strong dislike for all the shams and trivialities of life, which united with shyness to keep her confined to her home." Thus Mabel, following the lead of Austin and Vinnie, began the repudiation not only of her own experiences in the red brick house, but of all the floating rumors she had absorbed from her Amherst neighbors for a decade. If audiences were a little disappointed to be shown this rather humdrum figure behind the poems, they still enjoyed listening to and looking at the vivid Mrs. Todd, who in her usual choice of a severe black ensemble displayed an admirable touch of showmanship, and whose "every tone and gesture revealed not only the intelligent critic but the loving friend."

Her relations with Vinnie, even after the treachery of the year before, continued smooth for a time, but strain gradually and perhaps inevitably began to appear. Vinnie was "horribly ignorant" of the complexities of editing and publishing, Mabel complained, yet was constantly importuning her to hurry the work on the letters and further volumes of poems. For her part, Vinnie resented Mabel's giving time to other projects, notably an extensive rewriting of a book on eclipses by Professor Todd, and she may also have begun to feel the bite of jealousy: the young woman who had begun as a helper merely copying the poems, had somehow magnified herself along with Emily, thereby diverting a good portion of the reflected glory. Money matters, again perhaps inevitably, added to the growing estrangement.

The first volume of poems had gone through a dozen printings, and the second was performing almost as well. There had been no prior agreement on division of income—it had scarcely been thought necessary—and for their part in the work Mrs. Todd and Higginson had each been given a few hundred dollars, a considerably smaller share than Vinnie had retained for herself. When, early in 1893, it was definitely decided to issue a volume of the letters, Austin stepped in and suggested the income from it should go entirely to Mabel, since she would be doing all the work and Higginson had bowed out of the picture. This idea Vinnie contemptuously swept aside, insisting that her sister's "mind" belonged to her; it was not until a month or so before the *Letters* appeared that she gave in sufficiently to allow Mabel half the income. That the concession was not made with a good will is evident: shortly thereafter, as Mabel lamented, Vinnie was again indulging in "the blackest treachery," though the nature of the grievance still went unspecified.

For all the fuss made over royalties, it soon became apparent that the letters were not to share in the popularity of the poems, and to offset this disappointment, Austin determined to present the Todds with a piece of the broad Dickinson meadow, situated just across Main Street. Some years previously the Todds had acquired a large plot in this meadow from Austin and had built their house on it; the strip proposed as a gift adjoined that piece and was gratefully accepted by the Todds. But before the deed could be executed—the boundaries had already been marked off and trees planted as a dividing line—death intervened to cause delay. In the middle of August, after a month of vague physical distress, Austin succumbed to heart trouble, and six months passed with nothing further said about the land. Then, shortly after the manuscript for Emily's third volume had reached the publisher, and no doubt to Mabel's lasting surprise, Vinnie signed the deed.

Satisfied, her work on the poems completed for a time, Mabel departed on another trip with her husband, again to the Orient. When she returned late in October, she was in high spirits as she bustled happily among the collection of Ainu curiosities, garments of salmon skin, old lacquer and bronzes, "and a big and very lovely Jinrickcha!" that crowded the parlor. Awaiting her at home were pleasant tidings about the success of the third volume, which had appeared in her absence, as well as dozens of speaking invitations, most of them interested in Emily, but a few asking to hear of her travels and her opinions on everything from the village beautiful to the solar corona. There was also awaiting her the news—the not quite believable news—that Vinnie had brought suit to recover the strip of meadowland.

In papers served on the Todds, Vinnie charged that they had imposed on her by fraud and misrepresentation, that in signing the paper presented to her she thought she was merely promising to allow no building on the strip; she never meant to give the land away. When they had recovered from their stunned outrage, unable to conceive how Vinnie expected to sustain the charges in view of the fact that the deed had been signed in the presence of a notary, the angry young couple hit back with a countersuit accusing Vinnie of slander and demanding twenty-five thousand dollars in damages. Scandalized Amherst, sniffing something more than a disagreement over land in the air, prepared itself to enjoy the fireworks.

But it didn't quite come off. There were only just enough revelations to tease the attentive villagers, supplying them with little more than innuendo, as well as to frustrate the hopes of later researchers. The two suits reached court almost simultaneously, after a long delay, with the slander charge scheduled to be tried first. This upset the planning of the Todd lawyers who preferred not to anticipate their defense of the fraud allegation, and when they could not gain a continuance, they withdrew the Todd suit altogether. Vinnie's case was called immediately afterward, and for two days Amherst had its show, as the papers lengthily reported the goings-on in the Northampton court.

On the stand Vinnie met all questions with calm, even-handed denials: she had not known what she was signing; the notary, a lawyer brought along to the house by Mabel, had not made clear the nature of the document presented to her; she had never told certain neighbors of an intention to give the land away; she knew nothing about business dealings, in any case, and was not accustomed to handling such matters. The Todds countered with testimony supplied in affidavit by a Dickinson neighbor and friend, Dwight Hills: yes, Vinnie had mentioned "the conveyance of this meadow land to the Todds a good number of times"; he had even offered to handle the transaction himself if she decided to go ahead. It was Vinnie's response to this damaging assertion that made irreparable—if a final seal was needed—the breach between the two families. Under questioning she insisted that Hills had, in fact, counseled her to give nothing more to the Todds for they were—and her voice rang excitedly in the crowded courtroom as her composure momentarily erupted—"Leeches! Leeches! Leeches!"* Precisely what she might have meant by that was never brought out, since the lead was not pursued except briefly when Professor Todd took the stand. The original large plot of land which he had acquired from Austin and on which he had built his house, he testified, had also been a gift; he had paid nothing for it. No explanation of this was offered and for some reason none was requested, but the question hung in the air.

* *Springfield Republican*, March 4, 1898.

As everyone recognized, the case hinged almost entirely on the testimony of the notary who had signed as witness to the deed, and he was unable convincingly to establish Vinnie's full awareness of her actions. He had made everything clear, he insisted, telling Vinnie the paper was "a deed of land," reading out the boundaries and showing her where to sign. But it was only too obvious that Vinnie could still have been confused even while assuring him that she understood, and the newspapers duly reported that the notary's testimony "was not so conclusive as many had anticipated it would be."

Only once did the proceedings seem on the verge of more interesting disclosures. After the deed had been signed, the notary said, as they were leaving the house, Mrs. Todd had asked him to delay the official registration; she did not want it to become public knowledge just then. The reason she gave for making the request was a serious estrangement between Sue and herself. "If Mrs. Austin Dickinson discovered it was deeded to me," Mabel was quoted as saying, "she would make trouble, there would be a row, she wouldn't like it."* This brought some eager stirring in the court as it appeared that the wraps might be coming off, but that line of questioning was abruptly terminated and nothing more was heard about Sue. To the surprise of very few except the Todds, the decision, rendered a few weeks later, was in Vinnie's favor. The case was promptly appealed, but the Massachusetts Supreme Court, later in the year, declined a reversal.

Disbelieving and crushed, Mabel bundled all the Dickinson papers in her possession into a camphorwood chest, snapped the lock and did not look at them again for thirty years. Included were many of Emily's original letters, given or loaned to her for the 1894 volume, the manuscripts of perhaps four hundred poems, and many other letters and documents of prime importance to Emily's story. All of this material had been in her possession at the time Vinnie instigated suit, and it had never been returned. Mabel, in a mood to retaliate, simply possessed

* Bingham, *An. Broc.*, 355.

herself of it and in succeeding years neither mentioned her treasure nor gave it up. Her act went unchallenged because, within six months of the decision on the appeal, Vinnie herself fell ill—of heart trouble like her brother—and died in August 1899. Her portion of Emily's manuscripts also disappeared back into the obscurity from which they had come as, just before her death and for reasons of her own, she managed to hide them somewhere in the red brick house. She hid them so well, in fact, that they were not rediscovered for many years, despite what must have been an intensive search through the silent rooms by Sue and her daughter Martha. Thus in hatred and recrimination the publication of the poems came to an end, though more than half had not yet reached print.

Giving up their house in the meadow after the lawsuit, the Todds removed themselves from the vicinity of the Dickinson enclave and for more than a decade Sue and Mabel lived at opposite ends of the little town in prodigious disregard of each other's existence. The passing years brought the bruised and bitter Mrs. Todd some measure of resignation, but she was never able to forget or forgive; in her memory Vinnie ever afterwards rose as a gargoylish figure stripped of any attraction or interest she might once have had. Asked in later years for a description of Emily's sister, Mabel responded that Vinnie's mouth had been "perfectly hideous and full of false teeth . . . her skin was very white and wrinkled. Her face was repulsive—no half beauty left in it . . . her hands had grown-out joints and were always dirty . . . she dressed in queer quaint clothes."

Nor was Mabel ever able to comprehend fully what had impelled Vinnie to her action—at least she never spoke openly of the incident with anyone, not even, at any length, with her own daughter. Of one thing she was sure, however. Sue Dickinson, while she had held herself aloof from courts and lawyers, was not free of responsibility. Millicent Todd, trying some years after her mother's death to explain how it all could have happened, claimed emphatically that Sue had frightened and harried Vinnie into taking the step through the exercise of various small and subtle cruelties. That assertion is almost certainly true: there were others among Vinnie's friends who believed that Sue had held "some dire threat" over her sister-in-law's head. But Sue's real hold on the tough-minded Vinnie could not have been anything so mild as general harassment. It could in fact have had only one point of leverage, Emily herself, or more properly Emily's reputation.

In their younger days Sue and Emily had been very close, sharing in each other's hopes and ambitions. Sue had sympathized with Emily's first serious poetic efforts and had encouraged her early desire for fame. She undoubtedly knew the truth, if anyone did, about the rumors of Emily's hopeless passion—knew that Emily had indeed been in love, very much in love, with a married man and knew who that man was. But there was something more, something that would, if revealed, strike at the very root of Emily's fragile but growing reputation. Sue knew that the poetry—that wonderfully original poetry—had received a very strange birth indeed, and was, in sober truth, not entirely Emily's own.

· 2 ·

NOBODY KNOWS
THIS LITTLE ROSE

THE FIRST HALF of Emily Dickinson's life is little short of re-markable—not for anything it reveals about her poetic beginnings but for its sharp contrast to all that followed. During the whole of her adolescence and youth, up to the start of her twenty-sixth year, she was essentially no different from thousands of other New England girls of similar background and education. She displayed not even a momentary flash of rare or unusual powers and was unvisited by any premonitory stirrings of the visions that would later descend on the brooding sibyl of Amherst. From perhaps her sixteenth year she wrote poetry and during a decade of such effort produced only brief, pedestrian, limply sentimental verses. A physically unattractive girl, small-bodied and thin, with a pale face marred by thick, permanently pursed lips and an amorphous nose, her only discernible distinctions were a buoyant verbal wit and an exuberant liking for companionship. Twice she was in love, twice disappointed, and never in all this time did she dream that the world might become too trivial for her notice.

Only in one sole respect was there a hint of things to come: an irrepressible tendency to self-dramatization. Constantly she saw the world around her, neighbors, home and family, through hyperbolic eyes, arranging the elements of the scene to suit some obscure need, most often with herself occupying the foreground. Some of the friends of her youth, put off by the not always subtle posturing, recalled her as being somehow "unnatural." To others who took a more relaxed view of such foibles, she had seemed possessed of "a charm, a grace," they found difficult to define. It was an attitudinizing that in its nature, depth and duration far exceeded even the normal self-indulgence of youthful creative groping, and it argues some cause more permanent and outward. Perhaps it is no accident that her manner of settled pretense is first noticeable at about the time she was becoming warily conscious of her homely appearance—a factor that, according to her brother, played no inconsiderable part in her life.

To some degree it was her family's position in Amherst, secured after fluctuating through eight generations of Dickinsons, that allowed her the appropriate amplitude of setting for all the make-believe. Her father, a prominent lawyer, served for nearly forty years as Treasurer of Amherst College and this, together with his other interests, very early turned the Dickinson house into a spirited center of activity. Edward Dickinson was an ambitious man and before Emily had done with childhood he had already served two terms in the Massachusetts legislature and two more in the state senate. He was being mentioned for Congress when he bowed temporarily out of politics and gave his energies to business, eventually to become one of the wealthiest and most influential men in the district. From all appearances he was somewhat remote in personality, clinging to the old Calvinist philosophy all the stauncher as he saw it slipping from the grasp of many around him, but he was not the repressive tyrant—"cold and forbidding" is a frequent description—solemnly exhibited as a psychological foil for the poet. For Austin, Emily and Vinnie, throughout their youth, the Dickinson home according to Emily's own testimony rang with "the cheerful voices and the merry laugh." The man who could be so moved by an unusually

splendid aurora borealis that he excitedly set the church bells
to a clangorous pealing in order to arrest the town's attention,
as Edward Dickinson did, arousing only mild surprise in his
children, was hardly cold and rather a poor sort of tyrant.

In one of Emily's later letters there occurs a fleeting scene,
an affecting miniature tableau, that in its short compass and in
her way of telling it, reveals more of Edward Dickinson's relation to his home and children than volumes of inert argument.
Early in 1853 Austin left Amherst to enter Harvard Law, and
later in the month Emily wrote to remind him that their father
was anxious for letters. "He reads them once at the office," she
said, "then he makes me read them loud at the supper table
again, and when he gets home in the evening, he cracks a few
walnuts, puts his spectacles on and with your last in hand, sits
down to enjoy the evening . . . I do think it's so funny—you
and father do nothing but 'fisticuff' all the while you're at home,
and the minute you are separated you become such devoted
friends." If Mr. Dickinson seldom put into words the love he
felt for his family, it was nevertheless a constant, warm presence
in the home, pervading it as heat from an old furnace—occasionally inadequate perhaps, sometimes no doubt stifling, but
otherwise necessary, dependable and familiar. Emily he simply
accepted as the slightly puzzling personality she appeared to be,
and his ghost, let it be assured, will rest easy in these pages.

Of her mother little can be said; little indeed of a personal
nature is known of her. A good woman, mild yet serious, somewhat fussy and nervous of temperament, self-effacing and unim-
aginative, she seems to have had the misfortune of impressing
her daughters only as a model to be avoided. When Emily later
declared in an expansive moment that she was always in love
with her teachers, she was in reality voicing her disappointment
that her mother was so ordinary a person. It was a feeling she
was not at all backward about putting into words. "I always ran
home to Awe when a child, if anything befell me," she once
wrote an acquaintance at a time when her mother was still

living, "He was an awful mother but I liked him better than none." If either Dickinson parent exerted detrimental pressures on the elder daughter, then perhaps the role should be assigned the mother, in whom, despite the paucity of evidence, a certain lack of warmth seems detectable. This, combined with the disparity in the physical appeal of her daughters, may have produced in Emily some feeling of rejection; the bland ease with which she made known her feelings, even to comparative strangers, calls for some such explanation. But that, admittedly, is no more than a guess and Emily's outspokenness may in the end tell more about the daughter than it does about the mother, may in fact provide a comment on the often narrow sympathies of the creative mind. In any event, it was not until later years, with Mrs. Dickinson a helpless invalid in Emily's care, that her daughter was able to summon up any sense of closeness. By that time an emotional invalid herself, and no longer reaching toward a poetic identity, Emily was content with the security of loving and being needed.

It was not in the red brick house on Main Street, fittingly enough, that Emily spent these early years. She had been born there in 1830, at a time when the house was being shared with her grandfather's family, but at the age of ten had moved with her own family to another house on nearby North Pleasant Street. The Main Street house was sold soon after, seemingly passing out of Emily's life forever. Fifteen years later, however, it would welcome back its shy tenant, the return coinciding in neatly mystic fashion with her artistic awakening. Thus even fate would play its part in the making of a legend: the red brick house with something of grandeur in its severity, guarded by high hedges and darkened by surrounding trees, was much more suited to myth than the large frame structure, painted white, that presented its many-windowed side wall to the busy roadway.

From the new house, during seven or eight years, Emily and her sister went to school daily at Amherst Academy, distant only a few minutes on foot. She was a bright pupil, well-behaved but far from prim, and she often displayed an impish humor that convulsed her friends, most of whom were children of the college faculty. One of these, Abiah Root, luckily preserved many of the letters Emily wrote to her in this period and they frequently display her indulging in some of her earliest and most transparent dramatics. The two first became friendly in the summer of 1844, and when Abiah left Amherst later in the year to attend another school in Springfield, a steady correspondence ensued. Their personal contact had thus lasted only a few months, insufficient time to allow for any real knowledge of each other, and Emily took full advantage of her friend's sympathetic ear.

Once she described in excruciating detail a vigil she had kept at the deathbed of a friend, twelve-year-old Sophia Holland, an event that had taken place two years before she wrote of it. She had visited the girl often during that last illness, she explained, until "Reason fled and the physician forbid any but the nurse to go into her room," a denial which pained her greatly. When at length the doctor said that death was inevitable, he "allowed me to look at her a moment through the open door. I took off my shoes and stole softly to the sick room. There she lay mild and beautiful as in health & her pale features lit up with an unearthly smile. I looked as long as friends would permit me & when they told me I must look no longer I let them lead me away." The tragedy had been real enough, and Emily had been sufficiently depressed by it to be sent on a visit to relatives, but in this telling of it, the loved and lost friend has become a character in one of the sentimental novels of the day—and the fact that Emily was consciously indulging in a widespread nineteenth century convention heightens rather than diminishes the significance of her attitude.

The pose is equally evident in other discussions that took place between the two girls, particularly when it came to religion. At that time in New England, especially in the western portions beyond the liberalizing influence of Boston, religion remained a matter of transcendent concern and the need to declare a formal tie with the church was impressed even on children; youth was no bar to fervent discussions of "the great subject." Even admitting this, Emily's treatment of it was, to say the least, overwrought. It was a mention by Abiah of her own concern with these matters that brought a mournful admission from her friend that she, too, was anxious to submit, only that some vague impediment always intervened. The world, she knew, could never fill the "aching void" in her heart, yet sadly she was perpetually kept back from acceptance by "evil voices" whispering that there was time enough in the years ahead for a decision. One passage of such ruminations presents the young lady in a classically characteristic attitude, not by any means an isolated instance of the bogus introspection by which she entertained herself. "It is Sabbath eve," sighed the fifteen-year-old Emily,

All is still around me . . . I am alone with God, & my mind is filled with many solemn thoughts which crowd themselves upon me with an irresistible force . . . I think of the perfect happiness I experienced while I felt I was an heir of heaven as of a delightful dream, out of which the Evil one bid me awake and again return to the world and its pleasures . . . now I have bitterly to lament my folly . . . I feel that I am sailing upon the brink of an awful precipice, from which I cannot escape & over which I fear my tiny boat will soon glide if I do not receive help from above.

This soliloquy, in its entirety a fine melange of the words and phrases from all the sermons she ever heard, taken together with other passages similarly inflated, displays not a precocious tender concern with the things of the spirit but an invincible, bland disregard of them. Unable in her time and place to escape religion's demanding presence, she found it a handy framework in which to exhibit herself as the reluctant rebel—a pose that brought her the welcome attention of concerned friends and masked from any reproach her airy dismissal of Calvinist other-world preoccupations. It was a technique which she kept up for some years, though in diminishing effusiveness as time went on, and which was eventually to become the stuff of the mockingly irreligious poems of her early maturity. In more adolescent form this pose made its final appearance during the year she spent at boarding school in South Hadley, a town some ten miles distant from Amherst.

Mount Holyoke Seminary for Young Ladies, while it offered an unusual pioneering course in higher education for women, had been founded on religious principles. When Emily entered its doors in the fall of 1847, she was offered ample opportunity in highly conducive surroundings, to accept the comforts of religion. But as Mount Holyoke quietly surged with the daily effort to bring its two hundred and thirty-five students to a full realization of God's church, Emily hung back among those listed as "without hope," the impenitents, as they were brusquely labeled. Leader in the effort of conversion was Mary Lyon, founder of the school and a woman of wide sympathies who burned with the fervor of evangelism. At regular intervals she gathered the impenitents into the large main hall, spoke earnestly of the need to feel the reality of Bible truths and urged the girls to open themselves to the infusions of the spirit. Emily was among this number, since attendance was mandatory, but she felt no call, no increase of danger as her tiny boat continued to skim the awful precipice. At least once she contrived to teeter on the brink as a lone dissenter, unaccompanied even by the other impenitents. The details of the incident are cloudy, but it concerns a general Fast Day planned by the school for Christmas Eve. While participation in the observance was to be on a purely voluntary basis, it was expected that those still without hope would agree to take part, since the exercise was hardly a compromising one. In unexpected response, however, to Miss Lyon's confident invitation, Emily's hand was the only one raised in refusal, the action making her the focus of wondering stares from some thirty pairs of impenitent eyes.

Perhaps exhilarated by that miniature insurrection, a few weeks later she decided to refine the drama still further by appearing at a special session for those girls who were still without hope but who professed feelings of "uncommon anxiety." The meeting is usually ignored by those of Emily's critics who prefer their poet as an unreconstructed pagan, and happily clutched at by others who see her as fundamentally Christian. "We may not cross the threshold of the room where Mary Lyon and her brilliant pupil knelt side by side," remarked one biographer (who yet was able to discern the kneeling figures) and the fact unfortunately is true. There remains no hint of what transpired behind those doors. Emily can, however, be seen emerging from that room still enormously unconcerned: the very next day she gaily informed her brother that while many of the girls were "flocking to the ark of safety," she herself had not yet given in.

Thereafter the subject disappears from the surviving letters she sent from South Hadley. Only as the school year reached its close, and with it her attendance at Mount Holyoke, did she again indulge the feelings of abandonment she had come to find so stimulating. It made her tremble, she assured the more conscientious Abiah Root, when she realized how she had so blithely thrown away her opportunities. Still, even though friends begged and her own conscience supplicated, she found it impossible to "give up the world." Whatever her friends felt about Emily's reluctance, it caused no undue concern in her own home: of the five Dickinsons, though all were regular church-goers, only the mother had committed herself to membership. Chances for embracing religion were to be many in the years ahead, but Emily, while she frequently attended church with her family and was well acquainted with a succession of Amherst ministers, never took the step. Two decades later, when she had indeed given up the world and when existence for her had become a dark tunnel leading she knew not where, she would come to need the consolation she had earlier refused—*was* there a life after death?—*did* people who loved really meet in the hereafter? The questions were to become the burden of her middle years and her persistent apprehensive rummaging in the recesses of her own soul would produce no certain answer.

Through the rest of her time at Mount Holyoke she was preoccupied with her studies—chemistry, algebra, rhetoric, astronomy, with daily practice in piano and voice—and was more or less content as the witty focus of a little clique that delighted in her hilarious stories "invented on the spot." Only a growing trepidation over her personal appearance disturbed her peace. As early as her fourteenth year she had become acutely aware of her lack of beauty, managing usually to veil her references to the subject in banter. "I am growing handsome very fast indeed!" she noted hopefully in May 1845. "I expect I shall be the belle of Amherst when I reach my 17th year." But a short three months later, her talk of her looks was decidedly more sober and she concluded ruefully that she hadn't "altered any" and even different hair styles didn't seem to help. Between times, it appears she had been afforded a closer look at herself in a profile silhouette cut by one of the teachers at Amherst Academy and must have been painfully struck by the too-honest depiction of the protuberant mouth. At the end of the year, as she approached fifteen, she came to the depressing decision that she would never be pretty, in fact would always be less than plain. "My face has not changed, nor will it in time to come. I shall always remain the same old sixpence."

But for a while she continued to hope and before leaving Mount Holyoke could not resist the impulse to see if a camera might depict something more acceptable than the evidence of her mirror. The daguerreotype craze by 1848 was in full swing, photography having only recently been perfected, and when an itinerant artist set up shop opposite the school, Emily joined the girls excitedly lining up for portraits.* The result was disheartening. From beneath the glass in the little daguerreotype case there peered back at her an image with scarcely one good feature,

* Leyda, I, 134.

a nondescript face framed by severely straight hair parted in the middle and swept back to cover the ears. It was a face, as she must have recognized, verging on the ugly. Some, looking at the portrait a century later, have professed to feel a strange charm, especially in the dark, wide-set, quizzical eyes, but it was a charm not discerned by Emily. Her hair she was soon arranging in short curls low over her forehead. The picture she put away and never, it seems, showed it to anyone. During the rest of her life she never again faced a camera.

Her silent fears are reflected in a wistfully complaining letter she sent her brother soon after the encounter with the portrait. It is, to anyone who reads with the heart, pathetically revealing. Valentine week at that time was the occasion for a great flurry of cards and messages among friends, the more extravagant in style the better, and sent largely for the fun of it. But none, even of the lighter kind, reached Emily in South Hadley. "Every night I have looked and yet in vain for one of Cupid's messengers"; had *all* the Amherst young men, she inquires lightly, forgotten Austin's gifted sister? The letter concludes with a request that it be kept confidential since she would "feel badly" to have it shown. She was seventeen and she no longer cared to joke about being the belle of Amherst.

• •

In the fall of 1848 the unmarried young ladies of Amherst, daughters of the well-to-do, formed a Sewing Society in behalf of local charities. Twice a month they convened at six in the evening, usually at the Amherst House, a large hotel beside the Common, sewed quilts and curtains until eight and then prepared themselves to receive any young gentlemen who cared to drop in. These gatherings were "pretty mirthful times," Austin Dickinson decided after attending one, ". . . when I got there they were all out in the 'dancing Hall' playing 'Blind Man's buff' after which game there was some dancing." Emily, home from school for good, joined the circle along with half a dozen of her girl friends, all of them, quite naturally, drawn more by the socializing than by any deep concern for the poor. At the dancing and games she would have no fears of being neglected since she was well acquainted with five or six young men, all of them either chums of her brother or connected with her father's law firm. Consciously literary themselves, they admired Emily's wit, and liked the way she had of responding warmly to their fervent opinions on such contemporary writers as Carlyle and Emerson, their comments on Shakespeare or the venerable, still-living Wordsworth. There was nothing of a personal nature in these particular relationships, but it may have been at one of the sewing circle evenings that she finally did meet the young man who would provide her with her first tentative romance. It was a brief encounter, of no importance to the young man, in which Emily can be seen making the usual error of anxious young female hearts.

James Kimball, a senior at the college preparing for the ministry, was one of the leading literary lights of the school and he and Emily were good enough friends by Christmas for him to offer her a gift, a volume of poems. For something over six months she enjoyed his companionship, reading into it, it seems, much more than the naive young man ever intended, and when he evaporated after graduation in August, she still couldn't quite grasp the situation. Six months afterwards she can still be heard complaining about his silence. "I have written to *Belvidere*," she confided to a friend, calling him by his nickname, "and young 'D.D.' will feel some things I think—at any rate I intended he should." Kimball's silence, as it turned out, was to be permanent, though it was another few months before Emily decided to forget him.

During this same period two or three other young men, prompted by pedagogical instincts rather than any romantic tendencies, showed a gratifying interest in the improvement of her mind. (Amherst, for all its intellectual atmosphere, was still a small town; one had to do something those long evenings be-

sides circumnavigate the Common.) Benjamin Newton, especially, a twenty-eight-year-old law student in her father's office,
spent many evenings in the Dickinson house enlarging on such
current topics as Transcendentalism and the new social gospel of
Lydia Child—subjects which must have caused Mr. Dickinson
more than one sad shake of the head. Newton appears to have
been more interested in the radical thinkers of the day than in
pure literature. He must have been particularly attractive to
Emily's adventurous spirit—even, because of his advanced views,
a little exciting. Afterward she remembered him as "a gentle yet
grave preceptor, teaching me what to read, what authors to admire, what was most grand or beautiful in nature, and that sub-
limer lesson, a faith in things unseen." On the strength of this
statement and one or two other random references, Newton is
usually cited as the one who first awakened Emily's slumbering
talents. The obscure young man, who died less than three years
after quitting Amherst late in 1849, has thus been awarded a
unique place in American literature. He may indeed have
played some brief part in the broadening of her outlook, but if
his recommendations on what to read and admire differed in
any respect from what everyone else was reading, the evidence
does not reflect it. Along with the rest of Amherst, and the rest
of the country, Emily devoured such popular authors as Dickens,
Tennyson, and Longfellow, especially Longfellow, whose sentimental ditty *The Rainy Day* ("Into each life some rain must
fall" ran its most famous line) she was incessantly quoting. She
also indulged herself, as did everyone else, with the flood of the
more ephemeral literature of sentiment, sharing with her friends
her endless delight in it. Ralph Waldo Emerson, who had not
then come fully into his inheritance but whom Newton seems
to have had a fondness for, exerted no fascination on the Emily
of the eighteen-fifties. Benjamin Newton was undoubtedly an
estimable young man who gave Emily needed companionship,
but it was coincidence and nothing more, that has preserved his
name.

The first sign that something out of the ordinary was stirring in Emily occurs in a letter of spring 1850 to an old friend, Jane Humphrey. It is a long letter, full of the inevitable posturing, but halfway through a more sincerely personal note is inserted, is in fact abruptly flung on the paper; it is clear that she is confessing, even if a little guardedly, that she has taken a lonely plunge into unfamiliar waters. She longs to see Jane again, she says, so that she can tell her of the new hopes she has so boldly embraced:

Oh Jennie, it would relieve me to tell you all, to sit down at your feet, and look in your eyes, and confess what *you only* shall know, an experience bitter and sweet, but the sweet did so beguile me—and life has had an aim, and the world has been too precious for your poor and striving sister! The winter was all one dream, and the spring has not yet waked me . . . do you dream from all this what I mean? Nobody *thinks* of the joy, nobody *guesses* it . . .

Jane Humphrey had been close to Emily since their Academy days, Jane serving there one year as a teacher, and the two had spent many an afternoon sitting on the steps of the school in rapt discussion of their futures. This cryptic outburst could hardly have failed to elicit from Jane an inquiry as to what the "aim" was all about, what so ecstatic in the winter's dream, but unfortunately there is a gap in the surviving correspondence just at this point; Emily's next letter to Jane does not occur until two years later. Nor do other letters of the time offer any overt explanation, though there are some faint echoes in her letters to Abiah. "You are growing wiser than I am," she commends her friend, "and nipping in the bud fancies which I let blossom." Sometime, then, in the early winter of 1849–50 something happened which had a transforming effect on Emily and her attitude toward the future. That something, beyond any doubt, was her first encounter with the novel, *Jane Eyre.*

Published to immediate general acclaim less than two years before, *Jane Eyre* had become standard fare for the bright young people of Amherst, and in the fall of 1849 Emily had borrowed a copy from her father's junior partner. She returned it in December with a tiny bouquet of leaves and a brief note that expressed her pleasure in typical lefthanded fashion: "If all these leaves were altars, and on every one a prayer that Currer Bell might be saved—and you were God—would you answer it?" At the time she read the novel she had been home from Mount Holyoke a year and a half, and while she had mixed more or less contentedly in village life, she had been feeling all the while some lack, some emptiness in her existence, a mood not helped by the pairing-off that was in steady progress around her, nor by Kimball's ungallant disappearance. Dimly aware that she possessed unusual abilities, though uncertain of their exact nature, impatient to discern in her stars something of loftiness, grandeur, exaltation, in the pages of the Brontë novel she came upon herself and all her vague desires mirrored to the life.

Jane Eyre was depicted as being exactly Emily's age, a small, frail girl excessively plain of face. Reading the book, Emily's eager eyes could not have traced the following words without a grim concurrence: "At eighteen most people wish to please, and the conviction that they have not an exterior likely to second that desire brings anything but gratification." And only a few pages further on she would have come upon another of Jane's recurring lamentations on the same topic. Explaining that to offset her lack of beauty she always took special pains to be neat and presentable, Jane candidly admits her impossible yearnings: "I sometimes wished to have rosy cheeks, a straight nose, and small cherry mouth; I desired to be tall, stately, and finely developed in figure; I felt it a misfortune that I was so little, so pale, and had features so irregular and marked." Here was Emily herself in her secret moments, bemoaning what she had once called her "gypsy face," and her identification with Jane could only have deepened as she followed the high-spirited girl's adventures, of a type then unique in literature.

The graphically described death of Jane's friend, Helen Burns, would have taken Emily back to her own attendance at the bedside of Sophia Holland, and Jane's exuberant and often expressed rapture in the sights and sounds of the natural world would have raised passionate echoes in Emily's sensitive heart. It can be taken for granted that like most contemporary readers of the book—unspoiled by the clouds of later imitators—Emily thrilled to the wild figure of the lunatic wife on the third floor of Thornfield Manor. But what impressed her most and stayed with her, working its subtle confirmation of her own dimly felt ideas, was the boldly asserted belief that life held, or should hold, larger opportunities for educated women than cooking and housework and the cultivation of genteel minor talents.

When Jane stands on the roof at Thornfield and gazes out over the countryside beyond the sequestering hills, she voices aspirations that were already very much in Emily's thoughts, in words that Emily herself might have used as she stared from her window at the low outline of the distant Pelham range. "I longed for a power of vision," cries Jane as she casts her eye along the low skyline, "which might overpass that limit; which might reach the busy world, towns, regions, full of life I had heard of but never seen . . . the restlessness was in my nature; it agitated me to pain sometimes." Not being able at that point to fulfill the yearning, Jane takes refuge in "a tale that was never ended—a tale my imagination created, and narrated continuously; quickened with all of incident, life, fire, feeling, that I desired and had not in my actual existence." Jane Eyre, of course, manages finally to live up to all this intensity, no doubt quickening by her fictional example more than one of her young female readers. Women, she declares, "suffer from too rigid a constraint, too absolute a stagnation, precisely as men would suffer; and it is narrow-minded in their more privileged fellow-creatures to say that they ought to confine themselves to making puddings and knitting stockings, to playing on the piano and embroidering bags."

That staunch pronouncement echoed long and sonorously in

Emily's brain. Within a month or so of reading those words, she is complaining in a letter about the drudgery of housework and the narrowness of her Amherst neighbors, plaintively insisting that she inclines to far other things. "The path of duty looks very ugly indeed—and the place I want to go more amiable—a great deal." Many years later she was still able to remember the "electric" effect that Charlotte Brontë's story had produced on her,* and it is surely no coincidence that soon after reading it she severed her connection with the Amherst Sewing Society.

The aim she had found and the dream that had cast its golden haze over the winter was, of course, nothing less than a firm resolve to follow her already rising desire to be a poet. But the decision seems not to have come in a burst of dedication. Rather, hesitant and groping, it seeped into consciousness over a period of two or three months, finding expression at first in a general way—a heightened enthusiasm and a deepening discontent with the prosaic details of daily life. Beginning early in 1850 her letters take on an expansive cast and her accustomed soliloquizing becomes redolent of the emotional coloring of the style of *Jane Eyre*. Her high spirits bubble over into flights of sustained wit, in letters and valentines, where before this kind of playfulness had been thrown off in a sentence or two. In the midst of this euphoria, in February, she was presented with a surprise that must have delighted her: one of her valentines, a *jeu d'esprit* in prose addressed to a friend of her brother, found its way into the pages of the college magazine where it was introduced by the comment that the author, who remained anonymous, "must have some spell, by which she quickens the imagination." A small thing, inconsequential, yet coming when it did it seemed like an omen.

Though Newton had departed from Amherst, after first presenting Emily with a copy of Emerson's poems, she was not left without literary companions, particulary one Leonard Humphrey (the surname was fairly common in New England), a

* *Letters*, III, 775.

tutor at the college and former principal at the Academy where Emily had known him in her last year. Intensely intellectual, with high ambitions of his own, Humphrey was a frail, sickly young man of twenty-four who tended to be tongue-tied in groups and fiercely resented his social inadequacy, a combination of traits that in the perverse way of the era made him faintly romantic. With him Emily now arranged to continue her studies on a more formal basis; aside from a commendable desire to extend her knowledge, this action may have been an imitation of Jane Eyre's pupil-tutor relationship with the single-minded St. John Rivers. To a dog that Emily acquired about now she gave the name Carlo, the name of Rivers' setter in the novel, and she was soon referring to Humphrey as her "master," the designation Jane Eyre repeatedly uses for Rochester.

By April, perhaps encouraged by Humphrey, she was able to admit to herself at last that she did have an aim and her epistolary cry of joy to Jane Humphrey followed, though even then she could not bring herself to assume, even by anticipation, the name of poet. In a postscript to that letter she mentions that she still hasn't heard from Kimball and though rather hurt by his indifference, insists that she no longer cares: "Something else has helped me forget *that,* a something surer and higher." Amherst, during almost this entire year, was in the throes of a religious revival and many of the townspeople had responded, including Emily's own father and sister. But all this excitement left Emily supremely unruffled, shrugging off the hubbub and the questioning glances cast in her direction with the remark that she was "standing alone in rebellion and growing very careless." She had found something that transcended not only Kimball's indifference but the too-insistent call of the church and her own acute sense of personal deficiency. She had found poetry—the mask that would, as she fervently believed, transform her gypsy face.

Higher her ambition was, yet its realization hardly surer, as she recognized, and the transformation had still to vie with the annoying and often wearisome details of living. Though she floated rapturously through the year that followed her reading of *Jane Eyre,* she was brought to earth now and then by the inescapable bustle around her. In the spring of 1850, with Vinnie departed for her turn at boarding school, Mrs. Dickinson fell ill, and the burden of her care, as well the time-consuming task of running the house, fell on Emily. Resigned to this martyrdom, she plodded through her duties until one bright day in May Austin's friend, George Gould, arrived at the house to take her for a carriage ride in the woods, where there would be talk of poetry and life and all manner of misty musings. At the sink washing dishes when she heard his knock, she told her caller sorrowfully that she couldn't leave the house because of her mother. When Gould insisted that it would be all right, "the tears came into my eyes," and then, as she continued the story in a letter to Abiah Root, the little incident acquired the tensions of high tragedy:

Oh I struggled with great temptation, and it cost me much of denial, but I think in the end I conquered, not a glorious victory, Abiah, where you hear the rolling drum, but a kind of helpless victory, where triumph would come of itself, faintest music, weary soldiers, nor a waving flag, nor a long-loud shout. I had read of Christ's temptations, and how they were like our own, only he didn't sin; I wondered if *one* was like mine, and whether it made him angry—I couldn't make up my mind; do you think he ever did? I went cheerfully round my work, humming a little air till mother had gone to sleep, then I cried with all my might.

Six months later the tears came again, this time with better reason. Leonard Humphrey, on a short visit to his home in Weymouth, died suddenly of congestion of the brain and the news shocked all his friends in Amherst. Emily threw her own dismay into another studied letter to Abiah, prophesying that now there would be no sunshine or bird-song in the coming spring and promising to be out early herself in order to fill up the deficiency. "I shall love to call the bird there if it has gentle music, and the meekest-eyed wild flowers, and the low plaintive insect. How *precious* the grave, Abiah, when aught that we love is laid there, and affection would fain go too, if that the lost were lonely!" However, she guessed correctly that loneliness was not one of the problems of the lost and offered, instead, her fast-falling tears. They were the only tribute, she murmured, she could render her departed friend and tutor—then changed her mind and decided a short verse might be in order:

> Sexton! My Master's sleeping here,
> Pray lead me to his bed!
> I came to build the bird's nest
> And sow the early seed
>
> That when the snow creeps slowly
> From off his chamber door
> Daisies point the way there,
> And the troubadour.

Written as she entered her twentieth year, the poem arose directly from the sentiments expressed in the letter, and though Humphrey's death had indeed been a sad one, it was not the blighted hopes beneath the sod of which Emily sang. She could feel only her own sadness. Herself in the act of decorating the anonymous grave was the limit of her vision.

• •

On Amity Street in Amherst, a few minutes' walk from the Dickinson house, there lived the family of William Cutler, which included his young sister-in-law Susan Gilbert. One of the most sought-after young ladies in the town, Sue Gilbert was everything that Emily dreamed of being. Darkly attractive if not exactly pretty, she breathed an air of independence bred by an unsettled childhood and the early loss of both parents. Self-assured and at ease in company, she was a graceful and captivating talker, maintained a discriminating interest in the arts, particularly painting, and a passionate devotion to literature. She was also talented as a mathematician, so much so that one expert had advised her to develop the gift. The adjective most often used to describe Sue was "rare," and in her combination of qualities she seems to have been precisely that.

She had come back to Amherst from her aunt's house in Geneva, New York, in 1847, the friendship between her and Emily probably beginning the following year, perhaps through the attendance of both girls at the Sewing Society. The fascination Sue exerted on Emily was immediate, and on her own part, Sue was quite taken by Emily's articulateness, her flashing wit, and, beneath the breathless posturing, the fine sensitivity of her mind. But it was not only Emily who attached herself to Sue: the whole Dickinson family opened their hearts to her, treating her as one born to them. Vinnie at one point, though she already possessed greater physical beauty and conversational talents almost as lively, admitted that she wanted nothing more than to be just like Sue. The father showed her a particular deference of the same sort that he bestowed on his own two daughters, and Austin—who was among the two or three most eligible bachelors in town—lowered his sights on the girl soon after his graduation from Amherst College in 1850.

Emily continued friendly with the other girls of her circle, but with Sue she began to share something special, particularly after the experience with *Jane Eyre*. They walked much, talked much about books and reading, and before long concluded that they would make their assault on the future together, "a little destiny to have for our own," as Emily phrased it.* That the destiny concerned the writing of poetry is clear enough from the letters that passed between them in the following years, though the fact is not openly stated: they amused themselves, as Emily remarked, with "the fancy that we are the only poets and everyone else is *prose*." In an ebullient mood she declares

* *Letters*, I, 144.

her happiness in their shared belief that there was "a big *future* waiting for me and you."*

It is also abundantly clear that Emily's dedication was in large part sustained—if indeed it was not in some measure prompted—by Sue's own steady optimism, an indispensable quality not overly prominent in her friend's normal outlook. In September 1851, despite her family's opposition, Sue left Amherst for Baltimore where she had taken a teaching position in order to earn her own living. She was away for nearly a year, Emily sending her frequent lengthy letters that overflowed with her accustomed affection, but couched in unusually extravagant terms. To modern ears the incessant declarations of love and dependence sound almost unhealthy—until it is realized that this time *both* girls are indulging in fantasy. Before Sue's departure the two had pored lovingly together over the pages of Longfellow's recently-published *Kavanagh*, a sentimental story of girlhood devotion and village life in which two young women are drawn together by the mysterious power that mystically selects friends in youth. Taking long walks they mutually reveal their most secret hopes and exchange long, impassioned letters. "In a word," explains Longfellow, "they were in love with each other," but the relationship was no more than an innocent "rehearsal in girlhood of the great drama of woman's life."

Emily's letters to Sue were thus a conscious indulgence joined in by her friend. But the pose included some truth: without Sue's bolstering presence the future they had dreamed appeared far less certain, village life faded from the romantic glow it possessed in Longfellow's tale, and imagination itself began to droop. "When you are gone from me," Emily confessed, "all life looks differently, and the faces of my fellows are not the same they wear when you are with me. I think it is this, dear Susie; you sketch my pictures for me, and 'tis at their sweet colorings, rather than this dim real that I am used, so you see, when you go away, the world looks staringly and I find I need more vail."

* *Letters*, I, 195.

After a year's unhappy trial at teaching Sue gave up, returned to Amherst for good, and began once more to "poetize" in daily association with Emily. A second welcome surprise, in the meantime, had come to Emily when another of her valentines, a typical nonsense poem, turned up in the pages of *The Springfield Republican*, a newspaper of note. Again it was anonymous and again the editor introduced it with praise, actually inviting further contributions from the unknown author. All the signs continued propitious.

But neither girl for a moment entertained the notion that the pursuit of poetry should involve seclusion or any curtailment of social life. There were parties, candy-pulls, and dances to attend, sleigh-rides and sugaring-offs in season, and musical evenings at which Emily played the piano. There were lectures and concerts at the college and in the surrounding towns—Emily heard the touring Jenny Lind in Northampton and sniffed at her voice as no better than the home-grown variety. There was a village Reading Club which seems to have concentrated on Shakespeare, and in good weather there were frequent rides in the hills, both by carriage and on horseback.

The Dickinson house itself provided no refuge even if Emily had wanted one, for its doors were always open to a constant stream of visitors—numerous relatives, her father's associates, and the omnipresent young men from the college. During term time there were few afternoons or evenings which did not see two or three students, perhaps some older tutor or one of the budding lawyers from her father's office, come sauntering unannounced into the Dickinson yard. The names of these otherwise anonymous young gentlemen are enshrined in Emily's letters of this time, running through them like a minor refrain—Root, Storrs, Harrington, Howland, Emerson, Spencer, Thompson—all of them destined soon to fade from the scene, unaware of their brush with immortality, to be forgotten in later decades even by the Dickinsons themselves. Among all these faceless youths, however, there was one, Henry Emmons, who deserved a better fate than the relative obscurity he has found. Emmons lived to a great old age, dying in 1912 at eighty. If, in his last years, he secretly believed that he was the one who had broken Emily's heart, turning her to seclusion and poetry, it would have been understandable—not quite true, but within the limits of his knowledge, understandable. For Emily almost certainly had been in love with him and very probably had expected to become his wife.

Emmons arrived at Amherst College in the fall of 1850 as a freshman, but did not, it seems, make his first visit to the Dickinson house till the following fall, when he became friendly with Emily's cousin, John Graves, also a student. About a year younger than Emily, he had a bluff sort of handsomeness and was well-rounded in his tastes, being equally attracted to good books, fine horses and warm friends; devoted to the classics, he was also becoming an accomplished linguist.* To Emily he must have appeared perfect and their friendship was in full swing shortly after their first meeting. In early February she reports to Austin that she went for a ride "last evening with *Sophomore Emmons,* alone; I will tell you all about it when I write again." The condescending label she affixes to his name was only meant to hide her pleasure from her brother; a second mention a few days later to Sue in Baltimore is more honest: "I've found a beautiful new friend," she says, "and I've told him about dear Susie, and promised to let him know you so soon as you shall come."

Throughout that year and the next, Emmons' frequent presence in the Dickinson house is easily traced, as well as carriage rides and long walks with him, and it is now that visions of marriage, with its blisses and uncertainties, first begin to intrude in Emily's letters. Writing to Sue in the summer of 1852 she reports a conversation she had on the subject the previous evening with Sue's sister. In the middle of the letter, she breaks into a paean on the wedded state, couched inevitably in her own over-

* *New England Quarterly,* XVI, 1943.

blown language but at bottom obviously sincere. "Those unions, my dear Susie," she exults, "by which two lives are one, this sweet and strange adoption wherein we can but look, and are not yet admitted, how it can fill the heart and make it gang wildly beating, how it will take *us* one day, and make us all its own, and we shall not run away from it, but lie still and be happy!" The possible erotic connotation, no doubt unconscious, in the closing words of the passage, may indicate—without pursuing the implications too ardently—that her conception of such matters, at this stage at least, was a peculiarly passive one, juvenile in fact. The letter continues with a revealing mixture of ecstasy and apprehension:

You and I have been strangely silent upon this subject, Susie, we have often touched upon it and as quickly fled away, as children shut their eyes when the sun is too bright for them . . . How dull our lives must seem to the bride, and the plighted maiden, whose days are fed with gold, and who gathers pearls every evening; but to the *wife*, Susie, sometimes the *wife forgotten*, our lives perhaps seem dearer than all others in the world . . . Oh, Susie, it is dangerous, and it is all too clear, these simple, trusting spirits, and the spirits mightier, which we cannot resist! It does so rend me, Susie, the thought of it when it comes, that I tremble lest at sometime I, too, am yielded up.

It is no strain on conjecture to see this letter as marking Emily's first tentative, even frightened admission to herself that she was falling in love. Is she herself not the trusting spirit who "cannot resist!" and Emmons the mightier one? The fears she expresses are transparently those of a committed young woman only too ready to be yielded up but too uncertain of her appeal to overcome the doubts which plague her. There was little she could do, of course, about her personal appearance except to fuss with her hair and dress more becomingly—almost at the same time that Emily was admitting her doubts to Sue, Vinnie was telling

Austin, with sisterly latitude, that "Emilie's hair is cut off and she's very pretty."

Though he had no literary ambitions himself, and little talent in that direction, Emmons was addicted to the writing of occasional verse, and he and Emily were soon commenting on each other's productions: she thanks him for allowing her to see his "beautiful writing" and lends him in return a "little manuscript" of her own. Continually they exchanged books and discussed their reading, and for Emily it must all have seemed too grand, with love and literature present in equal parts. Both family and friends by this time were well aware of what was happening (a gratuitous assertion, but people are not so blind as scholars, looking back, incline to think) and probably sensed that something of a permanent nature was in the offing. Austin, writing from law school at Cambridge, expressed his approval. Emily, pleased at the approbation, replied that she was "glad you are glad that I went to ride with Emmons. I went again with him one evening while father was gone, and had a beautiful ride." Further family consent to the developing situation was expressed silently: as Chief Marshall of the important Amherst Cattle Show held in October 1853, Austin selected Emmons to be his aide.

At this juncture, in fact, Mr. Dickinson had probably begun to feel easier about the futures of both his daughters. Vinnie had already reached an understanding with another young man, Joseph Lyman, a friend of Austin's, and was waiting patiently for him to return from the south where he had gone to complete his education. Now Emily, to all appearances, was about to make a choice. But it all came to nothing. Lyman never returned to Vinnie and she never married. And Emmons, as he was nearing graduation in the late summer of 1854, became engaged to a girl from a nearby town.

Exactly what happened and how, is not clear; the available evidence, though tantalizing, is less than abundant. As late as January 1854 Emmons and Emily were still sharing rides, visits and books and were attending lectures together. For Valentine's

Day Emily sent him not one of her usual elaborately joking productions but a fancifully embossed sheet saying simply "Please, Sir, to let me be a *Valentine* to thee." Then for six months darkness settles down. When at length the two can be seen in contact again Emily is discovered making a valiant and determined effort to be nice to Emmons' fiancee, Susan Phelps, who had arrived in Amherst in August to attend the graduation ceremonies. For the obscure half-year between, only two seemingly unrelated facts are at hand, but these, if viewed in connection with events before and after, may complete the picture of lost hopes and broken promises—though the promises were perhaps no more than implied.

Emily's father, after a hiatus of some ten years, had returned to politics, winning election to the House of Representatives in December 1853. Early the next year, at about the time Emmons must have begun paying serious attention to Susan Phelps—a girl he had known for some undetermined length of time—Mr. Dickinson invited his family to join him in Washington for an extended visit. All but Emily eagerly accepted. She refused to go and arrangements had to be made for her to remain at home, with Sue Gilbert moving into the house to keep her company and John Graves appointed to look in each evening. The family— Mrs. Dickinson, Vinnie and Austin—departed early in April and were away about six weeks. No letters, whether from Emily to the family or the reverse, have survived from this time (a curious gap, since many must have been written) so that these six crucial weeks are nearly a complete blank.

Alone, the girls seem to have enjoyed themselves generally: the house, empty and noiseless, was a gloomy place, prompting nervous amusement in Emily and her companion as they managed to "frighten each other to death nearly every night." Some evenings were passed with Emily at the piano entertaining her cousin, John Graves, but whether her audience included Emmons at any time, or whether he came to the house at all, are points open only to surmise. Emily was, however, definitely in some sort of depression during a part of these weeks, though the specific reasons for it were never allowed to surface. A note written to Sue, which is undated but which has been assigned to this year, is marked by its opening words as relating to a time when the girls were together. More sober in tone than was Emily's custom, it hints at some primary dim disturbance behind what appears to be a trivial rift:

Sue—you can go or stay—there is but one alternative—We differ often lately, and this must be the last. You need not fear to leave me lest I should be alone, for I often part with things I fancy I have loved— sometimes to the grave, and sometimes to an oblivion rather bitterer than death—thus my heart bleeds so frequently that I shant mind the hemorrhage, and I only add an agony to several previous ones, and at the end of day remark—a bubble burst! . . .

The departed images of Humphrey and Newton, and some of the other friends she had recently lost to the grave, are in those words. But more than all the grave had claimed from her, she here laments the bitter encroachment of an earthly loss—the oblivion that had overtaken her three-years' idyl. It is the fast-fading image of Henry Emmons that dominates the thought in that passage.

Sometime in May or June the official news of Emmons' engagement reached Amherst. And it is here that the second of the two stray facts assumes a sudden relevance. John Graves, Emmons' good friend and the one who had been responsible for the introduction to Emily, became embroiled in a quarrel of unknown nature with Emmons and the association ceased.

Almost at the same time a letter arrived from Abiah Root, who had been out of touch for years, inviting Emily to come for a visit. The answer, read against the background of Emmons' engagement, takes on a more understandable meaning than that so often given to it: far from being the earliest definite sign of her ultimate withdrawal, it indicates only the wistful depression of a hurt spirit unable or unwilling as yet to banish regret. Calling herself "your quaint, old-fashioned friend," she thanks Abiah for the invitation, then overplays her refusal: "I thank you, Abiah, but I don't go from home, unless emergency leads me by the hand, and then I do it obstinately, and draw back if I can. Should I ever leave home, which is improbable, I will with much delight accept your invitation."

Bravely facing her loss, but moved by inevitable curiosity, during Commencement Week Emily asked to meet Sue Phelps. Emmons complied, a little unwillingly it may be guessed, and the two girls spent a day at the Dickinson house "very sweetly." After graduation Susan left town, but Emmons remained behind for a while, seeing Emily a number of times, and it was during one of his last visits that she was told of a reconciliation between Graves and Emmons. "Tears of happiness came shining in my eyes," she remembered, "forgiving one another as Jesus—us." When it was all over she poured out her feelings to Sue Gilbert who was away on a visit: Commencement Week had brought her much of sweetness, "much too that was dusty." She and Emmons had spent long hours alone in serious talk and had shared a farewell ride—then, almost as if she cannot stop the pen, she murmurs, "I shall miss Emmons very much."

While this is the last time his name occurs in her letters, it is not the end of the tale. Some six years later, shortly after Emmons' ordination to the ministry, Susan Phelps broke off their engagement. Hearing of this, Emily dispatched to the girl a one-line note quoting a passage from Isaiah: "When thou goest through the waters, I will go with thee." Thereafter, until Sue Phelps's death in 1865, Emily and she considered themselves intimates.

How crushing all this was for Emily will perhaps never be known. It is worth noting that she now began paying weekly visits to her minister, visits which for some reason displeased her brother and sister. Such a resort to a spiritual adviser was, to say the least, uncharacteristic, though there may have been simple enough reasons for it. On the other hand, far from disliking to

leave home, as she had told Abiah Root, she twice paid visits outside Amherst in the next six months. The first was a brief stay in
September with family friends in Springfield. The second was a
lengthy jaunt with Vinnie to Washington and Philadelphia, her
longest absence from Amherst to then.

Washington, where the girls arrived early in February and put
up at the famous Willard's hotel, was a revelation, Emily's first
mature experience of busy cosmopolitan society. They remained
for three weeks, mixing gaily with the other guests at Willard's
and being steered through a round of parties and meetings by
their father. To Emily it was all a wonderful blur of elegance and
grandeur, a pageant of "sweet ladies and gentlemen, who have
taken us by the hand and smiled upon us pleasantly." The names
of some of these people are known, but only one deserves to be
recorded, if only for the contrast of celebrities that it provides.
This was the Chief Justice, Roger Taney, with whom the Dickinsons shared dinner one evening and over whom the clouds of
the Dred Scott case had already begun to gather. If it is hard to
picture the dour Taney smiling, it is even harder to imagine what
he and Emily talked about, though it is on record that she did attempt one little joke. When a flaming pudding was brought to
the table she inquired of the austere Taney, "Oh sir, may one
eat of hell-fire with impunity here?"—which sounds very much
like a nervous effort to loosen up a stiff conversation. Of the two
sisters, it was Vinnie who blossomed most; she was remembered
as the center of a group at Willard's quite taken by her unique
wit and mimic talent. With all the excitement Emily, too, began
to feel "gayer than I was before," and the words indicate that a
search for just such an improvement may have been the whole
purpose of the trip.

Among the many novelties encountered, Emily's most memorable experience, a little surprisingly, was a visit to Mount Vernon. Two or three days before the interlude at the capital ended,
she and her sister joined an excursion party bound for Washington's home, and a couple of weeks later she described it for the

Hollands. In her narration, it should be noticed, both she and Vinnie have unaccountably regressed to the status of carefree little girls:

I will tell you how on one soft spring day we glided down the Potomac in a painted boat, and jumped upon the shore—how hand in hand we stole along up a tangled pathway till we reached the tomb of General George Washington, how we paused beside it, and no one spoke a word, then hand in hand, walked on again, not less wise or sad for that marble story; how we went within the door—raised the latch he lifted when he last went home—thank the ones in light that he's since passed in through a brighter wicket! Oh, I could spend a long day, if it did not weary you, telling of Mount Vernon.

The scene is daintily sketched, probably mentioned in the first place for the benefit of Dr. Holland who took an interest in such matters, but it hardly seems to be describing two young ladies approaching their mid-twenties. The child-pose, frequently noticeable in these years, was a mask Emily was not to discard until much later, to the disgruntlement of critics who, even while dealing with her weightiest utterances, have found their solemn interpretations stumbling over the litter of these childish moods.

Leaving Washington after the adjournment of Congress on March 5, the girls proceeded to Philadelphia where they had been invited to spend some time with the Lyman Colemans, old family friends. They arrived in Philadelphia on the same day, were still there on the 18th and undecided about when they would return home. The length of their stay, obviously not important in itself, becomes a matter of some moment because it was during this stopover that Emily, supposedly, met the married clergyman with whom, again supposedly, she fell instantly and irrevocably in love.

The Reverend Charles Wadsworth, forty years old, plain of face and diffident of manner, but powerful in voice and in his effect on those who heard him preach, was pastor of the Arch Street Church where the Colemans worshipped. That Emily attended the church with Vinnie and her hosts is probable, since there were at least two Sundays included in her stay and perhaps three. It is also possible that she was introduced to Wadsworth at the Coleman house, scarcely five minutes' walk from the church. But first-hand evidence covering this period is miniscule in any event, and Wadsworth figures in none of it. Only one of Emily's letters from Philadelphia, written on the evening of Sunday the 18th, has survived, and if she had encountered him by this time she was not moved enough to record the fact. The hypothetically fateful meeting may have taken place, of course, after the 18th, but whether or not there really was a meeting, one thing is certain: the innocent Reverend Wadsworth could never have dreamed of the particular style of immortality that was to be conferred on him by his parishioner's frail guest. In any case, by the last days of March the two girls had left Philadelphia and returned to Amherst. Five years were to pass before Wadsworth would put in his first definite appearance on the scene.

The red brick house on Main Street, in the meantime, had been reacquired by Edward Dickinson, and in November, redecorated, it stood ready to receive back its old tenants. For any family settled long in one place such a move becomes a hectic disturbance, and for Emily it seems to have involved even more complex feelings, chief among which was an unnamed, perhaps unnameable fear. But her report of the move at the time was lighthearted enough. "I believe my 'effects' were brought in a bandbox," she recalled, and the 'deathless me' on foot not many moments after . . . It is a kind of *gone-to-Kansas* feeling, and if I sat in a long wagon, with my family tied behind, I should suppose without doubt I was a party of immigrants!" Among the effects in that box, very probably, there was a bundle of manuscript, representing the fruits of her six years of dedicated poetic effort. As she settled into her new surroundings, arranging her things in the large bedroom on the second floor, perhaps she took time to look through those manuscripts. If she did, and if she read with an honest eye, she would have found little to encourage her.

Awash with mawkish sentimentality, festooned with all the excesses of the flaccid romanticism that had overpowered the age, the fifty or so poems that can be identified from this early period express only the commonplaces of the era in less than commonplace form. The simple quatrain, which she had modeled on Calvinist hymnology, was the height of her metric ambition and ability. Weakly conceived ruminations on life, love and death twine together in a helpless, ineffectual spiral of feigned involvement, all thickly overspread with a soporific blend of butterflies, sunsets, flowers, bees and birds. She asks

> Have you got a brook in your little heart,
> Where bashful flowers blow,
> And blushing birds go down to drink
> And shadows tremble so?

and asks it, presumably, without blushing herself. Gazing on her own image with tender self-pity—almost, the reader feels, with her head hanging to one side in true melancholy style—she broods:

> Nobody knows this little rose;
> It might a pilgrim be
> Did I not take it from the ways
> And lift it up to thee.
>
> Only a bee will miss it,
> Only a butterfly
> Hastening from far journey
> On its breast to lie.
>
> Only a bird will wonder,
> Only a breeze will sigh:
> Ah little rose, how easy
> For such as thee to die!

She is herself, of course, the neglected and forgotten little flower, still trudging wearily on her pilgrimage to the longed-for status as a poet. Wit and attempts at humor, of the kind that often sparkles authentically in her letters, also occur in this early work, but it is dulled by its transference to verse, becoming mere persiflage. There was hardly enough distinction in most of these early poems, in fact, to win them a place in the village newspaper, and there are signs that Emily, as she approached her twenty-sixth birthday, was only too keenly aware of her failure.

Yet, miraculously, within a year or so she suddenly began to produce an entirely different kind of poetry—concise, enigmatic, full of subtle insight and piercing commentary on the human condition, her vision enlarged to universal sympathies, her power of expression focused startlingly to flame. Every serious student of her work has noticed this abrupt metamorphosis, this astonishing assumption of wings. One of the most respected among them aptly remarks that it came "without warning or transition . . . badinage and nonsense are suddenly replaced by penetrating observation and pithy comment."[*] But like all the others who have attempted to interpret Emily Dickinson and her art, this critic, too, was unperturbed by the lightning change—more striking, surely, than the rapid development of Keats—and he sought no further for an explanation. In reality it constitutes the paramount mystery of her life.

How and when did this sentimental versifier, this admittedly clever but disturbingly precious, unprofound and often childish young woman, blossom into a poet of major accomplishment? From what secret resource did she so swiftly wring the power to produce work possessing, as one commentator put it, "almost total originality," work that would earn her wide recognition as perhaps the greatest of female poets? That, clearly, is a riddle worth the unraveling, and the solution, as it turns out, sheds light on much else that is dark and perplexing in the changeling of Amherst.

[*] Anderson, 5.

· 3 ·

AND SHATTER ME WITH DAWN

WHEN SUE GILBERT and Austin Dickinson were married in the summer of 1856 and moved into the house built for them next to the Dickinson mansion, Emily was not only delighted but relieved. For a time Austin had considered taking his bride west, where opportunities for growth were unlimited, and Emily had been faced with the dismal prospect of losing two of the small group of people who were most necessary to her. In the end, after a quick inspection trip to Michigan, enticed by his father's offer of law partnership and a new house, and perhaps with Emily's entreaties ringing in his ears, he had decided for the security of Amherst. "If God had been here this summer," Emily wrote a friend soon after the couple had set up housekeeping, "and seen the things that I have seen, I guess that He would think His paradise superfluous."

Yet for all her vicarious joy in the bliss next door, there was reason for melancholy within her own walls. Mrs. Dickinson, never robust, had sunk during the year into a chronic illness which for some time was to keep her in and out of bed and which cast a settled foreboding over the Dickinson hearth. And Vinnie, after a more or less patient five-year wait for the return of Joseph Lyman, and having turned down at least one offer of marriage in the interim, had finally learned that he was engaged to a southern girl. She had known Lyman ever since he first came to the house as a boy, Austin's bosom friend, and the unexpected news of his engagement brought on profound dejection. She did not give up hoping for a reversal of the situation, in fact, until Lyman's actual marriage some two years later. Afterward, when the die had been cast, all trace of the part Lyman had played in Vinnie's life was carefully wiped out (carrying along important documents relating to Emily) and it was only a chance discovery a century later —some papers in the possession of Lyman's descendants—that brought the story of Vinnie's heartbreak to light. The Dickinson house in the latter half of 1856, it can be seen, had become a rather somber place and Emily felt the full weight of the mood.

To Mrs. Holland at one point she confessed her low spirits. She had been reading the Bible, she said, and had come across a verse which told of a haven where "there were 'no tears' and I wished as I sat down tonight that we were *there* not *here*—and that wonderful world had commenced, which makes such promises." She had been familiar with the Bible from her childhood, but had always thought it, aside from its power of language, an "arid book;" now she began to see it as full of wisdom, shedding "great bars of sunlight in many a shady heart,"* her own especially. With the sadly contrasting fates of Vinnie and Austin in her mind, and herself facing a future of murky promise, she concluded that love, after all, seemed to be the answer to everything. "I had rather *be* loved," she told Mrs. Holland, "than be called a king in earth or a lord in Heaven," indicating that she may even have begun to question the value of her own long cherished literary ambitions. In October, making some effort to throw off their burdens, Vinnie and she together took part, for the first time, in the annual Cattle Show, Vinnie as one of the three judges of rye and Indian bread and Emily as an entrant in the same contest. (She won a second prize, but any suspicions of

---

* *Lyman Letters,* 73.

sisterly collusion should be weighed against her later admitted proficiency in the art.)

The letter to Mrs. Holland, written in August, offers the last certain glimpse into Emily's youth. Another letter of definite date, or even of any significance, does not occur for nearly two years, and there are no other sources of information. What she was doing, thinking, feeling between the summer of 1856 and the summer of 1858 remains provokingly obscure. The least-known period of her life, it is also the most important, for at the end of it she had at last become a true poet. Fortunately the clues for penetrating it are available and though they are circumstantial, they are neither doubtful nor difficult to follow. In fact it is quite incredible, considering the impressive and relentlessly expanding mass of Dickinson scholarship, that this trail has remained so long unobserved and unpursued.

It begins with a poem Emily wrote sometime in the latter half of 1861. The pertinent stanzas describe an awesomely pivotal experience:

> I think I was enchanted
> When first a sombre girl
> I read that Foreign Lady:
> The Dark felt beautiful
>
> And whether it was noon at night,
> Or only Heaven at noon,
> For very lunacy of Light
> I had not power to tell.
>
> . . . . .
>
> The days to mighty metres stept,
> The homeliest adorned
> As if unto a sacrament
> 'Twere suddenly ordained.
>
> I could not have defined the change:
> Conversion of the mind,

Like sanctifying in the soul,
Is witnessed, not explained . . .

First published in 1935, the poem expresses Emily's well-known feeling for the verse of Elizabeth Barrett Browning, but it says nothing about just when she first read the foreign lady, does not name the work that brought on her "conversion of the mind," or in what that conversion consisted. Mrs. Browning had enjoyed world-wide fame for fifteen years prior to her death in mid-1861 and in that time had produced a steady flow of volumes. Emily could have read her anywhere from the age of fourteen, and in fact could scarcely have escaped being aware of her in the ensuing years. Sue Dickinson was a very early admirer of Mrs. Browning, for instance, owned copies of many of her works, and continued as a devotee even when that lofty reputation began to descend with the fading century. In the first flush of the friendship between the two girls there must have been much fervent talk about the Englishwoman, but nowhere, neither in her letters nor in the reminiscences of her friends, can Emily be heard uttering anything like a cry of discovery. Not until after Mrs. Browning's death did she permit herself any overt reference to the inspiration she had received, and judging by the poem quoted it was of nearly apocalyptic dimensions. To successfully identify the particular cause and time of this event, then, should afford some higher ground from which to view the puzzle of Emily's mysterious growth.

A close reading of all thirty-two lines of the poem reveals at least one which possesses some promise of hidden meanings: "The Dark felt beautiful." What precisely did this word "Dark," used in so unusual a context, mean to Emily, and why should she describe the Dark as beautiful? A guess might be made as to the probable meaning, but guessing is not necessary, and in any case would almost certainly lead to a distortion by displacement of emphasis. The answer can be found in Emily's own writings: throughout her poetry she makes frequent use of the word, often capitalized and always in some symbolic sense. Generally, she means by it a state of vague but enveloping uncertainty about life, a condition of blind groping toward some unpredictable future. That fits well with the verse in question, and the poem, then, to state it precisely, is an admission that some particular work of Mrs. Browning had cast a powerful beam of hope into her life, dissipating some unspecified gloom and regenerating her faith in herself almost as if she had received sacramental rebirth. This summary does not, however, bring out the precise meaning of "conversion," which for the moment may be left in abeyance.

With that explanation, another poem written about the same time promptly links itself with the enchanted Dark:

> Ourselves were wed one summer, dear;
> Your vision was in June,
> And when your little lifetime failed,
> I wearied, too, of mine,
>
> And, overtaken in the Dark
> Where you had put me down,
> By someone carrying a Light,
> I, too, received the Sign.
>
> 'Tis true our futures different lay:
> Your cottage faced the sun,
> While oceans and the north must be
> On every side of mine.
>
> 'Tis true your garden led the bloom,
> For mine in Frosts was sown,
> And yet one summer we were Queens;
> But you were crowned in June.

These lines, written to Sue, commemorate two events that took place almost simultaneously, and the first can hardly be anything else than Sue's actual marriage. The second, clearly involving Emily, refers to some cloudy circumstance—characterized as a nuptial but with a difference—that came to her when she was "overtaken in the Dark . . . By someone carrying a Light." Unless she enjoyed such encounters on an annual basis, this must be another reference to the original enchantment. At first glance, admittedly, there seems to be some confusion in the poem. She says that while both incidents occurred in the same summer, her own fate overtook her "in Frosts," and implies that wintry skies presided. But there is no confusion and it is Emily herself who again supplies the clue to her real meaning. For poets, she asserts elsewhere, "summer lasts a solid year," and she repeats the idea even more emphatically in the line "summer has two beginnings," specified as June and October.

Where she picked up the notion of a year-long summer, or what she meant by it, is beside the point just now. Pertinent here is the fact that it indicates unmistakably the precise time she was overtaken by the light-bearer, or—to reduce Emily's phrase to its earthly significance—was jolted by a first reading of some work of Mrs. Browning's. Sometime shortly after Sue's marriage, then, in the early winter of 1856 to be exact, at a time when Emily was experiencing a heavy depression of spirits and doubts about her future, she read something that overwhelmed her with all the transforming power of a religious conversion, and that left her feeling from that time on as in some way betrothed. The trail need be followed no further; the enchanter has been uncovered. In late October or early November 1856, Mrs. Browning's long, blank-verse melodrama *Aurora Leigh,* was published simultaneously on both sides of the Atlantic.

Few literary works have set sail so gloriously as this peculiar novel-in-verse. Everywhere it was greeted with an extravagant chorus of praise; it sent the critics reeling in astonishment, a reaction heightened by the fact that its author was a woman. Mrs. Browning had shown herself a female Shakespeare, it was agreed; Walter Savage Landor admitted being "half drunk with it," and the eminent Ruskin giddily pronounced the book "The greatest poem the century has produced in any language." It went through three large editions in two months and lending libraries were swamped with requests. Today, and with good reason, it has sunk completely out of sight, leaving not a wrack behind, but that is another story: for Emily and her contemporaries it remained the central argosy of nineteenth-century poetry.

Scooping up all the froth of mid-Victorian sensibility, the 350-page tale relates the now familiar epic of a young woman's much-thwarted struggle for personal fulfillment. In spirit, the plot is quite similar to *Jane Eyre,* and it even borrows its denouement— the blinding of the hero in the burning of his own home—from the earlier novel. (The coincidence was perceived by Mrs. Browning, it is said, with pained surprise and much earnest explanation.) But in place of Charlotte Brontë's brave little governess, Mrs. Browning supplies a high-born, attractive, well-educated young woman bent on winning literary fame, who gives herself fiercely to her ambition and is apt to enter on lengthy discussions of art and the artistic life, as well as politics, the sorry state of society, and the distressing burdens of religious doctrine. Shutting herself off from all distractions, Aurora retreats to a garret in Kensington where she flings herself into a relentless scribbling that, it seems, comes near to bringing on a nervous breakdown:

> The rose fell
> From either cheek, my eyes globed luminous
> Through orbits of blue shadow, and my pulse
> Would shudder along the purple-veinèd wrist
> Like a shot bird. Youth's stern, set face to face
> With youth's ideal . . . I worked on, on . . .

After about three years of this ferocious application, Aurora wins satisfying recognition as a poet, and the rest of the story takes her—with eyes again firmly in their sockets and blood pressure under control—through a series of more or less dramatic encounters, culminating in her marriage to the lover she had rejected in the beginning.

Emily's reaction to *Aurora Leigh,* when viewed in the atmosphere of her own times and the universal response the book evoked, is not really surprising. That she was not able to see through the clouds of adulation to the book's pedestrian heart is of a piece with her habitual poor footing in critical matters; in this case, moreover, she found enthusiastic agreement on her own doorstep. Both Sue and Austin, along with the rest of literate Amherst, fell completely under the book's spell and it may even have been Sue who recommended Mrs. Browning's masterpiece in the first place. But that Emily was indeed enchanted by it, as she confessed, haunted and transformed by it, and was not merely exaggerating a memory, is a fact that can now be amply supported by evidence beyond her own words. It was at this time, for instance, or soon after, that she began to arrange her hair in imitation of Mrs. Browning's famous ringlets, a practice she appears to have followed at intervals through the rest of her life, and it was not much after this that a treasured picture of the woman found a permanent place on her bedroom wall.

There is even a small but rather neat bit of evidence in connection with her handwriting, the gradual changes in which have received so much attention. Aurora, speaking to her cousin, remarks:

> I know your writing, Romney—recognize
> The open-hearted A, the liberal sweep
> Of the G . . .*

The Harvard experts who studied Emily's handwriting twenty years ago, in the hope of extracting a workable chronology from the changes in it, without any knowledge of this passage in *Aurora Leigh,* spotted two capital-letter innovations which, they claimed, made their first appearance about 1856. The A, they explained with technical precision, had become "similar to lower case *a,* rounded but not quite closed." The G also had taken on a new shape, showing a "more conventional form, with double loop to left of upright." It is obvious from a glance at the original

* Bk. II, 1134–1136.

manuscripts that these changes may also be described, less technically, as open-hearted and liberal. And the same thing seems to have happened to the lower case letters *d, g,* and *y,* all three of which became more "sweeping" in 1856.

With some assurance it can even be suggested that Emily's impressions of *Aurora Leigh* were so strong and her thinking about it so constant that her dreams became crowded with symbolism from the book. A poem which now survives only in a transcript made by Sue, and is therefore undatable, relates a strange incident which clearly could have taken place only in a dream, and which in fact is so labeled. Up to now it has been interpreted as an overt sexual fantasy, with innocent Emily not fully realizing the channel her thoughts had taken. It opens with her discovering a worm in her room—which, be it duly noted, is described as "pink, lank and warm"—upon which she proceeds to tether it by a string. Then,

> A trifle afterward
> A thing occurred
> I'd not believe it if I heard,
> But state with creeping blood:
> A snake with mottles rare
> Surveyed my chamber floor
> In feature as the worm before
> But ringed with power.
> The very string with which
> I tied him, too,
> When he was mean and new,
> That string was there.

Emily shrinks from the sight as the snake inquires hissingly, "Afraid of me?" He slithers toward her:

> I flew,
> Both eyes his way,
> Lest he pursue,

> Nor ever ceased to run
> Till in a distant town,
> Towns on from mine,
> I set me down.
> This was a dream.

The startling metamorphosis of the intruding worm into a serpent of compelling attraction has led more than one bemused critic to declare the lines a lightly disguised portrait of the male organ in erection. And that, of course, opens the doors to all sorts of interesting speculation, particularly when the last line—"This was a dream"—is discarded as a weak effort by Emily to take refuge in the freedom of the unconscious. The investigator who has been most intrigued by this possibility has managed to convict Emily of the following sexual handicaps: a dread of masculinity mixed with jealousy of its privileges, simultaneous horror and awe at the thought of an erection, a wish to retaliate against the threat of penetration, and a bad case of penis envy. From that he announces that Emily's real problem was a particularly painful menstrual process which embittered her view of the whole universe by regularly reminding her that she was not a man. His argument, of course, is not so bald as this summary of it, but it is at best a trembly sort of thing, and in the end rests squarely on this poem for its effect.*

There can be no doubt that the verse describes a real dream, and that last, quite inartistic, line almost certainly does not even belong to it: it was probably added by Sue in an effort to explain what obviously needed explanation (the entire manuscript exists only in her hand) after a talk with her sister-in-law. That there thus may be some admixture of sexual fantasy in the lines is possible, since dream material frequently carries multiple significance. But the truth is that symbolic worms and snakes occur throughout *Aurora Leigh*, and there are even a number of references to the Lamia, that changeful demon of myth, with its glim-

* Griffith, 273–301.

Emily Dickinson at 17 (1848)
The only known portrait
Amherst College Library

Lavinia Dickinson
about 1856
Houghton Library

Mabel Loomis Todd
about 1885
Jones Library, Amherst

Susan Dickinson
about 1856
Houghton Library

Austin Dickinson
about 1856
Houghton Library

Otis Lord
about 1875
Houghton Library

Edward Dickinson, 1874
Jones Library, Amherst

Rev. Charles Wadsworth
Presbyterian Historical Society

mering "serpent-skin." Mrs. Browning's worms always stand for
the earth-bound spirit, while her snakes serve various illustrative
purposes, and Emily's poem thus becomes the record of a simple
wish-fulfillment dream. Though the specific elements that might
permit a fuller interpretation are now beyond recovery, it was
evidently connected in some way with her reawakened literary
hopes. The powerful, mottled snake perhaps represents the full-
blown poetic fame she yearned for, which, naturally enough, results in driving her from the cramping obscurity of her own house
and village to a "distant town"—probably Boston, then America's
literary capital. Being, in dream, thus compelled and driven by
success into a wider world than Amherst, any necessary repudiation of the old values, of the woman's traditional role, is without
guilt.

It is no cause for wonder that Emily should have dreamed
about *Aurora Leigh;* her reaction to it as a source of inspiration
has scarcely a parallel in the lives of other writers. Mrs. Browning
gave back to her, she says in another poem, the "perfect, paralyz-
ing bliss" of poetic ambition which thereafter loomed in her
mind as the "supremest earthly sum." She was struck as if by
lightning, maimed in spirit and robbed of her ability to enjoy
ordinary things, yet "loved the cause that slew." Playing on the
name Aurora, she says it was

> As if I asked the Orient
> Had it for me a morn,
> And it should lift its purple dikes
> And shatter me with Dawn!

Much later, looking back from a distance of more than twenty
years, she finally found the only adequate symbol for what had
taken place: *Aurora Leigh,* to her, had been the heavenly vision
that felled, blinded and converted St. Paul on the road to Da-
mascus.

True, it all gets to be just a little hysterical, but the very excess of Emily's passionate response prompts deeper curiosity. Though her liking for *Aurora Leigh* has been recognized before this, it was thought to have been a part of her general attitude toward Mrs. Browning, and it has always proved a mite embarrassing for those who wished she could have picked a worthier object of devotion. One investigator, searching for traces that could be linked to Emily's work, performed the brave task of reading through the book's eleven thousand lines and managed to turn up some fifteen isolated images, a few of them rather questionable, which Emily had worked into perhaps thirty separate poems. This result was about what might have been expected, since the two women were worlds apart in their approach to the poetic art, Mrs. Browning usually favoring the large utterance, and Emily restricting herself to the quick gasp or sigh. On this evidence, Emily's profound entanglement with *Aurora Leigh* seemed to be a purely emotional experience, rather like a child wandering in a lush forest, too overcome with its wild grandeur to disturb the flowers, yet insensibly absorbing its fresh odors and tones of light, here and there delicately caressing a petal. But another, more careful reading of Mrs. Browning's book reveals a situation that can only be termed staggering. Emily's business in that enchanted preserve was not nearly so innocent as it has appeared, nor did she bear home from it a mere posy; rather she determinedly returned again and again to appropriate armloads of its blossoms.

To a mind steeped in Emily's verse, attuned to the bare sense underlying its gnomic expression, the reading of *Aurora Leigh* is an amazing experience. From beginning to end of Mrs. Browning's book Emily's low, breathless voice is everywhere, tantalizing as the piping call of a gyrating, unseen bird. Now it is clear and close by, again muted and far-off; sometimes it blends with Mrs. Browning's occasional vigor, then drifts easily in harmonious counterpoint. On the very first page the tale's heroine remarks:

> I have not so far left the coasts of life
> To travel inland, that I cannot hear
> The murmur of the outer Infinite . . .

And Emily, snatching up the equation between geography and life, gives it a name and molds it to:

> Exultation is the going
> Of an inland soul to sea,
> Past the houses, past the headlands,
> Into deep eternity . . .

On the next page Aurora, describing her childhood, says

> I felt a mother-want about the world,
> And still went seeking . . .
> As restless as a nest-deserted bird
> Grown chill with something being away, though what
> It knows not . . .

And Emily's voice is heard in plaintive agreement:

> A loss of something ever felt I:
> The first that I could recollect
> Bereft I was, of what I knew not . . .

The same poem has the phrase, "fainter, too, as wiseness is," and on page three of *Aurora Leigh*, a few lines below the passage quoted, this line appears: "not as wisely since less foolishly." As each page is turned the echoes sound disconcertingly numerous and in Book I alone (of nine books) there clamor for attention no less than seventeen of Emily's poems. It is not a case of simple appropriation of images, but of poems painstakingly constructed in their entirety on suggestions—lines, phrases, passages—supplied by Mrs. Browning, either as restatements in the personal mode or as deliberate variations. Aurora, describing her debilitating life as a child in England, recalls that she almost died and explains:

> slowly, as one in swoon,
> To whom life creeps back in the form of death,
> With a sense of separation, a blind pain
> Of blank obstruction, and a roar i' the ears
> Of visionary chariots which retreat
> As earth grows clearer . . . slowly, by degrees,
> I woke, rose up . . .

Emily, coming across that passage, worried it until by a happy inversion of viewpoint, she found a way to make it stand as a poem on its own:

> Just lost, when I was saved!
> Just felt the world go by!
> Just girt me for the onset with Eternity,
> When breath blew back,
> And on the other side
> I heard recede the disappointed tide!

She was not always so subtle, however; when the opinion is offered that

> A death-heat is
> The same as life-heat, to be accurate;
> And in all nature is no death at all,
> As men account of death . . .

the best that Emily could do was to sketch the paradox in more detail:

> A death-blow is a life-blow to some
> Who till they died, did not alive become;

Who, had they lived, had died, but when
They died, vitality begun.

The similarity of phrasing in this peom helps the identification, but it is not often so easy. Usually it requires a sensitive ear,
depending entirely on memory, to catch a correspondence in
subject matter, after which a comparison makes the borrowing
incontrovertibly clear. Here, for instance, is the fleetingest of
hints, from which Emily built up one of her best and best-known
poems. Aurora observes:

> Even prosaic men, who wear grief long,
> Will get to wear it as a hat aside
> With a flower stuck in't . . .

Grief is one of the commonest subjects of poetry so it is not surprising that Emily handles it a number of times. But when she
writes

> I measure every grief I meet
> With analytic eyes;
> I wonder if it weighs like mine,
> Or has an easier size.

and then continues through nine stanzas to analyze the different
kinds of grief in the world, ending with the statement that it
affords some comfort

> To note the fashions of the Cross
> And how they're mostly worn . . .

It is easy to believe that she never thought of measuring anybody's grief until Aurora supplied her with that jaunty hat. Her
deftness in expanding on Mrs. Browning's throw-aways, however, did not always result in exceptional poetry. In one passage

where Aurora discusses the sympathy that should exist between lovers, she compares their emotional lives to clocks and says

> leave two clocks, they say,
> Wound up to different times upon one shelf,
> And slowly, through the interior wheels of each
> The blind mechanic motion sets itself
> A-throb, to feel out for the mutual time.

Even in Emily's day it had become almost trite to picture the human heart as a sort of mystical clock, but it was undoubtedly on the idea in this passage that she built her own sixteen-line description of two bashful lovers who fumble in each other's presence until at last

> those two troubled little clocks
> Ticked softly into one.

Another of her poems, one that pops up in every anthology and which is known to anyone who is at all interested in verse, is this:

> It dropped so low in my regard
> I heard it hit the ground,
> And go to pieces on the stones
> At bottom of my mind,
>
> Yet blamed the fate that fractured less
> Than I reviled myself,
> For entertaining plated wares
> Upon my silver shelf.

Emily was often among her own pots and baking pans and dishes, and was aware of that special shelf in every New England dining room where the best silver was kept, so she might easily have drawn that sparkling bit of homely philosophy from her own surroundings. Yet it is more probable that, in spite of

all her hours in the kitchen, dishes were nothing but dishes to
her until she read Aurora's remark about the excesses of virtuous
people:

> He set his virtues on so raised a shelf,
> To keep them at the grand millennial height,
> He has to mount a stool to get at them . . .

Emily's contribution to the working out of that image, aside from
her subtlety of touch in expanding it, consisted in dropping and
breaking the virtue-as-dish and that, indeed, may have come
from her own experience. Not to carry the point to absurd
lengths, it might be noted in passing that there *are* two or three
documented instances when she can be seen dropping or breaking dishes. Once when her father became annoyed at having the
same cracked plate continually set before him at table, Emily
took the offending crockery outside and smashed it with a ham-
mer, "just to remind herself not to do it again," as she announced
on returning.

Even a single word, when it linked itself to some germinal
idea, was enough to set her off. Once Aurora admits that she
does not have any desire to visit the graves of her parents, since
their spirits are elsewhere, and then proceeds to turn the thought
upside down:

> let me think
> That rather they are visiting my grave,
> This life here, (undeveloped yet to life) . . .

Develop was a word closely associated with the then new art of
photography as well as with a peculiar belief of the time that
grew from it (not entirely forgotten even yet) by which it was
thought that the last scene registered on dying eyes remained
printed on the retina, and could be recovered if only the correct
developing procedures were known. More than one early murder
mystery took its rise from that notion but Emily made use of it,

under the prompting of Mrs. Browning, in a different way. She pieced together a twelve-line poem depending for its entire force on that single idea and that one word. If this life is only a preparation for the next, she says, what wonderful sights await us

> When from a thousand skies,
> On our *developed* eyes
> Noons blaze!

She herself underlined the word to make sure that both its obvious and its inner meanings would not be missed.

Everyone agrees that one of the marvels of Emily's verse is the way she could pick out of the common experience just the exactly right symbols to express those penetrating insights she was so constantly able to achieve. A good example is this little effort in which she captures, using only eight lines, the reality of human growth:

> I stepped from plank to plank,
> A slow and cautious way,
> The stars about my head I felt,
> About my feet the sea.
>
> I knew not but the next
> Would be my final inch;
> This gave me that precarious gait
> Some call experience.

At one time or another most people have crossed a depression in the ground, or negotiated a stream, by means of a plank, Emily no doubt included. So her symbol for the life of daily things would seem quite naturally derived. Yet here is Aurora talking:

> As if I led her by a narrow plank
> Across devouring waters, step by step,
> And so in silence we walked on a mile. . . .

> Then she led
> The way, and I, as by a narrow plank,
> Across devouring waters, followed her . . .

Aurora and her friend are actually walking through the streets of Paris, but the planks are symbolic of the alternating emotional states of the women.

Emily's virtuosity now and again extended to boiling down a figurative thought which Mrs. Browning had strung out through some long soliloquy. Half of the first book of *Aurora Leigh* is taken up with Aurora's ruminations on the intellectual growth of her youth; spread through nearly six hundred lines is the following:

> I kept the life, thrust on me, on the outside
> Of the inner life, with all its ample room
> For heart and lungs, for will and intellect . . .
>
> . . . But I could not hide
> My quickening inner life from those at watch.
> They saw a light at a window, now and then,
> They had not set there . . .
>
> And so, through forced work and spontaneous work,
> The inner life informed the outer life,
> Reduced the irregular blood to a settled rhythm,
> Made cool the forehead with fresh-sprinkling dreams,
> And, rounding to the spheric soul the thin,
> Pined body, struck a color up the cheeks . . .

The entire setting for that thread would have been of utmost fascination for Emily, revealing as it does, or seems to, the actual intellectual progress of the book's author. It was after what must have been unusually close study that she carved the following replica of the statement, down to the metaphorical blood rising in the symbolic cheeks:

The outer from the inner
Derives its magnitude;
'Tis Duke of dwarf, according
As is the central mood.

. . . . .

The inner paints the outer,
The brush without the hand,
Its picture publishes precise,
As is the inner brand,

On fine arterial canvas:
A cheek, perchance a brow—
The star's whole secret in the lake
Eyes were not meant to know.

That sort of thing is simple needlework, however, to the tapestry she wove from two similar but widely separated passages, putting together a production that has piqued and baffled all the commentators—the favorite interpretation at the moment being, once again, sexual fantasizing. To appreciate Emily's full virtuosity the complete poem must be given:

I started early, took my dog,
And visited the sea;
The Mermaids in the basement
Came out to look at me,

And frigates in the upper floor
Extended hempen hands,
Presuming me to be a mouse
Aground upon the sands.

But no man moved me, till the tide
Went past my simple shoe,
And past my apron and my belt,
And past my bodice, too,

And made as he would eat me up
As wholly as a dew

Upon a dandelion's sleeve.
And then I started, too,

And he, he followed close behind;
I felt his silver heel
Upon my ankle, then my shoes
Would overflow with pearl.

Until we met the solid town,
No one he seemed to know,
And bowing, with a mighty look
At me, the sea withdrew.

As with the poem on the worm-snake metamorphosis previously quoted, this one also seems much like the record of an actual dream, and it is very possible that there are sexual elements in it—the masculine Tide removes the speaker's shoes, apron, belt and dress, then prepares to overpower her. If the experience really was a dream, it mainly represents another wish-fulfillment episode in connection with the hopes aroused by *Aurora Leigh*. On page thirty-nine of the original edition, Aurora is engaged in solitary dreaming about her future as a poet. Playfully making herself a wreath of ivy, she dons it, performs a few twirls with arms raised and suddenly finds herself facing her cousin Romney, who has come up unnoticed. She is lost in embarrassed confusion:

> Hand stretched out
> I clasped, as shipwrecked men will clasp a hand,
> Indifferent to the sort of palm. The Tide
> Had caught me at my pastime, writing down
> My foolish name too near upon the sea
> Which drowned me with a blush as foolish. . . .

The two begin to talk in earnest about the place of women in the arts, Romney claiming that women were not meant to be poets, while Aurora fiercely insists she will be nothing else. Nine pages later they are still at it, and Aurora bursts out:

> I have not stood long on the strand of life,
> And these salt waters have had scarcely time
> To creep so high as to wet my feet:
> I cannot judge these tides—I shall, perhaps.

Emily's poem clearly revolves around that last line, the concept of judging the tides, or in other words the achievement of artistic maturity. Where she got the dog, the mermaids, the frigates, and the mouse is an interesting if perhaps less pressing question. She owned a dog, of course, but Romney had one, too, which is mentioned with affection, and in one lengthy passage Aurora pictures herself, in her girlhood, as a mouse. That leaves the mermaids and the frigates for Emily, quite ample equipment for additional Freudian probing by those so inclined.

To pile one instance of similarity or borrowing (or plagiarism, but whisper it soft) on top of another is worthwhile only to a certain point, and where *Aurora Leigh* is concerned that point would seem to have been reached. It may be enough to state now what is a fact: in total at this moment at least sixty of Emily's poems can be related to distinct passages in Mrs. Browning's book, with echoes of at least an additional fifty hovering just out of reach.* Finally, her favorite symbol of the Dark, which continued intermittently to pervade her work for the rest of her days, was itself derived from *Aurora Leigh*. At the nadir of her emotional entanglements, Aurora mourns:

> My head aches;
> I cannot see my road along this dark;
> Nor can I creep and grope as fits the dark . . .

a usage which, to be fair about it, Mrs. Browning had probably filched from Keats' *Ode to a Nightingale*.

It is no longer necessary to wonder why the book produced such an impact or why Emily held it in such reverence. What-

---

* A complete list is provided in the Notes.

ever its shortcomings, it taught her at a stroke that poetry was more than metrical gush about nature; that it began with observa-ion in its acutest form and demanded the fullest use of whatever mental power was available. It convinced her that butterflies and sunsets are only occasionally tolerable in verse, and it provided her with the raw material of thought, which she had never been able to generate in her own mind, on which to practice. It had "converted" her. In that respect, one line in *Aurora Leigh* must have gone like an arrow to Emily's breast. After Aurora has won poetic fame, she is besieged by a steady stream of letters from admirers and would-be poetesses, the envelopes bearing

> Pretty maiden seals, initials twined
> Of lilies, or a heart marked *Emily,*
> (Convicting Emily of being all heart.)

For too long, the Amherst Emily knew, she and her verse had been all heart and no head. Now that was changing.

The dull worm that, in Emily's dream-room, suddenly became a thing of rare power and beauty is not so strange a figure after all. In Emily's skillful hands, Mrs. Browning's casual thoughts had become—so the sleeping brain hopefully insisted—new and scintillating creations.

· 4 ·

GET GABRIEL TO TELL IT

SUE AND AUSTIN had not been married long before their parlor was graced for an evening by the most exalted presence it was ever to know, affording Sue, especially, one of her most cherished memories. For a decade she had been poring over the works of Ralph Waldo Emerson, the essays as well as the poems, until he had become "a hero in my girl's heart; till there grew into my feeling for him almost a supernatural element." When she heard that he was to speak in Amherst and would actually be spending the night as a guest under her roof, she felt as if she were about to come face to face with the Old Testament. That this was not a mere chiming in with popular sentiment can be seen in the way many others in Amherst responded to the impending honor: Tickets for the lecture moved so slowly that a week before the event the price was reduced from twenty cents apiece to eight for a dollar. Emerson had not then achieved his ultimate stature as the beloved Concord sage and the public had to be reminded that he was a man worth listening to. "There are few people who can afford not to hear Emerson," the village paper urged in announcing the price-cut, "when they can hear him for twelve and a half cents."

The size of the audience that gathered in the Meeting Hall,

at the southwest corner of the Common, on the evening of December 16, 1857 has not been recorded, but if Emerson possessed the platform mastery with which he has been credited, he would not have bothered counting the house. Instead, he would have been busy singling out one sympathetic face among his listeners to which he could direct his remarks, and if so he could have done no better than to fix on Sue. With Austin beside her, as she ever afterwards remembered, she was "lifted into a fine glow of enthusiasm," buoyed by the radiant words that drifted silverly from the front of the hall in a provocative analysis of rural life, and it is not surprising that she was never quite able to bring to mind just what the master had said. At the lecture's close, the two waited for their guest and Sue felt "strangely elated to take his Transcendental arm" in a leisurely stroll past the Common and down Main Street toward home, Emerson discoursing all the while on poets and poetry.

With a few invited guests for stimulation, he later held forth for a few hours in the parlor, and the nearness of his steady gaze made Sue even more conscious of her privilege. "His manner in talking was very quiet," she recalled, "and he turned his gentle, philosophic face toward me, waiting upon my commonplaces with such expectant, quiet gravity, that I became painfully conscious that I was I, and he was he, the great Emerson." Emily took no part in the evening, though she was at home and, of course, thoroughly aware of the presence next door: on receiving Sue's later account of the occasion she agreed that it must have been like meeting someone who had come from "where dreams are born." While she did not go the few steps to meet Emerson, when he departed the next morning, his carriage passing her door on its way to the station, Emily certainly was—if anything in this world is certain—peeking from behind a curtain or over a hedge.

This incident, so minor in the general flow of things but of such surpassing grandeur in Sue's memory, must not be passed over, as it usually is, without a closer look. Why didn't Emily attend the lecture and join the company at her brother's house afterwards? Her feeling for Emerson's writings may not have been as intense as Sue's, but she had read him and undoubtedly held him in high respect. There was also Emerson's association with the memory of the dead Ben Newton, which might have stirred a desire to speak with the man who had meant so much to her early friend. Even simple curiosity might have drawn her: Emerson's enigmatic little poem, *Brahma*, had appeared in the November *Atlantic* and was just then in the process of being praised as subtle or ridiculed as silly. It had intrigued Sue, and with Emerson a captive by her fireside, she had ventured to inquire what the Sphinx-like stanzas really meant. Emerson, perhaps not wanting to spoil a good thing, had brushed aside her question with, "Oh, there is nothing to understand. How can they make so much fuss over it?" But the fuss was there and Emily must have been as piqued as the others.

During this period of course, she was in her first fine rapture over *Aurora Leigh*, her suddenly splendorous days stepping grandly to mighty meters. Most of the time she was huddled at the tiny writing table in her room, writing, rewriting and doing her best to avoid the distractions of social outings and incessant callers. The quantity of poems she produced on the work of Mrs. Browning—not to mention the original work that must have engaged her—would have required a prodigious amount of time, an expenditure of effort greatly compounded by her new awareness of the real magic latent in diction. Though she had always shown a deft touch in the use of words, Mrs. Browning's art seems to have vitalized her deeper sensitivities toward language, its elusive power and ineffable delicacies. There are words, she now admitted, "to which I lift my hat when I see them sitting prince-like among their peers on the page. Sometimes I write one, and look at his outlines until he glows as no sapphire."* But the finely wrought language of her deceptively simple

* *Lyman Letters,* 78.

quatrains was not thrown off in an odd moment here and there; it was the product of intense and long-continued striving.

There are definite signs that at some point she had set herself the exacting task of writing at least one finished poem a day. The plan produced "slow riches" as she acknowledged, and the results were uneven, but it went on relentlessly. Sometimes she worked late into the night, taking advantage of the unnatural quiet that reigned while the others slept. This nocturnal habit became so pronounced that her worried father, noticing the light in her room and her worn looks next morning, inquired about it. Informed by his daughter what was going on, with a good deal of understanding for which he is never given credit, he canceled the family rule about early rising and allowed Emily to sleep late. How long this arrangement held is a question, but it certainly went on for some time. Like Aurora, in these years Emily, too, must more than once have felt the pulse shudder along the purple-veinèd wrist.

Still, all of this would not have precluded an hour or two in Emerson's company, and curiosity about her stay-at-home attitude continues to nag. She was not ill, as far as can be told, nor is her shyness—the usual reason given—a sufficient answer. Neither was she entering on the first stages of her grand withdrawal, as some have claimed. Her avoidance of chance arrivals on her doorstep at this time, and her occasional refusals to go out were only a part of her sensible efforts to conserve her time for writing; she still met people when she felt so inclined, in her own home and outside. The notion that the Emerson incident was an early sign of reclusive tendencies stems largely from a few offhand statements by Emily herself which, as too often, have been snatched up to prove a contended point. When turning down an invitation from one neighbor, for example, she explained, truthfully enough, that she would love to pay a visit, "could I leave home or mother," but then she slipped behind her mask again and continued coyly, "I do not go out at all lest father will come and miss me, or miss some little act, which

I might forget, should I run away." What the note's recipient may have been led to think about Mr. Dickinson is hard to say; what Mr. Dickinson's comment might have been could he have seen that sentence can only be guessed. It was not the first time Emily had employed her unsuspecting father as a shield nor would it be the last.

There thus seems no obvious reason why Emily should have kept away from her Sue's parlor that evening and the little matter seems to be at a dead end. But biographers as well as nature may be uncomfortable with a void, particularly when it surrounds so interesting a personality, and this particular hollow may not be so difficult to fill. What kept Emily at home that night was probably a reluctance to face the man from whose works she had begun to reap an abundant harvest. For months she had been delving into Emerson's volumes, no doubt under the guidance of Sue, and she had written a goodly number of poems on themes and hints he supplied. From one of his favorite concepts, for instance, that of "compensation," she was to wring no less than a dozen different variations, and the probability is that fifty or more of her verses will eventually be found to have had their inception in Emerson's pages. The presently-known matrix of Emerson-Dickinson similarities, long ago recognized, is not a result of common background and airborne ideas, as critics are wont to believe, but of a careful, persistent culling.

The fact is, Emily very quickly expanded her horizons beyond *Aurora Leigh.* Late in 1857, for instance, she and Sue were reading with much delight Mrs. Gaskell's *Life of Charlotte Brontë.* This reminded Emily of another book that had lit up her life eight years before, suggesting it as a suitable quarry. She went back for another look at *Jane Eyre* and before she had finished with it, the old favorite had supplied her with material for at least twenty poems—again with another dozen echoing dimly just out of hearing. Three brief but convincing examples will be sufficient.

Here is Jane describing her first meeting with the self-right-
eous Mr. Brocklehurst: entering a room, she curtseyed, and
"looked up at—a black pillar!—such, at least, appeared to me, at
first sight, the straight, narrow, sable-clad shape standing erect
on the rug: the grim face at the top was like a carved mask,
placed above the shaft by way of capital." Meeting him again a
few pages further on, Jane sees him as "the same black column
which had frowned on me so ominously . . . I now glanced
sideways at this piece of architecture." From this came a poem
of Emily's that has been much admired for its originality, beginning,

> On a columnar self
> How ample to rely
> In tumult or extremity . . .

The second example has no specific word to link it to *Jane
Eyre* yet is equally obvious on a careful reading. After Jane becomes engaged to Edward Rochester, master of Thornfield, she
confesses: "My future husband was becoming to me my whole
world; and more than the world: almost my hope of Heaven. He
stood between me and every hope of religion, as an eclipse in-
tervenes between man and the broad sun. I could not, in those
days, see God for his creature of whom I had made an idol."
Deftly, Emily catches the thought, personalizes it, and repeats it
without elaboration in these terse lines:

> You constituted time.
> I deemed Eternity
> A Revelation of yourself;
> 'Twas therefore Deity.
>
> The Absolute removed
> The relative away,
> That I unto Himself adjust
> My slow idolatry.

In the third example she was able to bring some of her own dramatic sense to her work. Jane is here describing a sermon she has heard, just the sort of sermon Emily had listened to a hundred times in the village church:

It began calm—and indeed, as far as delivery and pitch of voice went, it was calm to the end: an earnestly felt, yet strictly restrained zeal breathed soon in the distinct accents, and prompted the nervous language. The heart was thrilled, the mind astonished, by the power of the preacher: neither was softened. Throughout there was a strange bitterness; an absence of consolatory gentleness: stern allusions to Calvinistic doctrines—election, predestination, reprobation —were frequent; and each reference to these points sounded like a sentence pronounced for doom.

Like most born Congregationalists, Emily enjoyed a stirring preacher. But it was in Jane's description and not in her own experience that she found the inspiration for another poem that has been identified as a cover for sexual day-dreaming:

> He fumbles at your soul
> As players at the keys
> Before they drop full music on;
> He stuns you by degrees,
> Prepares your brittle nature
> For the etherial blow
> By fainter hammers, further heard,
> Then nearer, then so slow
> Your breath has time to straighten,
> Your brain to bubble cool;
> Deals one imperial thunderbolt
> That scalps your naked soul. . . .

The thunderbolt may have come from some memory of an Amherst Sunday in church, of course, but the figure is hardly a stroke of genius. What definitely deserves mention is the keen eye that sees this poem as an outright attempt to depict the act of sexual intercourse, complete with the fumbling of amorous foreplay, rising excitement, orgasm and gradual subsidence. The idea shows, at any rate, how much dissimilar things may be like each other, or even better, how much the spirit is like the body. But that line of thought leads straight to the *Song of Solomon*, and in all of Emily's poetry, otherwise so full of Biblical allusion and imagery, there is not a single reference to that particular book of the Bible. And if the lines are even secondarily sexual in nature, then poor Emily must be judged ignorant on the subject. When does the driving excitement preceding orgasm allow an interim for the breath to calm and the brain to cool before the scalping?

From Mrs. Gaskell herself she appears to have taken only one hint, a small one, on which she built the slight but interesting, "I know some lonely houses."* But the book itself, the first real glimpse the public had been allowed into the curious lives of the Brontës, must have delighted her, especially when she saw how similar her own life and personality were to those of the Yorkshire girls. Though she could probably not have achieved sufficient objectivity to be entirely aware of it, Emily was actually a mixture, a strange combination of the qualities, physical and otherwise, of the two sisters, Charlotte and Emily. The stark personality of Emily Brontë was to intrigue her more and more as time went on, leading to some quirks in her own behavior that added to her reputation for queerness.

With *Aurora Leigh* and *Jane Eyre* identified as major sources on which Emily exercised her delicate depredations, it seemed likely that there might be other works that had been laid under siege, and the suspicion was soon confirmed. In the Dickinson family library, a not inconsiderable one judging from the number of volumes that are still preserved, there was a copy of Lydia Maria Child's *Letters from New York*, which Emily is known to have read. It is just the sort of book—the highly personal observations of an intense Transcendentalist reformer—

* *Life of Charlotte Brontë*, chap. 2, paras. 26, 29, 30.

that would have attracted the girl's searching eyes; a fairly short work, not badly written, if rather inclined to go soaring off into the empyrean. Through its first seventeen pages Emily's voice is absent or is so attenuated as to be beyond hearing, but suddenly within the space of four pages two of her most famous verses become audible. "There are other points," says Mrs. Child, "greatly differing from these, on which most American juries would be prone to convict me of insanity. You know a New York lawyer defined insanity to be 'a differing in opinion from the mass of mankind.' By this rule I am as mad as a March hare." This play of ideas caught Emily's attention and from it she produced one of those paradoxical, downright verses for which she was to become noted:

> Much madness is divinest sense
> To a discerning eye;
> Much sense the starkest madness.
> 'Tis the majority
> In this, as all, prevail . . .

Since the concept around which she wove those lines was not exactly new even then, and might have been found in any number of places, let the second example add its weight to the evidence. One day in New York, Mrs. Child says, she stood on the Broadway sidewalk watching a gaudy temperance parade march by, flying banners extolling the virtues of water, fire engines clanging, soldiers stepping smartly to the strains of martial music. The excitement made her heart leap up and (recalling that she had a book to write) she proceeded to draw deep significance, not from the theme of the day but from the military aspects of the scene. She loathed war, she assured her readers, then somehow got from that to the following outburst:

Whoso does not see that genuine life is a battle and a march, has poorly read his origin and his destiny. Let the trumpet sound and the drums roll! Glory to resistance! for through its agency men become angels. The instinct awakened by martial music is noble and true; and therefore will not pass away; but it will cease to represent war with carnal weapons, and remain a type of that spiritual combat whereby the soul is purified. It is right noble to fight with wickedness and wrong; the mistake is in supposing that spiritual evil can be overcome by physical means.

A hundred pages further on she describes a visit to Heaven (not by herself, she never went that far) and repeats the thought: "The spiritual combats and victories of our pilgrimage write themselves above . . . perhaps all lovely forms of art are mere ultimates of spiritual victories in individual souls." Emily was well acquainted with the temperance movement, which was as active in New England as elsewhere, and her father had frequently served with the Hampshire Temperance Society. She had also more than once heard martial music, but she had to wait for Mrs. Child's ruminations before she could write the famous

> To fight aloud is very brave,
> But gallanter, I know,
> Who charge within the bosom
> The cavalry of woe . . .

One of the curious things about Emily's work is the way individual poems keep presenting themselves in which there seems no traceable connection to the events of her own life, and which are devoid of any special merit. They seem to have been hardly worth the effort they entailed and leave readers wondering what prompted their composition, or what in the world provided the offbeat inspiration. Such, for instance, is the one about a hanging:

> Upon the gallows hung a wretch
> Too sullied for the hell
> To which the law entitled him.
> As nature's curtain fell

The one who bore him tottered in,
For this was woman's son.
" 'Twas all I had," she stricken gasped.
Oh, what a livid boon!

That would appear rather far removed from Emily's usual concerns, and without Mrs. Child's book no one would ever have known that Emily is here remolding an actual incident in which Mrs. Child was involved during the execution of the New York murderer, John Colt. Mrs. Child reports that she was in the crowd that gathered outside the prison on the day fixed for the hanging. As execution hour neared, a fire broke out, causing a delay in the festivities, and the account continues:

"What a pity!" exclaimed a woman who stood near me, gazing at the burning tower; "they will have to give him two more hours to live." "Would you feel so if he were your *son?*" said I. Her countenance changed instantly. She had not before realized that every criminal was *somebody's* son.

Emily based at least seven poems on material from Mrs. Child's book; this one she might just as well have passed by.

Hunting for the sources of a writer's ideas is a pursuit rewarding and fascinating to some, while it is often vastly annoying to others; which way a man jumps depends on his opinion of the value in the endeavor. In Emily's case, over the past couple of decades, there has been a marked tendency to brush off the occasional scholar who reports stumbling on something that looks very much like a borrowing. It is urged that all poets, all writers, borrow to a more or less extent, and that Emily's infractions in this regard should be accepted with the same understanding afforded to, say, Shakespeare and Coleridge, two other great minds who didn't stint themselves when it came to picking other people's brains. And Emily offended far less in this way, it is said, than almost any writer you care to name. What's a line or an image here and there? Throughout the bulk of her almost eighteen hundred brief poems she is still "wholly original" Emily. But what if Emily's case turns out to be not so ordinary? What if she frequently did not just pilfer lines and images for inclusion in some original setting of her own, but regularly squeezed and stretched her borrowings as she molded dough for bread? And what if the number of poems so derived should begin—as it has begun—to mount into the hundreds? What then?

• •

Whatever may have been her exact reason for avoiding Emerson, Emily found Sue's house at other times a congenial place where she could meet interesting people and relax from her household duties, the care of her mother and the pressures of composition. Before long, a narrow footpath, leading through the trees and shrubbery that separated the two houses, was trodden out by daily use and marked by the planting of moss along its borders. Emily was to spend a fair portion of the remainder of her life traversing that little path as Sue's home gradually became the center of her existence, and it was that path that took her one day in the summer of 1858 to a meeting with the man who would give her the pleasure of seeing her first serious poem in print.

Samuel Bowles, thirty-one-year-old owner-editor of the *Springfield Daily Republican,* had been friendly with Austin for a number of years and was one of the first guests to enter the new home. An impressive man, handsome, personable, of wide sympathies and friendships, he possessed a driving energy and a sure journalistic instinct that was to make his paper one of the most respected provincial organs in the country. It was by his own choice that he had clung to the more rustic station of his birth; having once tried life in higher circles as the respected editor of an influential Boston paper, he had voluntarily returned to Springfield in a search for more independent scope. A self-made man, lacking any real taste for pure literature or poetry, as he confessed, he now began shoring up this neglected side of his education, and it was this, in addition to congeniality of temperament, that drew him closer to the Dickinsons. In the literate, unhurried atmosphere of Sue's home, he frequently escaped the hectic burden of his Springfield office in order to rest and imbibe his friends' enthusiasm for the finer things. The most exciting literary discovery to which they led him was the poetry of the Brownings, chief among which, perhaps inevitably, was Mrs. Browning's masterpiece. Like all the others in the Dickinson circle, he fell an instant victim to its charms: preparing for a trip to Europe once, he wrote his friends that he would take with him only two books, *"Aurora Leigh* and the Bible."* The benefits of the friendship were reciprocal, for with Bowles there came to the Dickinsons a fresher and wider view of the world, and his admitted readiness to "hob-nob with any man, saint or sinner, in whom he found any likeable quality," supplied a needed corrective for the unconscious touch of snobbery indulged in by most of the Amherst gentry.

Emily recognized a kindred spirit and accepted him eagerly from the start, a reaction not a little heightened, it may be, by the fact that his paper ran a regular weekly column of original poetry, and also frequently used verse in the daily edition. She knew, of course—as many a modern critic has forgotten—that publication in a newspaper of such poetry as she was writing was hardly a goal to be eagerly sought. Newspaper verse was essentially different from true poetry, basing itself almost entirely on simple, accepted forms and speaking directly to the common heart on themes of the moment. It was nothing but metric journalism, and its practitioners, in a day when every educated person could throw off a couplet or a quatrain, were legion. Still, the *Republican* had some standing and was read religiously every day by the Dickinsons, as well as most of the people in western Massachusetts. Just to see a poem or two glowing on a printed page, no matter where it appeared, would

* Bianchi, *Face,* 283.

be something, a beginning at least, and Emily soon set about the task of catching Bowles' attention.

His first real visit took place in June 1858, after his wife Mary had suffered a stillbirth; a change of surroundings seemed called for and Austin's home was one of the stopping places, the two remaining for a few days. A note Emily sent after their departure expresses not only her delight in their company but raises the curtain on her own altered personality. This is the first letter of definite date following the note to Mrs. Holland of two years before and though the coyness has not been completely put away, she has wrapped herself in a more studied utterance:

I am sorry you came because you went away. Hereafter, I will pick no rose lest it fade or prick me. I would like to have you dwell here. Though it is almost nine o'clock, the skies are gay and yellow, and there's a purple craft or so, in which a friend could sail . . . I hope your tour was bright, and gladdened Mrs. Bowles. Perhaps the Retrospect will call you back some morning. You shall find us all at the gate, if you come in a hundred years, just as we stood that day. If it become of "Jasper" previously, you will not object, so that we lean there still, looking after you. I rode with Austin this morning. He showed me mountains that touched the sky, and brooks that sang like bobolinks. Was he not very kind? I will give them to you . . .

From first word to last the letter is a deliberate exercise, reflecting not only the stripped-down language of the verse she was writing, but also the effort to compel attention by cryptic phrase and sudden shift. Similar messages followed as she began to number the Bowleses among her chief correspondents, awaiting only the ripening of sympathies to uncover her growing pile of manuscripts. Now and then the messages were couched in poetry, little *jeux d'esprit*, intended to support the impression that here was a clever girl indeed.

Some other people who were to play a part in her life also

materialized about this time, and brief introductions of them here will do much to simplify some rather involved comings and goings. Her young Boston cousins, for instance, Louise and Frances Norcross, sixteen and eleven respectively, paid their first grown-up visits to Amherst in the autumn of 1858, the older girl making an instant hit with Emily when she confessed her own hopes of achieving a life above the commonplace. There was one October morning when the two families went out driving, leaving Emily and Loo in the dining room talking of poetry and deciding "to be distinguished." Writing after her cousin's departure, Emily recalled their talk: "It's a great thing to be 'great,' Loo, and you and I might tug for a life, and never accomplish it, but no one can stop our looking on . . . What if we learn ourselves someday!" The Norcross girls possessed some of the same eccentric tendencies as their Amherst relative but they had none of her talent and their importance to Emily's story rests on other than literary grounds. Unmarried, they lived out their lives in the Boston area, carrying on an intimate correspondence with their cousin for nearly three decades. Loo survived Emily by thirty-five years, long enough to see her raised to the distinction the two had yearned after, but at her own death she ruthlessly ordered the destruction of what must have been a huge accumulation of Emily's letters. A few selected passages from them had earlier been supplied to Mabel Todd, but no one had ever been allowed to read the originals, not even Vinnie. The most interesting things in these printed portions are three separate references to *Aurora Leigh,* oblique references, indicating the Norcross girls' close familiarity with the book. Nowhere else in the nearly one thousand extant letters Emily wrote after 1856 is there the least mention of Mrs. Browning's epic. That Loo and Fanny had secrets to keep about Emily's art is evident; that they may also have had information on other, more personal topics will appear for adjudication presently.

Also appearing, or reappearing, at this time was the problematic Rev. Charles Wadsworth, whose one-day visit to the

Dickinson home has earned him a more lasting fame than all his good works performed or sermons preached. No contemporary trace of the visit exists, but its date has been determined from incidental references in Emily's later letters, and there seems no doubt that it was the spring of 1860 that first brought the deep-voiced minister face to face with the poet in more than phantom light. It was a flying visit, however, and all that is really known of it is that Wadsworth had not, by any means, traveled all the way from Philadelphia to see a young lady. He had come north to call on a friend in Northampton, indicating that his presence in Amherst, a short carriage ride from the other town, may have been as much for the purpose of visiting another friend at the college as to see Emily. And when he left the Dickinson house that day, he did not show up again for twenty years.

Otis Lord, an old friend of Emily's father, also now first makes a sustained appearance. A noted Massachusetts lawyer, a sometime politician, and a resident of Salem, his appointment to the bench of the newly-formed Superior Court brought him once or twice a year into the Amherst vicinity as he presided in various surrounding towns. A man of outspoken nature, strenuous intellect, and a love of literature, Shakespeare in particular, he frequently dropped in at the Dickinsons', sometimes with his wife, and Emily always gladly put down her pencil or her baking pans to enjoy the stimulation of his forceful talk. While the others went for a carriage ride, she and Lord would have "their own adventures in conversation at home," which it seems, included much laughter. Lord's sense of humor tended to be of the old-fashioned variety and not all the Dickinsons appreciated it alike, but it suited Emily and she formed a habit of calling it "the Judge Lord brand." (The only sample of it that remains is the question he put to Sue's daughter on catching sight of her red-and-white striped stockings: "Are you intended for a tonsorial advertisement?") He and Emily formed a little clique of their own and many years later, after the death of Emily's father, they grew even closer as Lord assumed a paternal attitude toward his friend's children. When, finally, Lord himself lost his wife, he and Emily allowed themselves, according to present records, a December romance in which marriage was momentarily considered and rejected. By that time Lord, who was Emily's senior by eighteen years, was old and ailing, and Emily herself approaching fifty.

A last friendship which was begun at this time but which also did not assume importance until later years was that with Helen Hunt, an Amherst girl who had played with the Dickinson sisters as a child. With her husband, a lieutenant of army engineers, Mrs. Hunt revisited her old home during commencement week of 1860, taking dinner one evening at the Dickinson table. Emily was quite charmed with Lieutenant Hunt, a brilliant and inventive career officer who seemed destined for high places. He was sympathetic and witty, and Emily was to recall him as the most interesting man she had ever met. Five years after this visit Mrs. Hunt, crushed by the deaths in quick succession of both husband and son, turned to literature for consolation and a livelihood, and it was as far-famed Helen Hunt Jackson, poet, novelist and author of the memorable *Ramona,* that she would reenter Emily's life.

But visitors, no matter who they were, or how pleasant, Emily regarded as only interruptions in an endless parade of days devoted as much as possible to poetry. By now she had discovered that good ideas for the kind of verse she was developing—short, brilliant observations, set in delicately intricate patterns, like the illuminated capitals in old manuscripts—need not come from other poets or from established literary sources at all. Intensity or oddness of thought encountered in any chance connection, even simple facts when they were sufficiently out-of-the-way, could fire her to composition. In the pages of the *Hampshire Express,** for example, she read a casual paragraph headed "Ancient Books": "Dr. Rice of Leverett owns a work printed nearly three

* May 30, 1862.

hundred years ago in Germany. It is a large quarto volume containing a thousand pages and several hundred copper plate engravings . . . it is a very valuable relic of ancient science and engraving." And, calling on her imagination for further details, she turned that evanescent bit of intelligence into a twenty-eight-line poem beginning:

> A precious mouldering pleasure 'tis
> To meet an antique book,
> In just the dress his century wore . . .

Once it is realized how much of this sort of thing Emily was doing at this time, and when the mind of the investigator is honed for the job, the possibilities for tracking similar efforts begin to open up at an almost alarming rate. In April 1861, she sent a note enclosing a flower across to the other house asking, "Will Susan please lend Emily 'Life in the Iron Mills'—and accept blossom." The title she specified was that of a short story in the current *Atlantic*. Reading it now is a bit wearisome, filled as it is with exaggerated realism and heavy-handed social comment, and as the pages turn, no poem of Emily's suggests itself. Perhaps after all—the thought creeps in—she *did* sometimes read without rushing back to that little table in her room. Then on the last page, in a highly emotional denouement, Emily's whisper is suddenly audible. The hero of the tale, a downtrodden mill hand, is driven by his hopeless life to a single crime of theft and he is jailed. Unable to face life behind bars, he commits suicide. Emily wrote two poems on the subject of suicide, one of them about the time she read this story. It is unmistakably couched in prison imagery:

> What if I say I shall not wait!
> What if I burst the fleshly gate,
> And pass, escaped, to thee!

What if I file this mortal off—
See where it hurt me, that's enough,
And step in liberty . . .

When she finished reading "Life in the Iron Mills," would she have immediately returned the *Atlantic* to Sue or would she perhaps have browsed through the rest of the issue? It seemed probable that, like most people, she would have taken a further look, and there seemed nothing to do but follow her. At first, no echo. Then in a review of *Elsie Venner*, a novel by Oliver Wendell Holmes, this phrase flits into view: "The phosphorescent star-foam of wit and fancy." In no less than three poems written about this time Emily made judicious use of symbolic phosphorescence, and one of the few remarks preserved from her conversation—often cited in praise of her evocative language—was this observation on a local scholar: "He has the facts of learning but not the phosphorescence."

Not even the more transient prose of her youth can be exempted from possibility, as her reaching back for Mrs. Child's book indicates. In her twentieth year, for example, along with every other young woman in Amherst, she had been entranced by that epitome of the age of sentiment, Ik Marvel's *Reveries of a Bachelor*. To girls reaching maturity in the lingering atmosphere of Puritan attitudes the *Reveries* came as a light unto their souls, uncovering all sorts of emotional indulgence for vicarious enjoyment. Emily, Vinnie and Sue mooned over it so openly that Mr. Dickinson, grumpily comparing Marvel to the more substantial writers of his own youth, labeled it ridiculous. Some ten years later, in attempting to develop another idea from *Aurora Leigh*, Emily remembered one of Marvel's notions and used it as the setting for a ragged twenty-line poem in which she also made use of the phosphorescence symbol. Aurora, in talking of her restricted childhood, remarks that she was able to rise above it,

though certain of your feebler souls
Go out in such a process.

Emily tied that observation in with Marvel's psychological distinction between types of people: those who are, like sea-coal,
flashy, undependable, soon extinguished, and those who resem-
ble anthracite, slower-burning, steady, and with an intenser heat.
Having no one in particular in mind, she wrote:

> More life went out when he went
> Than ordinary breath;
> Lit with a finer phosphor . . .

To extinguish this anthracite type, she continued, requires

> A power of renowned cold,
> The climate of the grave,
> A temperature just adequate,
> So anthracite to live . . .

With the long-ago demise of Marvel's book no one remembered
his coal-people, and that "anthracite" in Emily's line puzzled
readers until one commentator picked up a copy of the *Reveries*.
With that, it became obvious what the line was supposed to
mean, but the fact that Emily, prompted by Mrs. Browning, had
constructed the whole poem on Marvel's distinction remained
elusive and there was much hunting for the mysterious party
supposed to be commemorated in the verse.

The temptation to mount a dogged pursuit of Emily through
all the more specific reading of these years is strong, and there is
no difficulty in determining much of what she was reading.
Among the more inviting works were Thackeray's *Vanity Fair*,
two or three of George Eliot's novels, the works of Coventry Pat-
more and Sir Thomas Browne, Theodore Parker's *Experience as
a Minister*, and even the *Imitation of Christ* (a gift from Sue).

Thomas De Quincey was one writer in whom she showed a lively interest and she must have found his unique and powerful mind quite congenial. His multitude of magazine papers, just then being gathered into volumes, may yet turn out a storehouse of Dickinson ideas. As one example, take a phrase in his lengthy article on Homer: "He talked to her in *italics*." That could not have been the first time any writer had employed the figure, yet Emily used the same symbolism, weightily, in a half-dozen poems at a time when her letters show her to have been attracted to De Quincey.

In addition to all this, there is her steady companionship with the other poems and prose of Mrs. Browning, Emerson, the Brontës, the monthly issues of the *Atlantic, Harper's, Scribners,* and the *Century,* as well as the ever-present newspapers. To repeat, the temptation to pursue her through this wilderness is strong, but it would be an infinitely tedious, mind-boggling task, requiring huge amounts of patience, time and effort. With the ground laid, the point established, further mere cataloguing of her subtle plundering is hereby resigned to others.

Through all these unrelenting days and nights of nervous effort, Emily relied greatly on Sue for an objective evaluation of her work, constantly dispatching to the other house copies of whatever she thought worthwhile. In some quarters there is a tendency, too innocently believing the assertions of the Todd forces, to deny the crucial part that Sue played, but there can really be no doubt of it. There still exist one hundred (out of many hundreds sent during her lifetime) of the copies made for Sue during Emily's first flurry of composition, and it shouldn't be forgotten that the two women were in daily contact. It was a matter of seconds for Emily to run over the little pathway clutching her latest achievement, excitedly anticipating Sue's opinion, and of these impromptu consultations there would have survived no record. One clear instance of their collaboration, however, does emerge from the mists of a century and it is enough to settle the matter.

In the spring of 1861 Emily began to rework a poem she had written a couple of years earlier. Sending the results to Sue, she ventured, "Perhaps this verse would please you better." The poem in question was the justly famous "Safe in their alabaster chambers," a marvelous evocation of the unutterable peace and finality of the grave (suggested—it is too good and well-known a poem to let this slide past without a nod—by a passage in *Aurora Leigh* alluding to the burial of Alaric the Visigoth). On reading it, Sue replied that she did not care for the second verse. "It is remarkable as the chain lightning that blinds us hot nights in the southern sky," she conceded, "but it does not go with the ghostly shimmer of the first verse as well as the other one . . . Strange things always go alone—as there is only one Gabriel and one sun . . . I always go to the fire and get warm after thinking of it, but I never *can* again."* A little while afterward, perhaps in a few days, Emily sent a new second verse, at the same time cautioning Sue against partiality in her judgment, that perpetual dread of writers who solicit criticism from friends. The note finishes with a remark that shows unequivocally—if further evidence is needed—the direction in which all her hopes were bent. "Could I make you and Austin proud," she murmurs bashfully, "sometime, a great way off,—'twould give me taller feet."

A more searching question about Sue's role in Emily's artistic life concerns whether she was entirely aware of how these poems, at least a large number of them, were being produced. That no contemporary proof exists is scarcely pertinent: until now Emily's massive rummaging has been unsuspected because somewhere along the line all sign of it was deliberately obliterated. But it is unbelievable to think that Sue could have witnessed the flood of verse from that busy pen, on subjects so varied and so unlike those Emily had handled in previous years, without having her curiosity aroused, the same curiosity felt by Emily's modern critics, only much more immediate and personal. In the face of questioning, Emily would hardly have dissembled, in fact would

* *Letters of ED,* II, 380.

have had no reason to do so, since she probably began the whole operation merely as a means of sharpening her technique, not until later coming to regard the resulting poems as legitimately her own.

Yet, despite such reasoning, the bothersome query remains: Did Sue in fact know what her sister-in-law was doing? Did she know that all the many books and magazines they so enthusiastically shared were being carefully combed by Emily and that her arresting little verses had enjoyed a double birth? The conclusive answer can be found in the one bit of real evidence to have escaped the holocaust that carried away so much else of interest, evidence that survived only because it happened to reach print before there was any need to cover up the past. On May 18, 1886, three days after Emily's death and just before Vinnie came upon the first box of poems, an obituary written by Sue appeared in the *Republican.* One passage referring to the poetry —unpublished, and for all Sue could judge, destined to stay unpublished—contains an unguarded admission that has slipped by entirely unnoticed. Emily was an avid reader, Sue wrote: "keen and eclectic in her literary tastes she sifted libraries to Shakespeare and Browning; quick as the electric spark in her intuitions and analyses, she seized the kernel instantly, almost impatient of the fewest words by which she must make her revelation." If that sentence was largely unintelligible to the *Republican's* readers at the time, and if it has remained inscrutable ever since, it is so no longer. (Small wonder that after Emily's death Sue hesitated for two years about publishing the poems, and then began thinking in terms of a limited private edition.)

By the end of 1860 Emily had become convinced that her apprenticeship was over; the shadow that crept over the land in November with the election of Abraham Lincoln failed to dim the sun rising in Amherst. When South Carolina seceded in the last days of the year, Emily was expectantly awaiting the appearance of one of her poems in the *Republican,* oblivious to the shudder passing through the country. Southern guns opened on Fort Sumter in April, and her sole recorded comment on the tragedy that ensued was this embarrassing flippancy: "I shall have no winter this year—on account of the soldiers—Since I cannot weave blankets or boots—I thought it best to omit the season." It was not just the season she omitted but the entire war; aside from her reactions to the deaths of one or two Amherst men, and two or three obscure verses, she resolutely turned her back on the conflict. Reading her letters of these years, it is easy to forget that the future of her homeland was in the balance. All that mattered now was the culmination of her own long and feverish struggle.

Three weeks after the Civil War began with the attack on Fort Sumter, the *Republican* in its issue of Saturday, May 4, carried eight poems, most of them anonymous. Four of them appeared on page six, all patriotic exhortations on the war, and four more on the back page, one on the war and three on general topics. The last of these, unsigned, was Emily's "I taste a liquor never brewed," a clever variation on Emerson.* Someone, either Bowles himself or an editor, had tamed the exuberance in two or three of the lines, dulling the piece a little in the process. Emily, for instance, had achieved the delicate rhyme "pearl-alcohol"; the editor was unable to accept so provincial a technique and rewrote —maimed—the line to achieve "pearl-whirl." Still, the poem retained most of its original force and was vastly superior to the other seven effusions that had been given place over it. But hindsight distorts everything, and it is necessary to read the verse in its contemporary dress, overshadowed by column after column of war news, advertisements and the usual hodge-podge of ephemera—so vital then, so forgotten now—to appreciate how Emily's forlorn little effort could have seemed no great revelation, could have passed unnoticed to die with the arrival of the next day's paper.

* Capps, 114–16.

Her triumph was confined to her own family, probably also a few friends and relatives, but convinced that she was on her way to fame, she reacted in typical fashion by exultantly dashing off three or four poems in celebration. "I'm ceded," she declared, adapting the country's troubles to herself, "I've stopped being theirs," and she goes on to explain her secession is for the purpose of choosing "just a Crown." Aurora Leigh had made much of crowns as symbols of artistic success, and Emily viewed the poem in the *Republican* as the first jewel in her own, her life suddenly brought to the full by "one small diadem." She calls for a trumpet and troops of the heavenly host to witness her coronation:

> Get Gabriel to tell the royal syllable,
> Get saints with new unsteady tongue
> To say what trance below
> Most like their glory show,
> Fittest the Crown!

Continuing the royalty theme, she surmises confidently that she is about to "wake a Bourbon," and had better get ready lest she appear with "the surprised air" of a rustic summoned by the Queen.

But her most typical and in its way most pathetic reaction to this first publication seems to have been a tender letter of gratitude to Mrs. Browning in Florence. This hitherto unsuspected probability—no, certainty—emerges clearly from an analysis of a poem that has caused much discussion because of the fact that it exists in two forms, one with feminine pronouns and one with masculine. Only the first few lines are needed here:

> Going to Her!
> Happy letter! Tell her,
> Tell her the page I never wrote!
> Tell her I only said the syntax,
> And left the verb and the pronoun out! . . .

Either this poem or a letter to which it may refer was to have been sent to Mrs. Browning, but she died on June 30, 1861, and Emily must have heard the sad news within a week or two. That the poem is connected with Mrs. Browning is easily shown: In the eighth book of *Aurora Leigh*, Romney is indulging in another of his frequent harangues on the meaning of life, in the course of which he manages to wring in a grammatical illustration of his theme:

> Is there any common phrase
> Significant, when the adverb's heard alone,
> The verb being absent, and the pronoun out?

The news of Mrs. Browning's death probably prevented the sending of the letter; among some elegiac verses that Emily composed on her in the latter months of 1861, there is one that opens with this admission: "I went to thank her, but she slept." That could mean either that a letter had been sent or was about to be sent when news of the death appeared in the papers; either way it clearly expresses Emily's disappointment at failing to set incense before a living idol. She did not feel the same intense sympathy for Robert Browning's works but did revere him as standing next the throne. With Elizabeth gone, she now changed the focus of the poem by switching the pronouns and either wrote Robert of her gratitude toward his wife or contemplated doing so. Perhaps somewhere in England or Italy, in a neglected cache of Browning papers, there is still a wistful note from a grateful young woman in Amherst.

It had now been almost five years since Emily began serious writing, and for each of those years she had averaged well over a hundred poems, probably discarding in the process an equal number as unworkable. Even admitting that a high proportion of these, say three quarters, had been cut from borrowed goods, and that many were inconsequential, her achievement still was impressive, particularly in its manipulation of language and its prosodic daring. Though she employed the simplest of forms—unquestionably because of a native incapacity for anything more elaborate—by using a novel species of muted rhyme and exploded grammar she was frequently able to make the old ballad and hymn stanzas quicken into something fresh and new.

For her success she had to pay an unexpected price. The long hours with books, magazines and newspapers; the close reading and writing in the dim glow of candle or lamp while the rest of the room was in darkness; the strain and pressures of continued mental agitation, all these reacted on her in the fall of 1861, bringing a frightening attack of eye trouble. Though there is no sign that the condition had progressed to any serious extent, the possibility of losing her sight just when she was reaching her goal filled Emily with dread. That she might never be able to read again was the only woe, she confessed, that "ever made me tremble,"* a confession that is even more understandable now in light of the use to which she put much of her reading.

The difficulty seems to have hung on for two or three months, and so depressed was she by its tenacity and its uncertain course that she withdrew into solitary brooding, avoiding callers whenever she could do so with grace and sometimes even when it appeared downright rudeness. Late in October, Sam Bowles, who was himself recovering from an illness, dropped in at Austin's house and inquired for Emily, probably also sending over a note suggesting she join them. Without answering the note she kept to her room, then the following day sent an apology: "Perhaps you thought I didn't care—because I stayed out yesterday, I did care, Mr. Bowles. I pray for your sweet health to 'Alla' every morning—but something troubled me—and I knew you needed light and air—so I didn't come." Whatever was the exact nature of the malady, her eyes were bad enough to put a stop to her writing for a while, and in her loneliness she began wishing for the sympathetic company of her young cousin Loo Norcross.

* *Lyman Letters,* 76.

When Loo regretfully replied she couldn't make the trip just then, the tears flowed.

Gradually the attack passed off, leaving no traceable damage. There was no extensive treatment, nor did the incident manage to get itself remembered by any of her family. The letters she wrote in the final months of the year (five manuscripts survive) bespeak healthy eyes. They are all in ink, showing her usual steady hand in small, delicate, firmly-traced characters. The fright she experienced was real, nevertheless, and not quickly forgotten, and out of it may have come the decision to wait no longer in her assault on the recognition that would make her brother's family proud and give her taller feet.

Sometime in December she and Sue came up with a plan for action. They would approach an established literary personality who could look at the poems objectively and who would have the necessary contacts to make things happen if he was impressed. There were a number of men who might have answered these requirements but one in particular seemed most suitable: Thomas Wentworth Higginson, well-known Cambridge man of letters, essayist, liberal reformer and friend of everybody who was anybody. What finally swung the decision in his favor was probably his public espousal of the cause of women's rights, a topic on which he was sincerely outspoken and perpetually active. (Why not Emerson himself, is the question asked today, with much shaking of heads. Probably because his objectivity was suspect, since he was now an acquaintance of the Dickinsons, and a cousin of his was married to an Amherst man friendly with the family.) Higginson must have seemed just right to the girls, and they had no doubt, of course, about his being impressed; that was taken for granted. Emily, wanting to get a prior look at the man to whom she was entrusting her future, asked Bowles if he could supply a portrait. Bowles answered that he had none and the matter dragged on into the early months of 1862, when Emily had the pleasure of her second appearance as a poet in Bowles' paper. *"Has girl read Republican?"* Sue inquired by note on the day of the poem's publication. "It takes as long to start our Fleet as the Burnside."—an allusion to the naval campaign then in progress under General Burnside on the North Carolina coast. "Our Fleet," of course, refers to the six hundred or so poems Emily had in manuscript, and Sue's easy use of the phrase sets to rest any smallest doubt of her total involvement. With the arrival about two weeks later of the April issue of the *Atlantic,* the dormant plan to approach Higginson was galvanized. The magazine contained an article by him, invitingly entitled "Letter to a Young Contributor," in which he discussed everything from the art of writing to the preferred manner of getting an editor's attention.

With Sue hovering at her shoulder—who can doubt it?—Emily sat down on April 15 and wrote a short note to Higginson, enclosing four poems. She did not put her signature to the note—that would have been too ordinary—but scribbled it on a separate card which she enclosed in its own envelope. As the days passed she felt a little nervous and began to wish she could fly to Higginson's house and peek through his window while he was reading her manuscripts. But in her heart there was no real fear. While waiting, her confident expectations overflowed into a number of happy little verses, all of them proclaiming that her Dark was at last about to change to brilliant day. Almost humming as she writes, she declares it is time

> to smooth the hair
> And get the dimples ready,
> And wonder we could care
> For that old faded Midnight
> That frightened but an hour.

· 5 ·

MY VERSE, DOES IT BREATHE?

IN A MILITARY recruiting office in Worcester, Massachusetts, thirty miles from Amherst, Thomas Wentworth Higginson was busy presiding over the induction of volunteers into the 51st Massachusetts Regiment. With the war a year old, he had become uneasy about doing nothing for the Union cause, and had accepted the position of recruiting officer, a post he regarded only as a beginning. In his spare time he was hard at work on books of military tactics and history, hoping soon to take a more direct hand in the conflict. Thirty-eight years old, with a semi-invalid wife, he had long been a staunch Abolitionist, had engaged in secret support of old John Brown, and was soon to undertake an historic assignment, command of the first Negro combat regiment. It was into this martial atmosphere that there floated, on April 16, a naïvely hesitant voice from Amherst:

Mr Higginson,
Are you too deeply occupied to say if my verse is alive? The mind is so near itself—it cannot see, distinctly—and I have none to ask— Should you think it breathed—and had you the leisure to tell me, I should feel quick gratitude—If I make the mistake—that you dared to tell me—would give me sincerer honor toward you—I enclose my name—asking you, if you please—Sir—to tell me what is true? That

you will not betray me—it is needless to ask—since Honor is its own pawn—

The spasmodic disregard for proper punctuation in the letter would not have bothered him, since it was a common failing among the educated in those days. When he found the same airy license in the four poems, however, he seems to have suspected that his correspondent was very young, and the impression could only have been strengthened by what appeared, on first reading, to be a serious technical ineptitude, particularly in the stumbling rhyme schemes. Still, he was immediately captivated by the spirited imagination that shone through the faults, and he answered within a day or two. While his letter no longer exists, it is easily reconstructed from Emily's later reply, as well as his own sentiments expressed elsewhere. Like a good editor experienced in working with promising young hopefuls, he first praised the applicant, saying there seemed genuine talent present, talent that could be nurtured. Then he quickly went on to advise against publication just yet. Freshness of concept and vitality of language, he explained, were not enough in poetry, there must also be form, for without it there was no perfection and no immortality. Some of her work was fresh, but it lacked finish; the rhymes, he pointed out, were sometimes exact, sometimes badly bent, and occasionally lost sight of altogether. Walt Whitman was a good example of this lack of finish—did Emily read Whitman, and had she been influenced by him? He closed by inviting his correspondent to write again and tell something of her schooling, reading, family and background. Perhaps also, he ventured, she might indicate how old she was?

Higginson's letter reached Emily's anxious hands about April 20, and the result was disastrous. Instead of being hailed as a mature artist ready to take a bow, she had been treated as if she were a talented child needing instruction. The weary hours of her five-year apprenticeship—the painful labor expended on each line and word, the careful effort to liberate meter and rhyme—

all flowed back on her now in a cascade of doubt and she became ill. Always the kind of person in whom emotional stress caused bodily breakdown, she took to her bed and stayed there for more than a month. This is proof enough, even if abundant proofs were not available elsewhere, of her essential immaturity. To pin all her hopes on the opinion of one man and to react so violently to an unfavorable reply is the mark of an incomplete personality; such things happen, of course, but not often to those who have passed the age of thirty and believe themselves whole. To the mature, in art as in life, a rebuff is unpleasant, not devastating.

About a week after being hit by Higginson's thunderbolt, she had recovered enough to prop herself up in bed and prepare a careful answer. Hurt, and thoroughly on the defensive, she penned a studied and blithely lying missive that allowed her to remain behind her mask and that was all too clearly intended to mantle her with the charm of strangeness. "Your kindness claimed earlier gratitude," she began, "but I was ill—and write today from my pillow." She thanks him for the "surgery" and bravely says it was not really painful. To all his questions she responds with outright lies, evasions and half-truths, maligning her parents in the process:

You asked how old I was? I made no verse—but one or two—until this winter—Sir—I had a terror since September I could tell to none —and so I sing, as the boy does by the burying ground—because I am afraid—You inquire my books—For poets—I have Keats—and Mr and Mrs Browning. For prose—Mr Ruskin—Sir Thomas Browne— and the Revelations. I went to school—but in your manner of the phrase—had no education . . . I have a brother and Sister—My mother does not care for thought—and Father, too busy with his briefs, to notice what we do—He buys me many books but begs me not to read them—because he fears they joggle the mind.

With all the wonderful pertness of a child trying to salvage its dignity in the face of a reprimand, she informs Higginson that two editors—not one but two—"came to my Father's house this winter—and asked me for my Mind—and when I asked them 'why' they said I was penurious—and they would use it for the world." Thus, even if Higginson didn't think much of her work, she pouts, there were others who did, though she felt no urgent need to explain that the editors in question, undoubtedly Bowles and Dr. Holland, were friends of the family, and their request for her mind a simple invitation to send another poem to the *Republican.*

This letter, addressed to an utter stranger, one to whom she is supposedly committing all her hopes in honest confidence, is nothing less than shocking, though it has always before been accepted with an indulgent smile. Here set in an intelligible framework of circumstance, it appears for what it is: not a witty rejoinder but the work of a badly wavering personality liable under stress to seek any shielding stance, to retreat in adversity to the familiar bower of her own soul, closing the shutters. That raw-nerve reaction is precisely reflected in another passage of the letter where she replies to Higginson's inquiry about her companions. The hills, the sundown, and "the noise in the pool at noon," are the items listed as preferable to flesh-and-blood, along with Carlo. She sent three more poems, said she was willing to learn whatever he could teach, and asked plaintively if such esoteric knowledge was "unconveyed—like melody—or witchcraft?" It was a hesitant request. If Higginson was right, if she had not in five furious years been able to reach artistic maturity, perhaps the secret would remain as elusive as a half-remembered tune or as imponderable as magic. Perhaps poets, like witches, really were born, and not made.

Through May and into June she continued much of the time in bed, writing an occasional letter to a friend, doing no work, only now and then tending her garden. Into the willing ear of Loo Norcross, following the death of a near relative, she pours a complaint that it is not always clear how life's anguish can receive adequate compensation. With Mrs. Holland she made an attempt to be lighthearted, but a flash of her deepest feelings escaped in spite of her, in words whose inner meaning, probably not caught by Mrs. Holland, is now unmistakable, words which must be among the saddest in literature. After some preliminary banter the letter takes a sudden twist and her heart overflows. "Perhaps you laugh at me! Perhaps the whole United States are laughing at me too! . . . I found a bird this morning, down—down—on a little bush at the foot of the garden, and wherefore sing, I said, since nobody *hears?* One sob in the throat, one flutter of bosom—'My business is to *sing'*—and away she rose!" The first chill cast over her by Higginson's letter had begun to dissipate and she was groping blindly for some reason why she, too, should continue to sing. Sue, of course, had quickly discovered the tone of Higginson's reply, and she consoled her sister-in-law with a reminder cast in the same mold. She is sorry for the shock Emily has received, she says in a note, but it must not be allowed to silence her; "If a nightingale sings with her breast against a thorn, why not *we?*"*

Higginson by now had been elected a captain in the 51st, and had also taken over the training of troops encamped near Worcester, yet he still found time for his pupil. He couldn't have deduced much about her from the second letter, though it probably told him she was older than he had suspected, and he must have wondered about the "terror" (the eye trouble, of course) and who the editors were. The same inner vitality was present in the three poems, however, and his first impression of originality and poetic force was deepened. He wrote once more about mid-May and (again inferring his reply from her later one) this time was careful to emphasize his very real admiration for her rare and original gift, quite aside from technical considerations, which after all could be learned. She was already a true poet, in the best sense, he assured her, but he also repeated his opinion that it might be better to delay publishing, since a little study could remove the blemishes.

On receiving this more emphatic commendation, Emily

* Ms. letter, Houghton Library.

promptly answered that she had known "few pleasures so deep as your opinion, and if I tried to thank you, my tears would block my tongue." That admission was made early in June, at the same time that her illness dropped away, leaving her feeling alive and well again. The thought of publishing, she lied to her teacher, had never entered her head; she was no shallow female pining for the applause of a worthless world. "If fame belonged to me," she assured Higginson grandly, "I could not escape her, if she did not, the longest day would pass me on the chase." Her only desire was to grow in her art and she prays that he will continue to instruct her. Higginson was willing to do so, even amid the turmoil of his military occupations, and two or three further letters with perhaps a dozen poems passed between them during the summer.

By now she had recovered fully and had begun to see that she had actually been accorded high praise by one of the country's leading literary arbiters. All was not lost. She was a true poet, even beyond those who flooded newspapers and magazines with technical niceties; true where it counted, in the bone. To Sam Bowles, who was traveling in Europe, she dashed off a report of the happy tidings that her six-year betrothal to the Muse had ended in marriage, even though the consummation of public recognition was still to be achieved:

> Title divine is mine!
> The Wife without the sign!
> Acute degree conferred on me,
> Empress of Calvary!
> Royal, all but the crown!
> Betrothed without the swoon . . .

How precise Higginson's advice may have been, and how much Emily took or was able or willing to take is beyond determination now. He used words like "uncontrolled" and "wayward," and seems to have suggested that she should try dropping rhyme altogether since she appeared unable to manage it with consistent ease. That was a point on which she would have been acutely sensitive, yet instead of seizing the opportunity to submit her theory of rhyme to discussion, she again drew back, dismissing the topic with a wave of her hand: "I thanked you for your justice—but could not drop the bells whose jingling cooled my tramp." (The image, seemingly so typical of Emily's colorful phrasing, was lifted whole from Aurora Leigh's reference to her writing as the ability to "jingle bells upon my robe.") During this time, in any case, Emily's letters show her quite content, even glad, to have Higginson analyze and admonish while she waited for his decision that it was time to publish. He was quite tolerant of her coyness, though at one point, struck no doubt by the Alice-in-Wonderland cast of her correspondence, and growing curiouser and curiouser, inquired if the pupil might have a photo handy. There was no photo, she regretted, but would a verbal description do just as well? She was "small, like the wren, and my hair is bold, like the chestnut burr—and my eyes, like the sherry in the glass that the guest leaves," a description that cleverly focuses on those features for which she was usually praised by people searching for a compliment.

Among most present-day critics there has grown up a peculiar convention, based on no evidence whatever, that Emily cared nothing for Higginson's opinion after his initial response, and only wanted someone to whom she could unburden herself—that her letters in reality were subtle exercises in mockery of her tutor. This idea, one of those convenient assumptions the critical mind is apt to prefer, grew from the supposed disparity between Emily's genius and Higginson's earthbound talents. But if words mean anything, and unless Emily was laboring under a mental handicap more serious than anyone has suspected, her cry for help was genuine:

Will you tell me my fault, frankly as to yourself, for I would rather wince, than die. Men do not call the surgeon, to commend—the bone,

but to set it, Sir, and fracture within, is more critical . . . if at any
time—you regret you received me, or I prove a different fabric to that
you supposed—you must banish me . . . To thank you baffles me.
Are you perfectly powerful? Had I a pleasure you had not I could
delight to bring it.

It was such characteristic phrases as that playful reference to
Higginson's being "perfectly powerful" that gave rise to the idea
that Emily from her Olympian height was merely toying with
the mortal Higginson. To those who believe it, what can be said?

Higginson seems to have heard somewhere (by now he must
have known that his correspondent was the daughter of Amherst's leading citizen) that Emily made a practice of avoiding
people and he inquired about it. Admitting that she did indeed
often find herself "shunning men and women," but declining to tie the habit to so mundane a thing as a writer's need for
isolation, she couldn't resist the opportunity for another flourish.
"They talk of hallowed things aloud," was her explanation, "and
embarrass my dog—He and I dont object to them, if they'll exist
their side." But her disdain for company was not so absolute as
she made it sound. At college commencement exercises in July,
for instance, shortly before she wrote those words, both she and
her dog had been surrounded by a houseful of people, including
Loo Norcross, the Hollands, relatives from Monson, Governor
Banks of Massachusetts, and Judge Lord, who had delivered the
principal address at the ceremonies. Despite the fact that her
spirits were still at a low ebb, she had mingled freely with these
guests.

Yet Higginson's asking about her shyness may have had a more
specific purpose. Among the first poems she had sent him there
was one that must have made him peer a little closer, the well-
known "There came a day at summer's full." This is, or seems
like, a very personal enshrinement of a lost love, a remembrance
of some mournful renunciation between two people who are kept
apart by some unnamed impediment. Higginson could hardly

have avoided connecting this verse with whatever it was he had heard, and Emily seems to have caught his drift very quickly. In plain words she corrected his unspoken surmise: "When I state myself, as the representative of the verse—it does not mean—me—but a supposed person." Higginson was thus the first, but not by any means the last, to draw inferences from that poem, so it may be as well to state here that Emily was, for once, telling the truth. The poem is nothing but an attempt to capture the renunciation scenes between Maggie Tulliver and Stephen in the final chapters of *The Mill on the Floss*.

The praise as well as the mild scoldings continued to flow from the Preceptor, and once he actually admitted that Emily's intricacies seemed now and then too deep for him—which led her to exclaim in happy disbelief that he couldn't mean it, that he must be joking. But it was she who was joking, not Higginson, for this same letter contains the most outrageous falsehood she ever uttered—one which may have been at the same time an unconscious effort to confess her dependence on borrowed seed, an urge perhaps quickened by Higginson's notice of the philosophic substance of her poems. "I marked a line in one verse," she says, "because I met it after I made it—and never consciously touch a paint, mixed by another person." This attempt at self justification probably intends to make a tenuous distinction between matter and language: ideas she could appropriate without dishonor, so long as she avoided the actual verbal tints of her sources. Having gotten that bit of shuffling off her chest, she then abruptly brought in the very person from whom she had borrowed the most. "Have you the portrait of Mrs. Browning?" she asks. "Persons sent me three—if you had none, will you have mine?" Consciously or unconsciously in that statement she was fishing for an inquiry from Higginson (why should so many people send her the Englishwoman's portrait?) which might have led eventually to disclosure of her methods. But he did not take the bait and the secret remained intact.

Of all American men of letters, great and small, Thomas Higginson, in a way, fell on the greatest misfortune. Never a writer of importance and sensibly aware of his journeyman status, he yet commanded a high and legitimate regard, as well as serving as one of the working cogs around which New England culture revolved. Today, solely because of his supposed wooden-headed handling of Emily, he is seen as a bumbling mouther of artistic rules and regulations who could not recognize a genius under his own nose. That verdict, even when pronounced in softer terms, is now general throughout Dickinson scholarship. But among all the surprising oversights of that same scholarship the most stupefying by far is the failure to take more than the most perfunctory look at the roll Higginson played in Emily's career. A more minute analysis of their relationship not only goes far toward exonerating Higginson, but also uncovers the hidden key to much of Emily's subsequent life. For the first time she is revealed as one more casualty of the Civil War.

The letter containing the mention of Mrs. Browning was sent in August, at a time when Higginson was engaged in training troops in the Worcester encampment, and also preparing to go south to his new command. When no answer arrived after a month or more of waiting, Emily inquired timidly if she had "displeased" her teacher, begging in some puzzlement, "But won't you tell me how?" and Higginson can easily be forgiven if he began to doubt the lady's awareness of current events or of anything outside her own affairs. But he had been ordered south and had no time to send even a brief reply. Unknown to Emily, he departed from Worcester late in November and was effectively removed, perhaps mentally even more than physically, from immediate concern with such things as rhyme and grammar. In this silence her fears began to kindle again: why didn't her Preceptor answer? Had he decided she was after all not worth helping? Had it all been an act of kindness on his part? By December, after five long months of trepidation, she was so thoroughly shaken, her faith in herself so undermined, that she took to her room, one day refusing to see Sam Bowles who was paying his first visit after returning from Europe. She had sent him a letter in August, along with the poem, when she felt sure that fame was just around the corner, a lengthy letter insisting how they all looked forward to seeing him again. Now, with Bowles in the parlor, she stayed behind her own door, unable in her depression to face him. Again she scribbled an apologetic note, again failing to specify any reason for her shyness. Vinnie and Austin were both present and probably went upstairs to see what was the matter. They had their curiosity left unsatisfied, and after Bowles' departure they "upbraided" their sister for her rudeness.

The entire year of 1863 passed without word from Higginson. Emily wrote him twice, once in January when she saw a story about his activities in the *Republican,* and again a few months later when his silence continued. The January letter, sent as it was to a man leading troops into combat, must be one of the weirdest messages ever to reach the front lines:

I did not deem that planetary forces annulled—but suffered an exchange of territory or world—I should have liked to see you, before you became improbable. War feels to me an oblique place—should there be other summers would you perhaps come? . . . Should you, before this reaches you, experience immortality, who will inform me of the exchange? Could you, with honor, avoid death, I entreat you—Sir—it would bereave   Your Gnome.

When that badly calculated bit of whimsy brought no reply, she sobered up considerably. The change in attitude was a natural result of her continued deepening frustration, but it was helped by a sudden death close to home, that of a well-loved uncle, the father of Loo and Fanny. The second note drops all pretense in favor of outright pleading:

You were so generous to me that if possible I offended you, I could not too deeply apologize. To doubt my high behavior is a new pain —I could be honorable no more—till I asked you about it. I know not what to deem myself—yesterday 'your Scholar'—but might I be the one you tonight forgive, tis a better honor—mine is but just the Thief's request—Please, Sir, hear 'Barabbas'

That was strong language, putting Higginson in Christ's place and making herself the criminal pleader for Paradise, but still no answer came, and if it all begins to appear more than a little amazing that Emily could be so obtuse about the reason for Higginson's silence, so wrapped in herself that she kept pulling and tugging at a man facing an enemy's guns, it is no more and no less than a simple fact. Underlying it, of course, was her need of reassurance, a desperate need which dimmed and subdued all the clatter of war to inconsequential background noise. In July, again unknown to Emily, Higginson was wounded by the concussion from an exploding shell and invalided home. Somehow she missed the *Republican's* report of that occurrence,* and her summer drifted by in "loneliness . . . too daily to relate," as well as a steady crumbling of spirit.

Emily's poetry, as is now abundantly clear, can never be taken as autobiographical without strong evidence to support the claim; too often she will be found parading in a rented costume. There is one poem, however, which fits the known facts so exactly that there can be no hesitation about its personal reference. It is a brief sketch, in twenty-four lines, of her whole life since the encounter with *Aurora Leigh* seven years before, and its final stanza unequivocally intones an elegy for the death of her poetic ambitions. Built around her memory of three different, epochal days, the poem is her valedictory to all thought of fame. The first day, she recalls, occurred in the cold of November when "hope it was that kept me warm." The second day took place in summer when fear "put icicles upon my soul." Those two days, beyond the shadow of doubt, refer to the glorious visions aroused by her reading of *Aurora Leigh,* and to the sick disappointment that followed her first contact with Higginson. The third day, which

* July 24, 1863.

occurred as she was writing the poem, was the most terrible day
of her life, the day on which her fears of failure enlarged to shat-
tering reality. It was

> . . . the day that I despaired;
> This, if I forget,
> Nature will that it be night
> After sun has set;
> Dark shall overtake the sky
> And put out her eye . . .

When she uttered that bitter cry, she had not heard from Higginson in eighteen months, a year and a half during which her
brooding had eaten away her never too firm confidence, leaving
her crushed and struggling beneath enormous self-doubt—years
later she was to tell Higginson that, to her, his mere approbation
was fame, its withdrawal "infamy." In a dozen or more poems
composed at this time, she continued the one-sided colloquy, at
one moment proclaiming herself as worthy of a crown, the next
insisting shrilly that public recognition didn't matter to a true
artist or again throwing defiance at Higginson's apparent indifference. Grasping for an idea in which to express her confused
and altered feelings toward her Preceptor, she snatched at a passage in *Aurora Leigh,*

> The music soars within the little lark,
> And the lark soars. It is not thus with men.
> We do not make our places with our strains . . .

and this time casting Higginson as Doubting Thomas the Apostle
who would not believe until he had felt the wound, she invites
him to rend the music-laden lark, herself, and witness the red
flow of authentic song:

> Split the lark and you'll find the music . . .
> Gush after gush reserved for you;

Scarlet experiment! Sceptic Thomas!
Now, do you doubt that your bird was true?

Aside from the poems there is no written evidence of the
turmoil that began to shake Emily in these final months of 1863.
There are no letters of definite date for the latter half of the
year at all, and the two assigned to this period, both to the Norcross sisters, are fragments lifted from originals now destroyed.
But there is on record one undisputed fact equal in significance
to any number of documents: her eyes began to trouble her
again, and they deteriorated so rapidly that a long series of treat-
ments was called for. The shock of her first setback had sent her
collapsing into bed. Now wild despair, corroding what she herself at this very time called "the glittering retinue of nerves,"
drove her to the shelter of incipient blindness. Without two good
eyes she couldn't compose, need not compose, nor need she offer
any excuse for giving up, neither to her own conscience nor to
anyone else. The light of her heart and the light of her eyes went
out together, and by April 1864, she was settled in the Cambridge boarding house of her Norcross cousins under the daily
care of a specialist. The Dark to which she had so confidently bid
farewell two years before now descended once more, no longer
just a symbol, but present in the reality of isolation from her family and of eye-coverings worn part of every day. In this misery
her thoughts turned repeatedly to the idea of existence in shadow.
Remembering how she had so lightheartedly dismissed "that old
faded Midnight," when she thought her morning of recognition
was about to dawn, she now saw herself as a homeless child no
longer afraid of the Dark:

> Good Morning, Midnight,
> I'm coming home;
> Day got tired of me . . .
>
> You are not so fair, Midnight,
> I chose Day,

But please take a little girl
He turned away!

•   •

The number of different Emily Dickinsons that critics over
the last half-century have been able to extract from her nearly
eighteen hundred poems has provided one of the more colorful
side-shows of American literature. In perfect good faith, through
cogent and sometimes sparklingly incisive arguments, she has
been presented, in whole or in part, as a Romantic, a Metaphysical, a Mystic, a Transcendentalist, a Puritan—and con-
versely, liberated by the break-up of social and theological
patterns, an irreverent rider on the tattered coattails of Puritanism. She has been identified as a genius who elevated authentic
American wit to exalted expression, a seeker of awesome sincerity
who turned her back on the shallow rough-and-tumble of her day
to suffer lonely Calvaries of psychic agony, a supreme ironist who
saw life as a delusion, a neurotic who crouched behind her bedroom door in a pathetic effort to arrest the passage of time, and so
on and on. This multiplicity of Emilys has led others to conclude that she was influenced by no particular aesthetic but
wandered as she listed, drawn only by the now-faint, now-pierc-
ing call of myriad humanity. With her mental elasticity and all-
embracing sympathy, it is pointed out, she was not above saying
one thing today and contradicting it tomorrow, and it is true, at
any rate, that inconsistency of attitude is only too evident
throughout her poems. "There is nothing within her purview,"
says one commentator, "toward which, in different moods, she is
not able to entertain two or three various and even contradictory
attitudes." But this fact, he continues, merely demonstrates that
she had a permanently illuminated (if not quite definable) "center of meaning" to which she always returned from her wander-
ings.* Another writer was able to find just the proper-sounding

* Chase, 135.

phrase to dignify the confusion: psychic reconnaisance. Thus the profundities piled up while the little lady herself receded further and further into the distance.

All this was inevitable. Given the bare, confused mass of the poetry, so charged with meaning but so completely detached from chronology and background, critics were driven into the role of archaeologists trying to unravel hieroglyphics in the pre-Rosetta days. The business was an endless, and endlessly fascinating, one, and it tended to curtail inquiry as to how it all had happened—how Shakespearean insight had so suddenly been born in the frail body of a New England spinster, how she had managed to see so much, so minutely, from behind her curtain. And it led them at last in their frustrated impatience to a tacit conspiracy in which it was agreed that the basic facts of Emily's life were all in, the sequences of her artistic growth pretty well settled, and it was time, for God's sake, to get on with the job of elucidating the poems.

There was, of course, only one highly industrious Emily, who took suggestion, as was said of Coleridge with much less reason, as a cat laps milk; who was possessed of extraordinary mimic powers and a preternatural gift of language remarkable for its condensed power to arrest, to stun. And it was, finally, through a fiercely dedicated use of this admittedly unbalanced equipment that she was able to steal, though belatedly, into the company of the immortals. That is the unavoidable conclusion dictated by the facts and the inescapable inferences from them. She is attributable to no school, or is attributable to all of them, because she took from one and all indiscriminately, in full consciousness of what she was doing. She contradicted herself because it was not thought that concerned her but the expression of thought, lack of system being of no consequence to her essentially unreflective mind. Most of her work fails because it did not rise up in the heats of her own imagination, but was taken cold from the printed page, transmuted and transferred, mechanically and without personal involvment, to her own breathless phrases and flitting stanzas.

A generation ago, indeed, there was one jeweler-eyed critic, R. P. Blackmur, whose close study of the poems led him to feel that there was something decidedly odd about them, something disturbingly out of plumb.* Believing, as everyone did then, that she was a monument of originality, he still could not accept her work as a major achievement. The technique, he felt, outweighed the content in some not quite definable way; the imagination had been "insufficiently fed into the words." Despite the undeniable force of the poems, they all seemed little more than "so many exercises in self-expression," given vitality by virtue of a natural aptitude for language. It struck him, in fact, that most of Emily's poetry—and the figure he chooses is amazingly apt—was "initially as near automatic writing as may be."

When Blackmur offered that opinion, he had not seen a certain little poem of Emily's in which she makes an outright confession of her methods, while trying to explain to herself what it was that had blocked her success. It was not published until 1945 and its full significance has never been discerned. Comparing herself to one of the flycatcher birds, she laments:

> I was a phebe, nothing more,
> A phebe, nothing less;
> The little note that others dropped
> I fitted into place.
>
> I dwelt too low that any seek,
> Too shy that any blame;
> A phebe makes a little print
> Upon the floors of fame.

There it was, her secret finally confessed in black and white. Written probably during the severe dejection of her Cambridge

* *Southern Review,* Fall 1937.

stay, those self-accusing words, taken in connection with all that is now known, make it incontrovertibly clear that the bulk of her poems came from those little notes—passing observations—dropped by other writers, and that Emily, like the phoebe or pewee feathering its nest, gave them a place and an existence of their own. Thus there has grown up the situation, undeniably verging on the ludicrous, in which critics discuss Emily's philosophy—when they are able to piece one together out of her kaleidoscopic utterances—by measuring her against the very writers from whom she picked up her ragbag notions in the first place. Usually adding nothing of her own to the notes she appropriated, or so little as to make no difference, she succeeded in creating an artistic anomaly unparalleled in the province of great literature, a true literary Sphinx, whose head does not belong to its body, yet which is implacably *there.*

Recently, one investigator drew up, for the first time, a list of Emily's recorded reading, with the intention of broadly settling the overlooked problem of literary influences. Though he gave only cursory attention to the listed works themselves, and eschewed close analysis, he still found himself juggling sources—mostly partial, as he assured readers—for nearly two hundred poems. Faced with this bundle of "influences," he was forced rather hesitantly to the conclusion that Emily had picked up many words, phrases and ideas from her reading, had even occasionally shaped an entire poem from it. In an equivocating summation he credited Emily's wide-ranging travels in literature with giving her only "vicarious experience and perspective," the poems remaining all the while her own "unique products."* Unique they certainly were, but perhaps not quite in the way this writer intended. The consummate language artistry she brought to bear on her sources is in itself a thing of wonder, and it compels a closer look, if possible, at the young lady plying her new-found trade.

Out of the total body of her work, it is generally agreed, there

* Capps, 5, 145.

are about three hundred poems possessing some interest, less than half of which might be called really fine achievements, and about two dozen of which rank as great, earning Emily her present niche among major writers. Though no pool has ever been taken, among those two dozen the following three would surely find a leading place: the hypnotizing "I felt a funeral in my brain," the deliciously atmospheric "Further in summer than the birds," and, perhaps the finest thing she ever wrote, "Because I could not stop for Death." Within the last five years sources, more or less partial, have been suggested for all three, and it is pertinent to inquire how much of Emily they contain, and how much of the source. Quotation is necessary but fortunately neither poems nor sources are of weary length.

Two of the poems, rather surprisingly, are indebted to Nathaniel Hawthorne—surprisingly, because Emily nowhere makes much of her countryman and the paucity of reference might easily encourage the belief that she had not read much of his work, in fact nothing beyond *The House of the Seven Gables* and that only because it was popular. But it was from one of his now overlooked short stories that, it has been claimed, she extracted the first of the group.* "The Hollow of the Three Hills" is typical if minor Hawthorne, telling a somber tale in which a young woman, separated from her home and family because of a sexual transgression, meets with the local witch in a glade where she is magically enabled to see and hear her far-off loved ones. Toward the end of the story, the woman, who is kneeling on the ground with her head resting on the old crone's knee, hears an ominous sound mixing with the witch's murmur:

. . . the knolling of a bell stole in among the intervals of her words, like a clang that had traveled far over valley and rising ground . . . stronger it grew and sadder, and deepened into the tone of a death bell, knolling dolefully from some ivy-mantled tower . . . Then came a measured tread, passing slowly, slowly on, as of

---

* *New England Quarterly,* September 1969.

mourners with a coffin, their garments trailing on the ground, so that the ear could measure the length of their melancholy array . . . there were revilings and anathemas . . . breathed against the daughter who had wrung the aged hearts of her parents—the wife who had betrayed the trusting fondness of her husband—the mother who sinned against natural affection, and left her child to die. The sweeping sound of the funeral train faded away like a thin vapor . . . When the old woman stirred the kneeling lady, she lifted not her head.

It appears that Emily—cutting away all the incidental details such as the witch, the symbolic setting, the nature of the transgression and the identity of the mourners—deliberately put herself inside the brain of the unfortunate sufferer and tried to reconstruct the harrowing experience from a personal angle. But instead of having the funeral announced by a bell, as with Hawthorne, she saved the tolling for a more dramatic function. By simply stating the primary fact of the passage as it appeared in Hawthorne's story, she achieved a striking first line and then kept skillfully within its framework for the remainder of the poem:

> I felt a funeral in my brain,
> And mourners to and fro
> Kept treading, treading, till it seemed
> That sense was breaking through;
>
> And when they all were seated,
> A service like a drum
> Kept beating, beating, till I thought
> My mind was going numb;
>
> And then I heard them lift a box
> And creak across my soul
> With those same boots of lead again,
> Then space began to toll,
>
> As all the heavens were a bell,
> And being but an ear,

> And I and silence some strange race
> Wrecked, solitary, here;
>
> And then a plank in reason broke,
> And I dropped down and down,
> And hit a world at every plunge,
> And got through knowing then.

If it is granted that nothing in that picture exceeds what is either stated or implied by Hawthorne, or is greatly beyond the power of a normal imagination taking the woman's place, then Emily's essential contribution is the transposition of the bell. It is this twist that suddenly raises the poem above itself, lending it unlimited vague associations and earning it much critical attention. This, then, is the touch of genius, the particle of originality in the poem? Perhaps to some extent, but it is more than probable that Emily is here remembering something else she had read, something of which the man who discovered the Hawthorne passage was not aware. In *Aurora Leigh* there is a scene in which the heroine boards a train for Italy, leaving behind her in England the man she loves, who is about to be married to someone else. Aurora falls into a deeply introspective mood in which she hears imaginary marriage bells tolling ever louder and louder. At last she envisions herself alone in a belfry surrounded by a multitude of bells,

> All clanking at me, in me, over me,
> Until I shrieked a shriek I could not hear,
> And swooned with noise,—but still, along my swoon,
> Was 'ware the baffled changes backward rang,
> Prepared at each emerging sense, to beat
> And clash it out with clangor . . .

The initial idea for Emily's poem undoubtedly came from Hawthorne, but the bell in his story did more than announce the ghostly funeral. It reminded Emily of Aurora's swoon amid the mad tolling of bells, supplying her with a fine denouement for her short verse, and accounting for line four of her poem—the "sense breaking through" being nothing else than Aurora's "emerging sense." Still, though Aurora swoons, she does not go crashing down through a plank, symbolic or otherwise. Emily's verse, quoted above, "I stepped from plank to plank," undoubtedly bears on this stanza, yet it is possible to go even one step further. Toward the end of *Aurora Leigh* a disillusioned Romney indulges in a long harangue of self-pity, and concludes:

> I stood upon my deed and fought my doubt,
> As men will—for I doubted—till at last
> My deed gave way beneath me suddenly . . .

Emily going through a plank in reason, Romney through his self-esteem: there seems little difference.

The poem is thus indebted as much to Mrs. Browning as to Hawthorne, but Emily's contribution, other than word artistry, is hard to pin down. In fact the feeling is strong that in this case at least, her achievement is almost accidental. In attempting to imagine for herself what the experience with Hawthorne's witch must have been like, she severed the mood from the setting, drew the psychological core from the human situation, and wrought greater than she knew. The best proof of this is the continuing wide disagreement over what the poem means. It has been taken as a metaphysical description of an actual funeral, a picture of the effects of grief, and a literal rendering of the onset of insanity —this last, of course, inevitably raising questions about the poet's own mental condition when she wrote the lines.

The second example from Hawthorne need not be presented at length. "Further in summer than the birds" is a straight transcription of a long passage in the introduction to *Mosses from an Old Manse*. The debt is undeniable and what Emily did was to pluck out the main thread, weaving it with delicate precision and perfect control of language into a memorable portrait of Indian summer.* Except for one unusual phrase she brought nothing of her own to the finished verse. That phrase—"a Druidic difference"—does not appear in Hawthorne and is really what gives Emily's poem its rounded perfection. It would be some sort of relief to find that she had thought that one up all by herself, but, alas, the ubiquitous Aurora again intrudes: twice in Mrs. Browning's book the word Druid is used symbolically. Once it is employed to describe the summer sun, which seemed

> On lurid morns or monstrous afternoons
> Like some Druidic idol's fiery brass,
> With fixed, unflickering outline of dead heat . . .

which is not quite what Emily made of the word but close enough. Hawthorne's cricket, moreover, generated three or four other poems for Emily, particularly the well-regarded "As imperceptibly as grief." Before she read Hawthorne, her use of crickets was casual and conventional.

The last of the three demands a more careful analysis, since it seems to have resulted from repeated attempts to embody a single unusual notion, the process of a soul passing from life to death. Emily's work is strewn with verses that speak to the reader from beyond the pale, but this is incomparably the best of them:

> Because I could not stop for Death
> He kindly stopped for me;
> The carriage held but just ourselves,
> And Immortality.
>
> We slowly drove, he knew no haste,
> And I had put away
> My labor and my leisure, too,
> For his civility.

* *American Literature*, May 1967.

We passed the school where children played
At recess in the ring,
We passed the fields of gazing grain,
We passed the setting sun,

Or rather, he passed us;
The dews drew quivering and chill,
For only gossamer my gown,
My tippet only tulle.

We paused before a house that seemed
A swelling of the ground,
The roof was scarcely visible,
The cornice but a mound.

Since then 'tis centuries, but each
Feels shorter than the day
I first surmised the horses' heads
Were toward eternity.

Probably the most praised and interpreted of all her poems, these lines, even so, have managed to keep the critics milling. Is the verse merely a finely witty miniature of a funeral depicted as a carriage ride in the country, with Death in the guise of a suitor? Or does it have some profound Blakean significance involving death, love and immortality? Is the somber carriage a wedding vehicle taking the Bride of Christ to her final rendezvous at the church-grave? Is the carriage life itself with Death at the reins and Immortality a not quite palpable third rider? Is Death, in fact, a welcome caller, or is he a malevolent seducer? The date of the poem's composition is unknown, but the final manuscript was written around 1863, which means it could have been done anytime before that. The date, as it turns out, is of first importance.

In the February 1860 issue of the *Atlantic* Emily read the conclusion of a serial tale in which the first person narrator, in the very last line, suddenly perceives that she has already been dead for twenty minutes.* The passing over has been so gradual and painless that she is enjoying her new state before she realizes that she has taken her final departure. The story had an electrifying effect on Emily, and when she returned the magazine to Sue, from whom she had borrowed it, she enclosed a fervent note: "Sue, it is the only thing I ever read in my life that I didn't think I could have imagined myself!" The remark is odd, since entrance into the after-life is the one thing even ordinary minds can picture, the one thing most people spend a good deal of time *trying* to imagine in an effort to clothe with reality that often troublesome concept. What Emily meant to say, but in her hurry didn't quite express, was that the *artistry* of the story had given her, perhaps for the first time, a thrilling perception of the soul's survival. The skill of the writer, the techniques of fiction, had on the instant made immortality more real for her than all the plodding assertions of reason and dogma. As that realization took firm hold of her mind—judging by the number of poems she wrote on this same theme—she tried over and over to transfer her exciting discovery to verse. But it was not until the work of two other writers somehow coalesced in her memory that she succeeded. And there is something satisfying in the fact that these two writers were man and wife, the Brownings.

It has only recently been pointed out that Emily's poem owes a debt to Robert Browning's "The Last Ride Together."† She owned a personal copy of the book, *Men and Women,* in which this poem appeared. It was published in 1856 and was probably a gift to her from Sue: the contents page bears pencil marks against a number of poems, which was Sue's usual way of indicating to both Emily and Austin those verses that had pleased her most. There is no mark against "The Last Ride Together," yet this was the poem that engaged Emily's attention beyond all others, for it gave her at last the perfect vehicle for capturing the idea

* H. P. Spofford, *The Amber Gods.*
† Capps, 88–89.

she had picked up in the pages of the *Atlantic*. Browning's poem is rather a long one—just over a hundred lines—and includes many elements extraneous to Emily's effort. What her questing mind caught out of it was the basic idea of an unending carriage ride, a ride that begins in time and continues into eternity. In the poem Browning has a rejected lover taking his lost love on a mournful farewell jaunt, during which he consoles himself with varied reflections on the meaning of life. At times his thoughts expand beyond the immediate surroundings:

> . . . it seemed my spirit flew,
> Saw other regions, cities new,
> As the world rushed by on either side. . . .

Toward the end there creeps in a hint that the brooding young man may have something drastic in mind (one must "have bliss to die with" he says ominously) and it closes with him wondering

> What if we still ride on, we two,
> With life forever old yet new,
> Changed not in kind but in degree,
> The instant made eternity,—
> And Heaven just prove that I and she,
> Ride, ride together, forever ride?

It would be worth a good deal to know just when Emily received her copy of *Men and Women*, and when she first read this poem. It might then be easier to trace the process by which she linked the unending carriage ride with a hitherto unsuspected passage in *Aurora Leigh*, in which occurs the transporting of a corpse between house and cemetery. While her letters of these years do mention Robert Browning a number of times, it is only in an incidental way, allowing no conclusions as to her reading. In any case, it was sometime after she read the *Atlantic* story— her imagination holding suspended the idea of a voice speaking

from both sides of the barrier—that there flashed together Browning's last ride and this picture from *Aurora Leigh*:

> Men carry a corpse thus,—past the doorway, past
> The garden gate, the children's playground, up
> The green lane,—then they leave it in the pit
> To sleep . . .

Perhaps it was the world passing by on either side, stated in both
sources, that brought the two into fusion. But that is only a
guess. In the end the catalyst remains unknowable.

The Brownings between them had thus given Emily her poem,
and yet something remains in the haunting lines that did not
come from either. It was Emily herself who made courteous
Death a real presence in that carriage, who saw the low-roofed
house and who surmised the true direction of the horses. In the
poem's first line she speaks from the world of the living. In the
second she dies without travail or full awareness of the terrible
fact. With consciousness unimpaired, she goes on to describe her
own funeral procession and the carefree depositing of her un-
wanted body in the grave. Then in company with Immortality—
Death stops at the tomb but the chaperon crosses the threshold
—she leaps lightly across everlasting centuries of bliss. Here, if
anywhere, her handling of borrowed ideas was truly inspired.
This once, at least, through the ultimate magic of her own words,
she had acquired the calm of faith, gloriously attaining in her
heart the one destination she could never perceive more than
fleetingly in her mind. In that rests the greatness of the verse and
its perpetual appeal, for the dilemma was not hers alone.

It was necessity, of course, that turned Emily into a phoebe,
that made her consciously and continuously indulge in the sort
of thing that most poets do unconsciously and intermittently.
She probably began it as practice but uncovered a fatal facility
as the bundle of manuscripts grew impressively in size, and she
had, or thought she had, the approval of no less an authority than

Ralph Waldo Emerson for what she was doing. In his long essay on Shakespeare, devoted entirely to displaying the thesis that great men draw freely on all that preceded them, he provided Emily with all the justification she needed. "Thought is the property of him who can entertain it," the sage asserted emphatically, "and of him who can adequately place it. A certain awkwardness marks the use of borrowed thoughts, but as soon as we have learned what to do with them, they become our own." That was all very well when understood in the framework of Emerson's general theme—the building of new structures on the foundations of the past—but Emily, in truth, took the words rather literally. And she capped her reading of the essay by snapping up two of its images to use in her own work.

Somewhere during those years a doubt must have crept in about the value of poetry so conceived and so written, but it was palliated by her exuberant feeling of impending success, submerged in the belief that she was on her way to winning a crown. The long interruption of her contact with Higginson allowed time for those doubts to surface, to erode the exuberance, to convince her that she had proved "a different fabric" to what he had supposed, at last to bring nightmarishly swimming before her mind all the hundreds of books, newspapers and magazines, the thousands of printed pages, the million words that had passed under her eyes and from which she had so assiduously picked out those little notes. On this day of despair, in this awful moment of recall—no direct evidence exists, or is needed, for its reality— she was driven to her final decision. She was not a poet but a scavenger, a clever scavenger, too inconsequential for either fame or blame. The poems were not really hers. To publish them would be a lie—and sooner or later someone would find her out. She would not publish; she would never publish. She had been preserved from a terrible error by the accident of Higginson's silence. "You were not aware," she told him later, "that you saved my Life. To thank you in person has been since then one of my few requests." She did eventually thank him in person, but by then had decided to say no more.

• •

As the months passed in the Cambridge boarding house, her aching eyes prevented her from writing much. She did now and then drop a letter to Sue or Vinnie or a thank-you note to some relative who called or sent flowers. The other boarders she viewed as irritations to be avoided, which left her spending a good deal of time alone in her room, a prey to uninterrupted brooding. In one of the first of her letters home she admits her melancholy, though of course she refers it only to the eye trouble:

It is a very sober thing not to have any Vinnie, and to keep my summer in strange towns . . . but I have found friends in the wilderness. You know 'Elijah' did, and to see the 'Ravens' mending my stockings would break a heart long hard—Fanny and Loo are solid gold, Mrs. Bangs and her daughter very kind, and the doctor enthusiastic about my getting well. I suppose I had been discouraged so long . . .

Sue, it appears, was urging her not to despair, to go on writing, and it may have been she who arranged for the publication of two poems in March in an attempt at encouragement: one in the *Republican,* and one in a New York paper, *The Round Table,* edited by an Amherst neighbor. Emily answered that by sending Sue the first stanza of a poem she had written some years before,* reaffirming her decision to remain aloof:

> The soul selects her own society,
> Then shuts the door . . .

During the summer a letter at last arrived from Higginson, the first in two years. He had been discharged from the military

* *Poems,* I, 225.

and was living at Pigeon Cove, Massachusetts, a few miles from Cambridge. But to Emily it no longer mattered. She answered him noncommittally, inquired about his health, said she had not known about his wound, asked if she would be able to see him, but enclosed no poems. Her wish to see Higginson was not new, but this time it may have had a purpose even beyond thanking him for saving her life. "I wish to see you more than before I failed," was the way she phrased it, and the "failed" probably meant as much in art as in health. If he had responded, would she have opened her heart to him, told him of her composing methods, sought his opinion on their legitimacy? No one will ever know. He did not go to see her and the correspondence lapsed for another eighteen months. When it did resume, it limped along for the most part on a single exchange of letters a year, in which Emily did not always enclose verse.

It was in his comparative neglect of his pupil from this time that Higginson may perhaps be judged culpable in a degree. He was always on the lookout for promising newcomers and did sponsor two or three young women writers who became well-known (including Helen Hunt). He now had in his possession some fifteen of Emily's poems, most of them clearly the work of an unusual talent, perhaps three indicative of something beyond talent. Still his interest dribbled away in the face of her own apparent loss of ambition, as well as what appeared to be her insuperable technical defects. He was never able to rid his mind of his Amherst correspondent, however, even amid the pressures of his own active and busy life, and he would later be one of the few permitted to visit her in her seclusion, the last outsider to see her plain. It was probably this long-delayed meeting with his shy pupil that finally taught him not to expect improvement in the form of her poems. Emily, as will be seen, staged a very special performance for this meeting, with the result that Higginson ever afterwards considered her "partially cracked." If he ever had any leaning toward acceptance of the eccentric technique in her work, all such inclination evaporated when he encountered the living eccentric.

Snow was on the ground when Emily returned to Amherst in November 1864, and the glimmering brilliance bothered her eyes, which weren't much better after her eight months of treatment, even the soft lights indoors making her squint. Ordered to rest, she did little but tend her garden for the first few weeks, only gradually getting back into the routine of the house. "I chop the chicken centres when we have roast fowl," she listlessly reported to Loo, ". . . then I make the yellow to the pies, and bang the spice for cake, and knit the soles to the stockings I knit the bodies to last June . . . Mother and Margaret are so kind, Father as gentle as he knows how, and Vinnie good to me." Even with all this solicitude her aching eyes cast her into a mood of settled misery, and with the coming of the new year she was eager for a return to Cambridge.

Now thirty-four years old, suffering emotional exhaustion and without any driving purpose to fill up her days, it would seem that her perpetual midnight had fallen in earnest, that no further darkness could overtake her. But her real night had only just begun. She had fallen in love, and the man she loved was married.

· 6 ·

THUNDER IN THE ROOM

ALL THE FAVORITE candidates for the role of Emily's great love
are now on stage, and it is time the auditioning were begun.
To some it may appear well past that time since, at this point in
the narrative, Emily has written most of her poetry, has made
her anxious bid for fame and has retired from the field in despair, all without the least stimulus from the uprooted heart of
legend. That view so completely contradicts everything that has
been believed to the present, and its exposition involves such a
twisted tale that a somewhat extensive treatment is called for.
In the process, it is hoped, there will unfold the manipulations
of certain nervous hands that attempted to bury the truth forever.

Counting the rampant village gossip of Emily's day, and the
equally pervasive literary gossip since, there are at least a half
dozen names that at one time or another have seriously been
suggested as the man she loved. In addition, there are a few
nameless personalities identified only as a Boston Lawyer or a
disappointed student. Some writers, impatient with this conjec-
tural merry-go-round which always hampers serious study of her
work, more recently have solved the problem by coyly suggesting
that there may have been no lover at all. The mysterious gentle-

man darkly reflected in the poems, they say, could have been the coinage of Emily's own starved heart and fertile imagination, the village rumors only the inevitable consequence of her retired spinsterhood. A few go even further and insist wildly that whether there was a real lover or not is a question of no importance—but this attitude only demonstrates the utter frustration into which the whole subject has driven Dickinson biography.

That there were rumors in town about Emily's love life is true, though even if her neighbors had ignored her, the publication of her poems would have made the topic central to her story. The initial volume, under the heading "Love," contained eighteen poems with such intriguing first lines as "That I did always love" and "I cannot live with you." The second volume offered sixteen additional love verses, some of them with such outspoken beginnings as "I gave myself to him" and "Wild nights! Wild nights!" These were quite enough to provide Amherst tongues with knowing corroboration, and contemporary reviewers with matter for speculation, but the third volume provided still another batch on the same theme, in one of which the poet announced boldly that she was "Proud of my broken heart." Thus, when the publication of the poems was halted in 1896 there were on record nearly sixty of these little lyrics depicting a somber tale of lifelong yearning. It was partly this fact, no doubt, that led the publishers to risk issuing Emily's letters, since notoriety of one kind or another could have been the only reason for expecting sufficient public response to the correspondence of a local minor poet, no matter how enchanting her epistolary style. But eager readers of the letters found nothing in them to confirm or deny the existence of a lover.

The first definite sign of fire behind all this smoke came from a member of her own family, and thus was received by the public as infallible. Emily's niece Martha in 1914 brought out a fourth volume of the poems, stating in a brief introduction that her aunt, contrary to the usual assumptions, had "bewitched" many Amherst males, among them college boys, tutors, law students, and even the prospective husbands of some of her girl friends. More pointedly, yet with becoming reticence, she asserted that her aunt had engaged in one full-blown affair of passion "whose tragedy was due to the integrity of the lovers, who scrupled to take their bliss at another's cost." That sentence, if it didn't add much to the picture, at any rate served to keep the talk alive, but another decade passed before Martha felt free to say any more. When she did speak again, she pulled out all the stops, concealing only the name of the man involved:

All that was ever told was a confidence to Sister Sue, sacredly guarded under all provocation till death . . . it was instantaneous, overwhelming, impossible. There is no doubt that the two predestined souls were kept apart only by her high sense of duty and the necessity of preserving love untarnished by the inevitable destruction of another woman's life. Without stopping to look back she fled to her own home for refuge . . . but only a few days later Sister Sue looked up from her sewing to see Lavinia, pallid and breathless from running, who grasped her wrist with hurrying hand, urging: "Sue, come! That man is here—Father and Mother are away, and I am afraid Emily will go away with him!" but the one word he implored Emily would not say.*

The affair concluded, according to Martha, with the dejected lover dramatically separating from his family and burying himself in the west where he soon died, presumably of a broken heart. Emily continued to live on in the old house, the only reminder of what might have been hanging on the wall of her room, "a picture in a heavy oval frame of gold—unexplained." It was the Rev. Wadsworth that Martha had in mind, of course, though even the most cursory investigation would have shown her the impossibility of fitting him into the pattern of facts she had divulged. And the oval portrait, as she must have known, did not find its way to Emily's wall until many years later.

* Bianchi, *Life,* 47.

Martha's information had come through Sue and it had been accepted unquestioningly. In the other house, however, Vinnie had been spreading a different tale. With the arrival in 1930 of the centennial of Emily's birth, two biographies heralded a renewal of interest in her work. One of these put forth Austin's friend George Gould as the lover, a claim based on the sworn statements of two Amherst women who had long been close to Vinnie. Gould was the man, these elderly women insisted, named by Emily's sister in confidence to them. It was only Mr. Dickinson's stern opposition to this youth, they said, that had prevented a marriage, and it was on the break-up of this affair that Emily had bid the world goodby. The other biography widened the search by identifying the lover as Lieutenant Hunt, the husband of Emily's girlhood friend, a thesis that lacked even hearsay evidence to sustain it. Both hypotheses were soon disintegrating under critical attack, but the search for Emily's lover had now been launched in earnest.

The next voice to speak up was that of the seventy-four-year-old Mabel Todd, at length aroused from her brooding, and it was she who placed the Rev. Wadsworth squarely on center stage. Bringing out a new edition of the *Letters* she added portions of the correspondence that had previously been suppressed, letters Emily had written to Wadsworth's friends, the Clark brothers, after the minister's death. This new material revealed her sadness at Wadsworth's passing as well as a certain depth of affection for him. The nature of that affection, however, was almost transparently the reverence of a religious supplicant toward a spiritual counselor (clouded somewhat by Emily's usual hyperbole) and it was noticeable that she had known nothing of Wadsworth's personal life. A casual, uninfluenced reading of the suppressed matter leads only to the conclusion that Wadsworth, through some special knack, had been able to bolster the religious faith of his timid charge, especially with regard to the truth of immortality. Still, there were phrases referring to him as her "dearest earthly friend," and a man "whom to know was Life," and these prompted Mabel to push the inferences to their limits. "Just what shade of tenderer feeling to ascribe to her attachment," she asked, "who would presume to guess?" When she wrote those words, Mabel was in possession of other unpublished papers that documented an overlapping attachment to a quite different man, but that revelation was to be reserved to her daughter.

The evidence, such as it was, for supporting the reality of some sort of love affair, and of the Wadsworth claim in particular, was augmented when Martha in 1932 published her book *Emily Dickinson Face to Face*. She had always known, she said, of her aunt's renunciation of the man she loved, could recall overhearing as a little girl the low-voiced conversations "when my mother and her sister Mattie were speaking together of the sacrifice of her young romance." Sue and Austin had a horror of gossip, she remembered, and they had impressed on their children from the first that their reclusive relative was not to be discussed with outsiders, though this did not save the children from being questioned on the street by acquaintances and even strangers. When Martha as a sensitive ten-year-old complained about such rudeness, she was directed by her father to "tell them you don't know. Don't say a word more." The true situation was known not only to the immediate family, Martha insisted, but to some relatives and close friends as well. Emily, when visiting in Philadelphia on her way home from Washington, had met and fallen in love with Wadsworth: "The definite renunciation followed a brief interview in her father's house, and left a permanent effect on my aunt's life and vision." That was the story Martha had believed all her adult life, having heard it from her parents, her aunts Vinnie and Mattie (all of whom were dead before Martha began to speak out) as well as from two or three unnamed sources close to the family. She went to her grave holding the Wadsworth version yet she, too, even more than Mabel Todd, had been aware of another love that had brightened

Emily's last years, a love which, as she was well aware, had overlapped the supposed lifelong passion for the minister.

With the appearance in 1938 of the first truly worthwhile biography of the poet, Wadsworth became the official lover—or loved one, since nobody cared to admit that he might have reciprocated to the extent claimed by Martha. Under critical molding Emily's dramatic self-sacrifice was tacitly set aside and Wadsworth cleared of all implication of being the instigator. The great love became nothing more than a hopeless hope on Emily's part, an interior, unvoiced, lifelong turmoil in which no word or look of Wadsworth's played a role—from her twenty-fourth year, in other words, Emily was a frustrated amorous neurotic. No one was quite comfortable with that spectacle, but it nevertheless held until Millicent Todd finally disturbed the contents of her mother's old camphorwood chest.

Thirty years had passed since the day following the lawsuit when Mabel Todd had snapped the lock on the mass of Dickinson papers in her possession, angrily appropriating property not her own. Ever since, she had painfully turned aside all her daughter's questions about the Dickinsons, thereby engendering in Millicent an attitude of awe toward the mysterious contents of the old-fashioned chest. When Dickinson interest began to boom, Mabel at last permitted her fifty-year-old daughter (by then, Mrs. Bingham) to view the treasure. "With thumping heart I turned the key," Millicent recalled, "and for the first time heard that little tune. What I might find within I did not know. I looked and caught my breath. For there, before my eyes, were quantities of Emily's poems. How could they have kept quiet so long? With such inherent vitality it seemed as if they must have shouted lying there in the dark all those years."* It was not only the poems that made her catch her breath, for she also turned up a number of other fascinating documents, three of them love letters which, if they did not shout in the dark, have not ceased to clamor since their publication.

* Bingham, *Bolts of Melody*, Intro., vii.

All three letters were written to someone Emily called "Master," but they contain no indication as to who that Master was. The handwriting places them within the eighteen-sixties, thus neatly fitting into the presumed general pattern of the love affair. That Wadsworth might have been the Master remained no more than a possibility, and close study of the carefully circumscribed language soon brought a cloud of suspicion round the handsome head of Sam Bowles. Half a dozen writers, combing through Emily's poems and correspondence, engaged in a minute analysis of her relations with the dynamic editor and concluded that here at last was the culprit. Emily had been infatuated with the married Bowles, it was said, had offered both her poems and herself to him only to have both items summarily declined, whereupon she retreated behind the hedges in hurt and embarrassment. The theory rested on much convoluted reasoning, selected half-truths, and assiduous overlooking of bothersome facts, but it was an interesting suggestion and Sam Bowles was given place beside Wadsworth. That this turned Emily into something of a Jezebel didn't seem to faze Bowles's supporters: all the while Emily was supposedly chasing the editor she was in friendly, even warm, correspondence with his wife. In any case, Mrs. Bowles at this time was more worried, with some reason, about a certain Maria Whitney as a rival for her husband's affections.

That Bowles should have drawn attention was inevitable from the first; he would have been given his turn at the honors even without the Master letters. The only surprising thing is that their discovery did not produce a perfect rash of candidates. Using the same shaky methods that have been expended on the Bowles theory, any number of men might qualify. The long-forgotten Henry Emmons comes first to mind, and it would be no trick at all to accumulate a dossier in his behalf. Emily's cousin John Graves and her father's law partner Elbridge Bowdoin, would require but little additional effort. Joseph Lyman offers a fairly large target as well as a more sensational angle, and an obscure family friend in a nearby town, the Rev. John Dudley, would not be above suspicion to an easy-going analyst. Lieutenant Hunt and George Gould could be brought back into the race, and even Thomas Wentworth Higginson himself, though the mere hint of such a thing would probably have struck him dumb, might be promoted to the rank of Master.

Underlying all such efforts, however, would be a judicious slicing up of Emily's poems into slivers of autobiography, and of all dubious undertakings that is supremely the most doubtful. While there must be autobiographical elements here and there in the poems—what poet has avoided that?—the bulk of Emily's work consists of personalized borrowings unrelated to her own life. Even those comparatively few poems which do seem to carry a personal tinge have proved, wrapped in symbolism as they are, woefully misleading to investigators. This is especially true of those verses which revolve on the "wife" and "marriage" themes, all of which in reality identify Emily as a poet and are built on the marriage-to-the-Muse convention first expressed in the lines composed at the time of Sue's marriage, "Ourselves were wed one summer." In such poems, indeed, Emily did write her literary autobiography, all the way from the ecstatic flowering of her ambition late in 1856, to the misery of her deep despair some seven years later, but they are worthless in any attempt to probe the love affair. Where the more general love poems are concerned, they are less than worthless, and one example from many that might be presented should settle the matter. The following lines are invariably cited by every writer treating the love disappointment and, admittedly, they do seem quite pertinent:

> He put the belt around my life,
> I heard the buckle snap,
> And turned away imperial,
> My lifetime folding up,
> Deliberate as a Duke would do

A kingdom's title deed;
Henceforth a dedicated sort,
A member of the Cloud . . .

Whether those words have any application to Emily herself must
be judged in the light of the hitherto unknown fact that the lines
were suggested in their entirety by one of the most emotional
scenes in *Jane Eyre,* and were topped off by a suggestion from
Mrs. Browning. In the novel, Jane comes near accepting an offer
of marriage from a man she does not love and describes her critical moment of wavering in these words: "All was changing ut-
terly, with a sudden sweep. Religion called—Angels beckoned—
God commanded—Life rolled together like a scroll." In the end
she refuses, a denouement with which Emily also concludes her
poem. The Cloud in which Emily claims membership (however
that is supposed to work) came from Aurora Leigh's designation
of her blinded lover as "My Cloud," as well as from the subsequent explanation of the title:

> if a cloud came down
> And wrapped us wholly, could we draw its shape,
> As if on the outside, and not overcome?

It was from these two love scenes, famous in Emily's day, that she
drew her poem, the initial spark probably coming from the life-as-
a-scroll simile. If anyone cares to insist that it still may contain an autobiographical substratum, no further words are likely
to dispel the notion.

It becomes clear that any attempt to get at the secret of Emily's
broken heart must begin by sweeping to one side her entire body
of verse, wholly removing it from consideration. After surer
ground has been attained through other avenues, if some of the
poems demand attention, they may be permitted to offer their
cautious corroboration. And as matters stand now, the Master
letters still provide the best hope for breaching the wall of
silence that has been so elaborately erected. Veiled as they are,

cryptic as they appear, they must contain a revealing slip somewhere, since even the most careful hand will falter in simultaneous expression and concealment—and Emily, penning these
letters in dejected privacy more than a century ago, never
dreamed that one day they would come before the inquisitive
eyes of a world that had more facts about her life to draw on than
any of her contemporaries.

One question about these letters which probably can never be
answered is how they managed to survive at all. According to
Millicent Todd, they were found among Emily's manuscript fragments, and since they were, as she thought, rough drafts, she felt
they had most likely been discarded and ultimately forgotten.
Whether fair copies had been made from them and sent is not
known. Austin, sometime in the early 1890's, gave them (that
is, loaned them and died before he could repossess them) to
Mabel when she was preparing the volume of Emily's letters.
His intention was that Mabel should pick out such impersonal
passages as might seem appropriate and not, of course, to print
the whole of them. She did extract a number of short phrases,
dating them 1885, though she certainly knew from internal evidence that the letters belonged to a period some twenty years
earlier.

To begin with, none of the letters is strictly a draft. Two were
final copies in which Emily made changes after completion; the
third was begun as final (though in pencil) and turned into a
draft at the bottom of the second page when she changed her
mind about wording as she copied. They are usually printed complete with bracketed alterations, which makes for very bumpy
reading and even acts as a bar to Emily's full meaning. Since the
changes are mostly innocuous, the letters are set down here, so
far as possible, as Emily wrote them first. They bear no dates and
their probable sequence has been determined on the basis of content and handwriting, though that, too, remains uncertain. The
one that seems to be the earliest is also the shortest and least compromising.

Dear Master

I am ill, but grieving more that you are ill, I make my stronger hand work long eno' to tell you. I thought perhaps you were in Heaven, and when you spoke again, it seemed quite sweet, and wonderful, and surprised me so—I wish that you were well.

I would that all I love, should be weak no more. The Violets are by my side, the Robins very near, and "Spring"—they say, Who is she—going by the door. Indeed it is God's house—and these are the gates of Heaven, and to and fro, the angels go, with their sweet postillions—I wish that I were great, like Mr. Michael Angelo, and could paint for you. You ask me what my flowers said—then they were disobedient—I gave them messages. They said what the lips in the West say, when the sun goes down, and so says the Dawn.

Listen again, Master. I did not tell you that today had been the Sabbath Day.

Each Sabbath on the Sea, makes me count the Sabbaths, till we meet on shore—and whether the hills will look as blue as the sailors say. I cannot talk any more tonight, for this pain denies me.

How strong when weak to recollect, and easy quite to love. Will you tell me, please to tell me, so soon as you are well.

That, salutation and all, might have been written to any of Emily's male acquaintances, since the references to the sun, the Sabbath, the sea, and even love, are precisely the sort of thing she customarily sprinkled over her correspondence. It is in the second letter that the surprises come thick and fast.

Master.

If you saw a bullet hit a Bird and he told you he wasn't shot, you might weep at his courtesy, but you would certainly doubt his word. One drop more from the gash that stains your Daisy's bosom, then would you *believe*? Thomas' faith in anatomy was stronger than his faith in faith. God made me, Sir, I didn't be myself. I dont know how it was done. He built the heart in me. Bye and bye it outgrew me, and like the little mother with the big child I got tired holding him. I heard of a thing called Redemption which rested men and women. You remember I asked you for it—you gave me something

else. I forgot the Redemption in the Redeemed. I didn't tell you for
a long time but I knew you had altered me. I was tired no more—

> No rose yet felt myself a'bloom,
> No bird yet rode in Ether.*

So dear did this stranger become that were it or my breath the alternative, I had tossed the fellow away with a smile. I am older tonight,
Master, but the love is the same. So are the moon and the crescent.
If it had been God's will that I might breathe where you breathed,
and find the place myself at night, if I never forget that I am not
with you, and that sorrow and frost are nearer than I, if I wish with
a might I cannot repress that mine were the Queen's place, the love
of the Plantagenet is my only apology. To come nearer than Presby-
teries, and nearer than the new coat that the tailor made—the prank
of the heart at play on the heart in holy *holiday*—is forbidden me.

You make me say it over—I fear you laugh when I do not see, but
"Chillon" is not funny. Have you the heart in your breast, Sir, is it
set like mine a little to the left, has it the misgiving if it wake in the
night, perchance itself to it a timbrel is it, itself to it a tune?

These things are reverent, Sir, I touch them reverently, but persons who pray dare remark our "Father!" You say I do not tell you all
—Daisy "confessed and denied not."

Vesuvius dont talk, Etna dont—one of them said a syllable a thousand years ago, and Pompeii heard it and hid forever. She couldn't
look the world in the face afterward I suppose. Bashful Pompeii!
"Tell you of the want"—you know what a leech is, dont you, and
Daisy's arm is small, and you have felt the horizon hav'nt you, and
did the sea never come so close as to make you dance?

I dont know what you can do for it, thank you, Master, but if I
had the beard on my cheek, and you had Daisy's petals, and you
cared so for me, what would become of you? Could you forget in
fight, or flight, or the foreign land? Couldn't Carlo and you and I
walk in the meadows an hour, and nobody care but the Bobolink and
his a silver scruple? I used to think when I died I could see you, so I
died as fast as I could, but the "Corporation" are going too so Eternity wont be sequestered at all. Say I may wait for you, say I need go

* *Letters,* II, 234, prints these two lines as the close, following the
original, but overlooking the small crosses that indicate ED's intention.

with no stranger to the to me untried Country. I waited a long time, Master, but I can wait more, wait till my hazel hair is dappled and you carry the cane, then I can look at my watch, and if the day is too far declined, we can take the chances of Heaven.

What would you do with me if I came "in white"? Have you the little chest to put the Alive in?

I want to see you more, Sir, than all I wish for in the world, and the wish, altered a little, will be my only one for the skies. Could you come to New England this summer, could you come to Amherst, would you like to come, Master?

Would it do harm, yet we both fear God. Would Daisy disappoint you—no, she wouldn't, Sir, it were comfort forever just to look in your face, while you looked in mine—then I could play in the woods till Dark, till you take me where sundown cannot find us, and the true keep coming till the town is full. Will you tell me if you will? I didn't think to tell you, you didn't come to me "in white" nor ever told me why.

If there were ever any serious doubts about the reality of Emily's love affair, then that jumbled outpouring should set them at rest. Clearly addressed to a single flesh-and-blood individual, the letter was obviously written in response to a letter received. She is talking to someone she has known for some time, and with whom she is on terms of easy, even lighthearted intimacy; someone moreover to whom she unhesitatingly confesses both her love and her impossible wish to be his wife. It is a correspondent, finally, who knows her as "Daisy," a name never applied to her by any of her known friends. The third Master letter (written in pencil where the first two were in ink) contains still further surprises. It pulses with unspecified agitation, a state which has to some degree stripped away her mask, leaving her tremblingly unprotected.

Oh did I offend it. Didn't it want me to tell it the truth. Daisy, Daisy, offend it, who bends her smaller life to his, meeker everyday, who only asks a task, something to do for love of it, some little way she cannot guess to make that Master glad.

A love so big it scares her, rushing among her small heart, pushing aside the blood and leaving her faint and white in the gust's arm.

Daisy, who never flinched through that awful parting, but held her life so tight he should not see the wound, who would have sheltered him in her childish bosom, only it wasn't big eno' for a Guest so large—*This* Daisy grieve her Lord—and yet she often blundered. Perhaps she grieved his taste—perhaps her odd, backwoodsman ways troubled his finer sense. Daisy knows all that, but must she go unpardoned—teach her, Preceptor, grace—teach her majesty. Slow at patrician things, even the wren upon her nest learns more than Daisy dares.

Low at the knee that bore her once unto royal rest, Daisy kneels a culprit. Tell her her fault, Master, if it is small eno' to cancel with her life, Daisy is satisfied, but punish, dont banish her—Shut her in prison Sir, only pledge that you will forgive—sometime—before the grave, and Daisy will not mind. She will awake in your likeness.

Wonder stings me more than the bee, who did never sting me, but made gay music with his might wherever I did go. Wonder wastes my pound, you said I had no size to spare.

You send the water over the dam in my brown eyes.

I've got a cough as big as a thimble but I dont care for that. I've got a tomahawk in my side but that dont hurt me much. Her Master stabs her more.

Wont he come to her, or will he let her seek him, never minding so long wandering if to him at last.

Oh how the sailor strains, when his boat is filling. Oh how the dying tug till the angel comes. Master, open your life wide, and take me in forever. I will never be tired, I will never be noisy when you want to be still. I will be your best little girl—nobody else will see me but you—but that is enough—I shall not want any more—and all that Heaven will be will disappoint me because it's not so dear.

It appears very much as if Emily's unknown correspondent has put his foot down about something, and an interim guess might be an interdiction on further letter writing. Perhaps Emily's letters were becoming incautiously frank and disturbingly frequent, and Master has suggested a cooling-off period;

that seems the likely import of her plea that he not "banish" her. The prime fact to be noticed regarding all three letters, though, is that they are replies, and as such can hardly be mere imaginary exercises. The most striking revelation they contain, the one that would seem to furnish the best handle for an investigator, is her assumption of the name Daisy, but aside from the poems, that clue, disappointingly, leads nowhere. While in a number of verses she does appear to identify herself with the flower, that evidence is not at this point admissible.

Of the three letters, it is the last that was written in the least guarded mood and which carries a number of the most inviting references. Among these, one in particular attracts the searching eye because of its implication that Emily and Master had, at least once, enjoyed a degree of physical contact beyond a handshake. While begging her Master's pardon for the unnamed transgression, she confesses: "Low at the knee that bore her once unto royal rest, Daisy kneels a culprit." Though there is no great difficulty in imagining Emily on the lap of any one of the candidates in some fumbling moment of tenderness, in view of her known character and the atmosphere in which she lived, such a liberty in whatever circumstances would be surprising. Beyond that, it is a strange admission to be recorded so openly where the writer is otherwise taking such pains to shield herself from accidentally prying eyes.

The short sentence does not appear to reveal much: on Master's knee Emily found royal rest, or as she corrected the phrase, "wordless" rest. By tracing the times and circumstances of each candidate's known visits to Amherst and the Dickinson house, it can be seen that all would have had an opportunity for this intimacy, although the Rev. Wadsworth in the setting appears not only out of character but a fairly fast worker. Yet there is one man—the idea intrudes with an abrupt clarity—to whom the words can apply in a sense entirely divorced from their evident meaning. At the time Emily was born, Otis Lord was a young student at Amherst College, a classmate and close friend of one of the favorite Dickinson cousins. He graduated when she was a year and a half old, and for a few months thereafter read law in the Springfield office of a friend of her father's. It is thus certain that he would have visited the Dickinson house more than once during Emily's first two years, and might easily have held her on his knee as a "wordless" baby. Otis Lord—the man who was frequently in Amherst during the presumed period of the love affair and who, though eighteen years her senior, found Emily to be a particularly sympathetic spirit; the old family friend to whom she turned for comfort in the last years of her life—in what way, exactly, does he fit into the story?

• •

Readers of the 1894 *Letters* encountered Lord's name twice, mentioned incidentally as Mr. Dickinson's friend, and that was the role assigned him by all writers for more than half a century. That he was also friendly with Emily seemed a fact of little moment. Martha Dickinson's brief reference to the two, however, showed their relationship to be somewhat more than casual; it was given moreover, whether by design or accident, in a context relating to the 1860's. "Judge Otis P. Lord of Salem," she wrote in the first biography of her aunt, "was her father's friend, but into his childish heart of rigorous justice Emily flashed as an unconscious aurora on a polar night and their friendship was of the most deep and lasting quality."* Coming from such a source, that was an admission of some weight, yet despite all the flurry about Emily's lover that surfaced in the 1930's, Otis Lord remained an obscure figure until 1954, when Millicent Todd reached once more into that compendious chest.

In that year she published a number of highly personal letters that Emily had written to Lord, all within her last decade. They established, beyond the slightest question, that the two had enjoyed a belated love affair, and they contained, as well, strong hints that marriage at one point was contemplated. So intimate,

* Bianchi, *Life*, 68.

so unexpected was this correspondence that Millicent felt constrained to apologize for making it public, and she preceded it with an admonition from the Old Testament: "Put off thy shoes from off thy feet, for the place whereon thou standest is holy ground." The decision to go ahead had been a struggle, she said, after a long life spent "within the shadow of the Dickinson family," and she did so only because the new information might help toward a better understanding of the poet. At last, when it had all been sifted, the Lord episode was relegated to a disappointingly minor position, of importance only to the latter years in which Emily had largely ceased writing. However much Lord had meant to Emily, he concerned her critics not at all.

The picture of the affair that emerged was uncomplicated: the death of Mr. Dickinson in 1874 had thrown his always dependent daughter on the ready sympathy of his friend, and the death of Lord's wife some three years later brought the two lonely souls together for mutual comfort and sustenance. That is the way the story took its place in Dickinson biography and the way it is presented today. But as a matter of fact, even the most hurried glance at the details indicates that a great deal more was involved than a simple December romance. Even by themselves the letters, to an objective mind, show that a passionate attachment was already in progress some years before the death of Lord's wife.

The earliest one, written within a year of Mrs. Lord's passing, if taken solely as the expression of new love between a recent widower of sixty-five and a spinster of forty-seven, is truly amazing in its youthful fervor. If viewed, on the other hand, as the joyful, unanticipated resurrection of dead longing, it assumes a pathetic rightness. "My lovely Salem smiles at me," she wrote. "I seek his Face so often—but I have done with guises. I confess that I love him, I thank the Maker of Heaven and earth, that gave him me to love—the exultation floods me. I cannot find my channel, the creek turns sea at thought of thee." It was no platonic or imaginary or one-sided romance; the frankness of her sexual remarks reflects a stormy renewal of physical desire that is almost incredible in its naïveté. The following, referring to a stay by Lord at the Dickinson house, was composed before Mrs. Lord had quite settled in her grave:

To lie so near your longing—to touch it as I passed, for I am but a restive sleeper and often would journey from your arms through the happy night, but you will lift me back won't you, for only there I ask to be—I say, if I felt the longing nearer, than in our dear past, perhaps I could not resist to bless it, but must, because it would be right. The "Stile" is God's, my Sweet One—for your great sake, not mine—I will not let you cross, but it is all yours, and when it is right I will lift the Bars, and lay you in the Moss—You showed me the word. I hope it has no different guise when my fingers make it.

The present reluctance to assign the origins of this emotional flooding to a period when Mrs. Lord was still living is understandable, but the time is well past when such diffidence has any meaning. Assuming that Emily was in love with Lord before the death of his wife, and that he may have encouraged her, it becomes necessary to determine as closely as possible when those feelings first took root. The best way to begin will be with another and more minute look at the Master letters.

Every reader, by now, will have spotted a small but telling phrase that fairly leaps from the third letter, a phrase which has previously seemed mere hyperbole, but which now assumes new and large significance: *"This* Daisy grieve her Lord . . ."￼ The possible relevance of that may be conceded and set aside for the moment, while an attempt is made to compare the Master letters with the actual correspondence Emily carried on with Lord. What similarities, in thought or phrase or symbol—of the private sort and which do not appear anywhere else—can be gleaned? No less than half a dozen such links, of a kind that preclude all chance of coincidence, come to light. In addition, there are a number of others that might be cited, but they are of a more abstruse quality.

Perhaps the most interesting of the items is the one in which she assumes the character of Peter, the Apostle who denied the Lord. "Why did you distrust your little Simon Peter," she inquires banteringly of her Salem friend, "you said you didn't but she knew you did." In the second Master letter she also identifies herself with the Apostle, but indirectly, by reference to the incident of Peter's denial of the Lord: "You say I do not tell you all —Daisy 'confessed and denied not.'" This pose, which she assumes nowhere else, turns on a pun, of course, and there are two other clear instances of such punning on Lord's name. To Lord himself she quoted the words of the Good Thief, "Lord, remember me when thou comest into thy kingdom." Later, referring to something Lord said, she observes that she has kept his "Commandment." With those examples in mind, the cryptic remark in the third Master letter—"She will awake in your likeness"— gives up its meaning. Unless it is a pun on the name of Lord it makes no sense at all. In view of all this, there need be little hesitation over the real import of the phrase mentioned above, "*This* Daisy grieve her Lord . . ." Thus both the second and third Master letters contain hidden references to the name of the man Emily is known to have been in love with later in life.*

Equally strong, perhaps even more so, is an unusual passage of symbolism that occurs in both an acknowledged letter to Lord and the third Master letter. In each case she takes on the character of a rustic supplicant begging the grace of forgiveness from a monarch. "Our life together was long forgiveness on your part toward me," she tells Lord, "the trespass of my rustic love upon your realms of ermine, only a Sovereign could forgive—I never knelt to other." And, almost as if more than a decade did not separate the two passages, to her Master she can be heard in precisely the same strain. She knows she has often blundered, she admits: "Perhaps she grieved his taste—perhaps her odd, backwoodsman ways troubled his finer sense. Daisy knows all that,

* For the three phrases addressed to Otis Lord in this paragraph, see *Letters*, III, 664, 754, 861.

but must she go unpardoned—teach her, Preceptor, grace—teach her majesty. Slow at patrician things—even the wren upon her nest learns more than Daisy dares. Low at the knee that bore her once unto royal rest, now Daisy kneels a culprit." This request for pardon supplies still another link which, by itself, might warrant little regard, but which in conjunction with the above is pertinent. Alluding to Lord's function as a judge, Emily asks, "Will you punish me? 'Involuntary bankruptcy.' How could that be crime? Incarcerate me in yourself—that will punish me." Of Master she begs to be told what her offense is, "but punish, don't banish her." Lastly, to both Lord and the Master she writes of love and religion, twining the two topics in a rather distinctive way. She admits to Lord that her love for him has strengthened her belief in God: "I know Him but a little, but Cupid taught Jehovah to many an untutored mind." To Master she confesses: "I heard of a thing called 'Redemption,' which rested men and women. You remember I asked you for it—you gave me something else."*

But if Lord was the man to whom the Master letters were sent, and thus the married man with whom Emily was in love, when and under what circumstances were those letters composed? Undated as they are and containing no reference to external events, they offer scholars nothing to rely on but their handwriting scale, a tool which cannot place them any more precisely than somewhere between 1859 and 1865. It was in the former year that Lord took up his duties as a judge of the Superior Court, bringing him at least once a year thereafter into the vicinity of Amherst. During 1864–65 Emily spent those sixteen months under an eye specialist's care in Boston, and there Lord could have visited her even more freely and frequently, both from his home in Salem and from his duties at the Boston Court House. Suspicion naturally settles on the residence in Cambridge, when Emily was out from under the watchful eyes of

* For the three phrases addressed to Otis Lord in this paragraph, see *Letters*, III, 728 and II, 615, 617.

neighbors and family, particularly when it is recalled that next to nothing is known of those lonely months—and her hosts, the Norcross sisters, it bears repeating, did away with the very documents that might have afforded some light. The most persistent searching through the whole imposing mass of Dickinson books, magazine articles and personal papers turns up nothing in the way of concrete evidence that Lord was accustomed to visiting Emily in Cambridge, yet there does exist one vital clue, and in some minds it will stand as all the evidence needed.

Otis Lord, in addition to his formidable forensic and legal talents—he was one of the ablest common law judges in Massachusetts history—also possessed a deep appreciation for literature. As a student at Amherst College he helped to found its first literary society (and delivered a graduation speech in which he argued that there was no conflict between science and religion).* Later, however, under the pressure of work his literary interests narrowed to Shakespeare, and his abiding love of the plays became a byword among his friends. Following the death of his wife, when he and Emily made more or less open acknowledgment of their friendship, one of Lord's first actions was to supply Emily with a concordance to Shakespeare, and the two of them thereafter in their letters used a code based on the plays to transmit personal messages, many of them sexually oriented (a single line would be cited as the beginning of the indicated passage). Now Emily is known to have read Shakespeare as early as her twentieth year, if not before, yet her mature appreciation of him dates from the fall of 1864, immediately following her return from the first stay in Cambridge. Aside from sundry bits of outside evidence to support this claim, sufficient proof exists in Emily's own words. Soon after returning, she began spending time in the garret with a volume of Shakespeare. Poring over the parting scenes in *I Henry VI* she was so moved that, as she told Loo Norcross, "the rafters wept." Another letter is more explicit. When the Boston specialist allowed her to go home, giving her

* Alumnae file, Amherst College.

permission to use her eyes for reading again, she compared her release to the "open sesame" of Sinbad, and continued:

How my blood bounded! Shakespeare was the first . . . I thought why clasp any hand but this? Give me ever to drink of this wine. Going home I flew to the shelves and devoured the luscious passages. I thought I should tear the leaves out as I turned them. Then I settled down to a willingness for all the rest to go but William Shakespeare.*

With one or two inconsequential exceptions, all the many Shakespeare allusions in her letters date from this time on, and it was in this same period that she fashioned her first poem from him, a straight transcription of one of the sonnets. What could have occurred in Cambridge between April and November to cause this delayed awakening, this sudden and total surrender to Shakespeare's genius, a reaction usually associated with the blossoming of the sensitive juvenile mind? Was it perhaps that in Cambridge Otis Lord had spent many hours reading his favorite works of literature to her, plumbing new depths of meaning, Emily all the while listening with covered eyes and dawning comprehension? And was it in this secluded intimacy that an affection of many years ripened to love? Satisfactory answers to those questions must remain—at least until some forgotten piece of paper is extracted from some other dusty attic—in the realm of the unprovable. In the meantime, this much can be said: the records of the Massachusetts Superior Court, Suffolk County, show that Lord in both 1864 and 1865 remained in Boston for the fall sitting, something he did only one other time in his entire first decade as a judge. For approximately the last six months of each of those years he was never very far from the Norcross boarding house at 86 Austin Street, Cambridge. The Court House in downtown Boston and the hotels where he would have stayed while court was in session were about fifteen minutes away by carriage.

* *Lyman Letters,* 76.

There is one further, admittedly tenuous but nonetheless interesting clue available. According to Emily herself, a passage in *Hamlet* for which Lord had a particular fondness was the description of Ophelia's death. Read with Emily in mind, the words become a touching reflection of her own story as a failed poet, even including an indirect reference to a crown. Lord's liking for it just possibly may have arisen from talks between himself and Emily regarding the still-recent adventure with Higginson and the lingering hurt it gave the young woman. In the play, the Queen explains how Ophelia went alone to a brook, from the edge of which grew a willow tree:

> There on the pendent boughs her coronet weeds
> Clamb'ring to hang, an envious sliver broke,
> When down her weedy trophies and herself
> Fell in the weeping brook. Her clothes spread wide,
> And, mermaid-like, awhile they bore her up;
> Which time she chanted snatches of old tunes,
> As one incapable of her own distress . . .

When Emily identified that passage as a favorite of Lord's, she did so by quoting from it the four words, "an envious sliver broke." Why, it may be asked, did that particular phrase stick in her mind? *Sliver* is one of the rarest words in Shakespeare, occurring only twice, once as a noun and once as a verb. It is at least possible that Emily's memory of it may have had an unconscious connection with its other use, which is in *King Lear*, a play she is known to have read. The context in which it appears is not relevant, only the lines themselves:

> She that herself will sliver and disbranch
> From her material sap, perforce must wither . . .

If Emily did have those lines at the back of her mind, they might have reference to her either as a poet or as a woman, but perhaps both at the same time, for if the trail followed so far is the true one, then her abandonment of the pursuit of fame pretty nearly coincided with the start of her hopeless love for Lord. And in both cases she found herself sadly disbranched from the living tree.

The attraction between the two, for it does seem to have been mutual, could have had its remote origins at any time from the early 1850's on. After graduating from Amherst College and spending a few months in the Springfield law office, Lord went to Harvard, where he took a law degree, then settled in Ipswich, a few miles north of Boston. He married in 1843, moved to Salem the next year, entered politics soon after (probably in this way renewing his friendship with Emily's father) and by 1854 was Speaker of the Massachusetts House of Representatives. After a bid for a seat in Congress in 1858 miscarried, he accepted appointment to the Superior Court, where he was to serve well and faithfully for fifteen years. His earliest traceable return to Amherst after graduation was to attend the 1852 class reunion, though it is likely that he had been more than once in town during the intervening years. He was probably there in November 1853, was certainly there in July 1857—when Emily, recall, had just fallen under Mrs. Browning's spell—held his first session as a Superior Court judge in the neighboring town of Northampton in October 1859, and after that was often within visiting distance.

Emily, it appears, was not only Lord's friend, but his wife's as well, at least in the beginning. Elizabeth Lord was an Ipswich girl, reportedly a woman of some beauty and devoted to her husband. The couple had no children, though there was at least one child born shortly after their marriage who did not survive. The two women probably met first in June 1860, when Mrs. Lord accompanied her husband to Northampton and together they dropped in at the Dickinsons' for dinner. A brief record of the day, which shows that Mrs. Lord had not been much in Amherst before this, is available in her diary:

Fine clear day—Got ready & started with Otis for Amherst at ¼ to 9.
Fine ride rather cool thick shawl necessary, buggy top down—Called
on Bina & sister, found them about as usual. Went over the colleges
with Mr. Dickinson, dined with him found his wife & daughter
pleasant back to N at 5½.*

The "Bina" mentioned in that account was Zebina Montague,
Emily's cousin and Lord's old classmate. A few months after
this visit, Emily sent Lord a note, enclosing a flower for his wife,
and apologizing for her delay in returning some book: ". . .
shall send 'Little Jennie' as soon as I know where the Owner is.
Am much ashamed to have kept it so long." Writing this note in
the fall, she hesitates to dispatch the book because, it seems, she
doesn't know in what town Lord is holding court; he was also
making a second unsuccessful run for Congress at this time and
was probably seldom at home.

In the summer of 1862 Lord was very prominently in Amherst
as one of the two principal speakers at the college commencement, the other being Henry Ward Beecher. On the morning of
July 10, he spoke with passion to a large audience about the war
then raging ("Our duty to posterity, to humanity, and to God is
to suppress this rebellion. We must spare no pains! though it cost
rivers of blood and millions of treasure and make a wilderness
of the South!") and later in the day attended a class reunion.
That evening with his wife he joined the reception under way
at the Dickinson house. Emily was there, handing round the tea
and making a brave attempt to conceal the grief she still felt over
Higginson's cool initial response to her poetry. It was scarcely
more than a month, in fact, since she had gotten back on her
feet after spending six weeks or so brooding in bed, and it was
just at this time that she had signified to Higginson her willingness to keep trying. "I had rather wince than die," was the way
she had expressed her renewal of purpose, and it is possible that

* Leyda, II, 10.

Lord, during the couple of days he spent in Amherst, had a hand in convincing her that for an artist some amount of wincing was necessary and good.

Lord did not attend commencement the following year but was within reach at least once, and the first Master letter may have been sent this spring as Emily's mood of dejection over Higginson's silence deepened. It does not speak of love, only great affection and a kind of mournful dependence. "Each Sabbath on the sea," she murmurs, "makes me count the Sabbaths till we meet on shore." Exactly how Lord would have been expected to take that remark is a slippery question, and it is cited here principally to spotlight its connection with a later event, which will unfold in due course.

If the two met again in the fall of 1863, as they probably did, Emily would hardly have been able to hide the downward path her life had taken—the threat of blindness, the total collapse of her poetic ambitions, the day of despair about which she wrote so savagely. That Lord went out of his way to comfort her while she was in Cambridge, to read to her in an attempt to revitalize her spirit, does not after all seem like such a wild guess. And here, at last, may be cited the first of the poems in which there seems to be concealed some personal memory. Without insisting on the accuracy of the suggestion but merely noting that the handwriting of the manuscript places it about 1864, and that the verses are unrelated to any known event, the following lines are offered as possibly preserving Emily's later recollections of happy hours with Lord in Cambridge:

> I learned, at least, what home could be,
> How ignorant I had been
> Of pretty ways of Covenant,
> How awkward at the hymn
>
> Round our new fireside, but for this,
> This pattern of the Way;
> . . . . .

What mornings in our garden guessed,
What bees for us to hum,
With only birds to interrupt
The ripple of our theme,

And task for both when play be done:
Your problem of the brain,
And mine some foolisher effect,
A thimble or a tune.

The afternoons together spent,
And twilight in the lanes . . .

Perhaps there is no need to belabor the hints in those lines: the "pattern of the Way" might mean many things, but it punningly echoes the Bible's description of the Lord as "the Way, the Truth and the Life." The "problem of the brain" assigned to the visitor is a fitting description for legal work, and the "thimble or a tune" fits Emily's two pursuits when allowed to use her eyes, sewing and scribbling away at her manuscripts. Also worthy of mention is the fact that the Austin Street boardinghouse had a "luxuriant" garden to one side.*

At the end of her first eight-month-period of treatment, was there an "awful parting" with the man who had companioned her loneliness and who had restored her joy in literature—the parting reflected in the third Master letter? After dragging through a heavy winter at home, she returned to Cambridge again in April 1865, once more remaining through the fall, and for this entire time only two letters survive out of many that must have been written. Both are brief and general, both to her sister, and one of them is incomplete. While she was in Cambridge two events of national importance occurred—the Civil War ended and Lincoln was assassinated—and one personal event of a significance that can only be guessed: Judge Lord rescinded a previously announced decision to resign from the

* Pollitt, p. 195.

bench of the Superior Court.* Nothing else is known of that intended resignation, just the bare fact of its being withdrawn, but it may find its explanation in a passage of the second Master letter. If Master were in her place, Emily had inquired, "could you forget me in fight or flight or the foreign land? . . . Could you come to New England this summer, would you come to Amherst . . . ?" In 1865 Lord was a robust fifty-two years old, financially well off, and with no children to make him hesitate about military service. He did turn in his resignation, may have informed Emily of his intention of going south to join the fighting—and then the war ended.

Home in Amherst again, Emily's eyes were still not cured, or even much improved. She anticipated a third stay in Cambridge, at any rate, and the plan was not abandoned until sometime in the spring. Her reason for deciding against going up for further treatment, as she lightly tossed it off to a friend, was the implied selfishness of her father, who objected to her going again to Boston because "he is in the habit of me." (It was to Higginson that Emily sent that bald statement, and it is small wonder that when the two men met Higginson came away with a distaste for the reserved parent of his pupil.) Whatever her real reason for not going—a guess would not be difficult in light of the third Master letter—Emily remained at home in 1866, treating the eyes herself with the help of a book written by the Boston specialist. She never afterwards approached the Boston area nor did she ever again leave Amherst.

• •

During the decade that preceded Emily's fateful residence in Cambridge, then, the attraction between her and Otis Lord slowly built to its culmination, softly stole on both parties unawares, until Emily, in Martha's phrase, "flashed as an unconscious aurora on a polar night" into the susceptible heart of Lord. What, if anything, do her poems have to say of all this?

* Leyda, II, 97.

Could such deeply tangled emotions have escaped preservation in verse?

Strewn throughout the large body of poems that belong, in general, to the mid-1860's, there are literally dozens that fit themselves into the pattern here uncovered, linking with both Lord and the Master letters. A long chapter would be needed for the proper detailing of all this, and since the verses are offered only as corroboration of a thesis that must stand or fall on quite other grounds, a sampling may be sufficient.

One poem, in which Emily asserts that the countenance of "the Lord" obliterates everything else in the world, has this outright reference not only to her illness but to her failure as a poet, and Lord's gentle encouragment:

> O poor and far, Oh hindered eye
> That hunted for the day;
> The Lord a candle entertains
> Entirely for thee.

Poems whose theme revolves around the face of the beloved, in fact, total at least a half dozen, all of them easily referred back to her clear preoccupation, in both Lord and Master letters, with the countenance of the loved one.

It was probably not long before she went to Cambridge that she wrote the following invitation, though it could also have come after that first parting and during the brief year or so when she indulged herself in the rosy glow of love, unwary of the future:

> The Judge is like the owl
> I've heard my father tell;
> And owls do build in oaks,
> So here's an amber sill
>
> That slanted in my path
> When going to the barn,

And if it serve you for a house,
Itself is not in vain . . .

The judge in this case, admittedly, is unidentified and Emily may indeed have known more than one such official. Yet there is proof of a sort that she was thinking of Lord in these lines, proof that leaps across the wide gap of years separating this verse from her later acknowledged love for him. In the Dickinson collection at Harvard there is a small card bearing a picture of a bright-eyed owl. Surrounded by floating clouds, against a sunset background, the owl sits high in the heavens on a crescent moon, looking down on the earth. Along the top edge of the card, written in ink in an unknown hand, there is this message: "To cheer your lonely hours." The lower right-hand corner of the card bears a copyright date, printed in infinitesimal type, of 1884. It was in March of that year that Otis Lord died.

There are three poems in which the speaker explicitly compares herself to a daisy, and it may have been from these that the name in the Master letters arose. Two of them are veiled, playful allusions, but the third provides the clearest link that could be asked between Daisy and the man from Salem:

I tend my flowers for thee,
Bright absentee!
My fuchsia's coral seams
Rip while the sower dreams.
. . . . .
Globe roses break their satin flake
Upon my garden floor,
Yet thou not here
I had as lief they bore
No crimson more.

Thy flower be gay
Her Lord away!
It ill becometh me;

I'll dwell in calyx gray,
How modestly alway,
Thy Daisy
Draped for thee!

More than once Emily's penchant for punning on the name of the man she loved brought her to the verge of accidental confession. The following lines, for instance, are so obviously addressed to some Lord who was *not* the Lord of Heaven, and whose home was an earthly home, that any of her family seeing them must have been led to wonder. But they were never shown to anyone, it seems, and were published only in 1945 after spending a half century in the Todd chest:

You love the Lord you cannot see,
You write him every day,
A little note when you awake
And further in the day.

An ample letter how you miss
And would delight to see,
But then his house is but a step,
And mine's in heaven, you see.

That Emily and Lord corresponded during the years before the Cambridge stay, as well as for a while afterward, is probable; that many of the letters contained poems or were notes in verse can be shown by an interpretation of the most puzzling sentence to occur in the Master letters. While wishing she could be closer to her Master, Emily bemoans the fact that she may not approach nearer "than the new coat that the tailor made," and the import of that phrase has baffled everyone, though the letter has been available for almost two decades. Yet the Master obviously was expected to understand it, indicating that the words bore some known and special relevance for both. Whether Lord was a reader of *Aurora Leigh* cannot be said, yet that is where the answer lies, for in that poem Mrs. Browning equates the writing of poetry with the bestowal of clothing. Plant a poetic thought deep enough in any man's heart, she says, and you have done more for him "Than if you dressed him in a broad-cloth coat."* Thus Emily's phrase is a complaint over the meagerness of verse-notes as channels of affection between her and Master.

There are many love poems not displaying any evidential linkage to Lord which yet arrange themselves effortlessly in the pattern. One which may hold the record of Emily's very first rapturous upsurge could very well have been written after Lord's commencement 1862 visit:

> I got so I could hear his name
> Without, tremendous gain,
> That stop-sensation on my soul,
> And thunder in the room;
>
> I got so I could walk across
> That angle in the floor
> Where he turned so, and I turned how,
> And all our sinew tore . . .

It appears that Lord was now and then too busy to write, or perhaps he was only being the more cautious of the two. This little verse, written on a small slip of paper, was wrapped around the stub of a pencil:

> If it had no pencil
> Would it try mine,
> Worn now and dull, sweet,
> Writing much to thee;
> If it had no word
> Would it make the Daisy,
> Most as big as I was
> When it plucked me?

* Bk. VI, 221–24.

Eight simple lines, not even intended as poetry; Emily in penning her note fell perhaps accidentally into stanza form, little
caring what she wrote. It was merely a request for a letter. Yet
in that relaxed moment she inadvertently again gave up her
secret. The one to whom she is writing, she says, entered her
life at a time when she herself was hardly bigger than a daisy.
Only one man, of all the men she knew, was acquainted with
her from birth; only one could have plucked her—picked her up—
as a man picks up a flower. Here again, in an unmistakable echo
of the Master letter, is the young student, Otis Lord, holding
Emily as a baby on his knee.

· 7 ·

GREAT STREETS OF SILENCE

IT WAS AFTER returning from the second stay in Boston that Emily began fading into the shadows. The tendency to hover near her own doorstep, which had been steadily deepening under the influence of her poetic dedication, now quickly became more pronounced and at last found words. "I do not cross my father's ground to any house or town," was her pontifically firm reply to an invitation from Higginson that she come up to Boston. Thus the inward turn, while less than sudden, still was not the gradual, decades-long drift often claimed, and it was moreover in some part deliberate. With it came a significant heightening of the queer behavior that the villagers had before shrugged off as allowable independence in one of their own. It is now, for the first time, that Emily can be seen playing her various versions of hide-and-seek.

Late in 1866 or early the next year, there arrived in Amherst the wife of a family friend from the Dickinsons' childhood days, a woman of whom they had fond memories. She was invited to the house for what should have been a warm welcome, but instead of being offered a seat in the parlor she was led upstairs and shown into the back bedroom. A connecting door stood slightly ajar and next to it there was a chair. On the other side of the door, out of sight, sat Emily. "The conversation was carried on," the visitor afterwards recalled in some amusement, "without either seeing the other's face." What reason Emily gave for this mode of greeting an old friend, or if she gave any at all, is not known. The visitor must have made at least a tentative inquiry, of Vinnie if not Emily herself, but if she received an explanation, she neglected to note it down, and no amount of guessing can supply an intelligible one now. What conceivable reason could there have been, what normal excuse, for the action? Emily had no scars to hide—no outer ones.

In any case, that was only one of a number of such incidents that began at this time to build toward the ultimate legend, some of them slightly bizarre and some that seemed mere quirky indulgence. Annie Holland, for instance, teen-age daughter of Emily's good friend, on one of her infrequent visits to Amherst dropped in to pay her respects to the woman who wrote those unusual letters to her mother. When she entered the hall, a soft voice called her into the dimly lit passageway beside the stairs, where she was offered a choice between a glass of wine and a rose. The girl preferred the rose, whereupon Emily told her to wait while she went to pick one. "She seemed very unusual," Annie remembered, "and her voice, her looks, and her whole personality made an impression on me that is still very vivid." Some of the neighbors, meanwhile, were smiling over a little note that had reached the wife of a newly arrived professor: Emily would like to see and greet the woman, the note invited, if she wouldn't mind coming to "the foot of the back stairs by moonlight, alone." Whether she was entirely serious about the place and time of rendezvous, or whether the invitation was accurately reported, may be doubted (the original of the letter is missing) but some rumor of it would have gone into the growing accumulation of village tales.

It was only shortly after this that there took place the stealthy nocturnal visit to the new church, an incident which seems to have been an Amherst favorite since it was one of the first stories heard by Mabel Todd on her arrival. The new edifice stood on Main Street, diagonally across from Austin's house. It had been started and completed largely under Austin's impetus, and the dedication speech had been delivered by his father, so that it was probably her family's enthusiasm about the project that moved Emily's curiosity. Late one moonlight night when the streets were deserted, with her brother beside her, she went as far as the vestibule and looked in, but would not cross the threshold to the place of worship proper. That happened in the fall of 1868. The event marks, as far as can be told, the last time that Emily for any reason put foot outside her father's grounds. When next she passed beyond the hedges she was being carried to the cemetery.

However much she succeeded in veiling herself at other times, the annual commencement receptions given by her father still brought her briefly into the light. Quite fortuitously, an early eye-witness account of her manner at these affairs is extant; it seems to relate to 1867, a year otherwise devoid of record. John Burgess, a senior at the college, later renowned as a scholar, was among the graduates who swelled the reception crowd that year. As he recalled Emily's presence among the billowing skirts of the ladies, the stiff-collared men and the tinkling teacups, she "seemed more like an apparition than a reality. At a moment when the conversation lagged a little, she would sweep in, clad in immaculate white, pass through the rooms silently curtseying and saluting left and right, and sweep out again."* The probability is that, if it had not been for her father, she would have remained in her upstairs sanctuary at such times; he seems otherwise to have accepted his daughter's growing peculiarities. For her to abstain from the company with a houseful of people, below, however, would have led to all kinds of mischievous talk, and that he was understandably not prepared to suffer. Wisely he provided this one safety valve for both Emily and her neighbors.

It is the mention of the white dress in the Burgess account

* John Burgess, *Reminiscences of an American Scholar*, 61.

that especially arrests attention. Was it assumed thus early for just such occasions, with less dressy outfits worn on ordinary days, or had she indeed by this time adopted white as a perpetual garment? And what, getting down to the fundamental question, did the white mean for her? On this topic, one point must first be covered which may seem trifling but which in fact is of some importance and yet is always overlooked. Emily could not suddenly, or even in a short time, have banished color from her wardrobe without betraying definite evidence of what she was doing. In her day, particularly for women of her class, dresses were made to order by seamstresses who came to the house, measuring, cutting and sewing for the most part under the patron's eye. Clothes were almost never bought ready-made and dressmaking sessions were not frequent, usually taking place on an annual basis. Women, even as men, wore their clothes year in and year out, repairing them as necessary. After Emily decided to use nothing but white, whenever that was, she would have required perhaps two or three years in the ordinary way to accumulate a sufficient number of white garments to permit uninterrupted daily use of them. The alternative would have been an extraordinary dressmaking flurry of gossip-generating proportions, and no hint survives anywhere in the town's memory of this, even under the enticements of the pervading legend.

As late as 1862 Emily describes herself as wearing an all-brown oufit, so that if white began its encroachment on her closet in, say, 1866, it might have been 1870 before she was able to forswear color. Thus it appears that she may have inclined only by degrees to white, continuing with color a good deal of the time. With that conclusion, a rather different complexion comes over the whole matter, since it obviates any precise, conscious moment of decision, any clear-cut reason for the action. Yet there exists one small bit of evidence, almost accidentally preserved, which modifies such trim reasoning by showing that at some moment Emily did employ a special seamstress for the making of white dresses.

The evidence consists of a stray, undatable newspaper clipping recounting an interview with a certain "Miss Marian" then aged ninety-three and living in an old ladies' home. For twenty years, the story said, Miss Marian had resided in Amherst, making a living with her needle. Sue Dickinson had been one of her regular customers, but once she had spent "a whole week" sewing at the other house, the only time she had ever worked there.

"Did you sew for Emily?" the interviewer inquired.

"Oh, yes. Yes, I sewed for Emily. White dresses. All white dresses," was the answer.

But didn't Emily use any colors at all, she was asked.

"I made white dresses for Emily," Miss Marian responded. "I don't think she wore any colors."

During her week at the house she didn't see Emily until the last day, she said; the fittings had been made on Vinnie. At lunch before her departure Emily came to the table attired in one of the new frocks. "She talked to her sister and she talked to me. But she was quiet. Before her sister and I were through she asked to be excused and went upstairs."

The clipping yields no information as to when this week occurred, though it fits easily into the decade of the seventies, the very time when the village legend about the "white-robed recluse" was coming to flower. Perhaps it was the talk of Miss Marian herself, with the knowing agreement of other Amherst seamstresses, which provided the town with the inside information that fixed attention on the white garments. (Another source would have been Maggie Maher, the Dickinsons' young Irish servant, who was just then becoming acquainted with the household. What Maggie saw and heard each day of interest would almost certainly, knowing the Irish, have found a place in the evening's conversation with her parents, brothers and sister, all of whom the young woman had brought to Amherst from Ireland. From that little circle stories would have spread, carrying who knows what accretions of detail.) Some rallying point, in any case, would have been necessary to meld the fitful rumors, since Emily's rare appearances could have given little impetus to talk about what she wore. A good week's sewing, however, could probably have produced no more than two or three dresses, so Miss Marian's teasingly brief memory may reflect only the ultimate moment when Emily did away with any remaining colors.

As to the exact reasons for that singular decision, in the present state of the records it remains the one element firmly beyond the power of analysis to lay bare with finality. Her family never mentioned the subject and, incredibly, no one seems to have inquired, even during the years of her first notoriety when her brother and sister were still living. Since then, critical pronouncements have tended to link it with the poetry as a symbol of whatever aesthetic was being favored by the particular writer: renunciation of fame, artistic independence, purity of purpose, renewed spiritual orientation of heart—the choice is wide and free. It has also been tied inevitably to the love affair, in which case the white becomes a pledge of virginity, a shroud reflecting a mild death wish, or the robe of St. John earned through adversity. Since neither jot nor tittle of evidence can be offered as proof for any of this, everyone is entitled to his own guess or to any mixture of the existing ones.

There is only one spot of sure ground, and it is there that the probe must begin: the white robes are connected, obviously and inseparably, with her reasons for withdrawal. They are a direct reflection of the state of mind that made her pull back from life, another way of expressing whatever it was that made her seek the dark of the hallways. Thus in order to get at her reasons for wearing white it is first necessary to determine the exact nature of the forces that drove her into retreat. The argument that explains this as a natural recourse for a New England spinster— almost every town had at least one such, it is claimed—does not come near supplying the answer. It is not the withdrawal merely, but the degree and most particularly the style of it, which sets Emily apart from all the other old maids who had outlived their family grandeur. True, as with these others, it was a surrender, but in this case it was the grudging capitulation of a rarely ebullient heart.

At bottom, of course, it was a sense of futility, a dead weight of disappointment that stole away Emily's former delight in companionship. Erosion of natural feelings by the steady sweep of untoward events is no new thing in the world, and in that she was precisely akin to other women of the reclusive sisterhood. But with Emily there were unusually high aspirations involved, exceptional sensitivities and a very real degree of genius. The sudden crash from such heights would have been enough to jar the heart out of even a sturdier frame. There was fierce pride, too, perhaps in a way linked to her consciousness of that "gypsy face," a pride that would not allow itself to be made captive, that would retreat only with flags flying. She had failed as a poet, so she thought, and had somehow fallen in love with a man she could not have. Fulfillment of mind and heart were now beyond her; for all practical purposes, as the world counted those purposes, her life was over. " 'Tis a dangerous moment for anyone," she wrote later, "when the meaning goes out of things and life stands straight, and punctual, and yet no signal comes. Yet such moments are. If we survive them, they expand us, if we do not—but that is Death, whose if is everlasting."* Facing her own moment of danger, she did not have the internal stamina to survive without large concessions and it causes hardly a ripple of surprise to find that in two poems written about now she sees herself as a nun.

The perpetual, year-long summer of the poets, hymned so gaily and with such expectation so short a time ago, had ended for her and she knew it:

> 'Twas here my summer paused;
> What ripeness after then,
> To other soul or other scene?

* *Letters,* III, 919.

No other scene but only her own home could solace, no other soul but Lord's.

It was her old strong sense of the dramatic that came to her rescue, her innate ability to reorganize external facts to suit her own interior designs. Forced by circumstance to give up, hers would be a defiant surrender; on the ramparts she would still ostentatiously flaunt a standard. What form that standard might take she perhaps learned from *Aurora Leigh*. At one dejected stage in her artistic career Aurora declares she would rather take her part "With God's Dead, who afford to walk in white,"* a pronouncement which leads back to the famous white robes of *Revelations*, worn by those who had suffered most and who had been justified by their suffering. Symbolic white was nothing new to Emily, in any case, nor to anyone else who had grown up in the Calvinist tradition, and she made repeated use of it in her poetry during the years when she still looked for fame—in the second Master letter she had made it stand for "spirit," a reference that the tradition-minded Lord would have readily grasped. Curiously, perhaps inevitably, at the time she gave the symbol substance it entirely vanished as such from her verse.

The white dresses, then, represented both defiance and reassurance. In part they were a sign to the world at large, and to her neighbors in particular that in accepting defeat she did so on her own terms, retaining her spirit free and untrammeled—certainly she anticipated the talk that would gather round her unusual habit. More importantly, they were a pledge to her own heart that, as her physical boundaries shrank and her social outlook diminished, she would suffer no contraction of her mental horizons. That reading of the facts, while not susceptible of proof, seems likely, and it is supported to an extent by her own words and those of her niece. "I should think a faded spirit must be the most dreadful treasure that one could possess," she wrote in the depths of her seclusion, and it was Martha who later

* Bk. II, 101–02.

assured the public that her aunt's buoyant spirit had suffered no sea change, had even at times ascended to "arrogance."

Behind the white dresses lay no single instant of apocalyptic decision, only the persistent groping of Emily's acute sense of drama. And it was transparently this same tendency that gave rise to all the other quirks. From her side of the half-open door, from the shadows of the hallway or through a curtain, she was able to view a world that was in many ways a delightful reversal of the one to which she had been accustomed. Not being a part of things, she saw how the perspective changed, the pieces and coloring shifted. She saw how people who had taken her for granted, perhaps dropping an eye of pity on her now and then, quickly became intrigued when she was no longer to be seen. The friend who turns away, she once noted, is "resonant with mystery," and in another verse she pointedly observed how an unnative charm comes over a face "imperfectly beheld." The trick was, she concluded, to keep the veil draped just right. By the simple act of walling herself up in the pleasant confines of her father's house, by carrying the ordinary spinster's retirement one step further, she was able to gain just such a veiled, elusive attraction.

The sorry part of all this, the part she did not foresee, was the retribution exacted by long continued pretense. Nothing is clearer than the fact that while she began her retirement with the deliberate cultivation of armoring strangeness, she came to the end some twenty years later suffering from actual personality disruption. In time, by infinite gradations, she became what she pretended to be, not awaking to her predicament until it was too late: as Sue was the first to note, she ended by hating her peculiarities and shrinking from any notice of them. Though it is impossible now to trace fully the steps in that inexorable slippage, by a lucky accident one of its more arresting scenes still stands out, cameo-like, clear and detailed against the faded background of those undifferentiated years.

In 1870 Thomas Higginson, who now pictured her, in his own phrase, as dwelling in a fiery mist shot through with luminous flashes, paid Emily his first visit. To her old mentor on this occasion she offered an appealing performance, so much so that he came away convinced that she was somehow both ingenuous and devious at the same time, and not a little unbalanced. While the part she played at this meeting, despite Higginson's reaction, was largely a manufactured one, easily under Emily's control, it is apparent that he was at least partially correct in his estimate of her mental equilibrium. By this time she had indeed begun to cross the line. The meeting can be reconstructed in satisfying fullness because Higginson took the trouble to make some notes for his wife about the "remarkable" encounter.

Having business in Amherst, he wrote Emily early in August saying he would like to pay his long contemplated call, and received her eager agreement. At noon on the 15th he arrived in the town, slumbrously peaceful in the meridian heat, put up at the hotel and sent another note by hand announcing his presence. "I will be at home and glad," Emily promptly replied, adding that his coming seemed nothing less than "incredible." The following morning Higginson climbed the stone steps to the house, was admitted by Maggie and shown into the parlor, which struck him as "dark & cool & stiffish." While the servant disappeared with his card, he cast his eye around the room. Besides books, engravings and an open piano, he spotted with pleasure two of his own most recent works on conspicuous display. After a few moments' waiting in the silence, he heard footsteps "like a pattering child's" and looked up to see a small figure of a woman glide through the doorway, her attire consisting of an "exquisitely clean white pique," and a blue shawl. Floating up to Higginson, she held out two day lilies, whispering "These are my introduction," and her manner of offering the flowers impressed the visitor as incongruously childlike. The face of the woman before him was exceedingly plain, he saw, without one good feature, its lack of definition accentuated by the two tight bands of reddish hair pulled back from the forehead. (Mrs. Browning's ringlets, evidently, had been discarded along with the literary ambition.)

The lilies accepted, Emily spoke again, her voice even softer: "Forgive me if I am frightened; I never see strangers and hardly know what I say." But once they were seated the talk began to flow from her in a steady stream as she responded for an hour or so to Higginson's hesitant and slightly awed questioning. At intervals she paused to observe that her guest looked tired, or to ask that he do some talking instead of her, then readily recommenced when he demurred. Though his notes on the conversation, which purport to give her actual words, were thrown down in random snatches that night and on the train the next day, careful analysis of them supplies a good idea of how the hour went. It is no wonder that Higginson felt strain, was aware of "an excess of tension," and concluded that Emily for some reason had deliberately kept him at a distance.

Much of the time she talked about herself; that, in any case, is the leading impression created by Higginson's notes and in the circumstances would have been quite natural. Now and then she perked the conversation up with one of those forthright challenges at which she had become so adept—her constant delight in her ability to draw a "what?" from listeners is obvious, and she didn't hesitate to practice on this captive audience. "Is it oblivion or absorption when things pass from our mind?" was a thrust that in those pre-Freudian days must have given Higginson pause. Throughout the interview this intellectual earnestness was wonderfully maintained, though once or twice her natural wit threatened to burst the bubble. In the course of remarking on the glories of the mental life, for example, she deftly slipped in a typical flashing aside which, perhaps predictably, whistled past Higginson's bemused head. "How do most people live without any thoughts?" she asked. "There are many people in the world (you must have noticed them in the street). How do they live? How do they get strength to put on their clothes in the morning?" The visitor noted down her words in all serious-ness, not bothering to spotlight that delicious *you must have noticed them in the street*, but perhaps he was indeed very tired. And just as her poetry frequently contradicts itself, she managed during the hour to negate that view of people who thrive with-out thought. "I find ecstacy in living," she replied to some ques-tion of Higginson's, "the mere sense of living is joy enough," but then she failed to explain why such overblown emotionalism might not be adequate for others as well.

She also rehearsed the story of her literary life, a good part of it fable, as Higginson was to discover in dismay many years later. After reading her first book, she told him, she found her-self exclaiming in raptures, "This then is a book!" As a precocious child, she might very well have said something like that, but in recalling the moment for Higginson she couldn't resist rounding it out with "and there are more of them!" This early enthusiasm, she went on, had been sadly dampened by her father, who pre-ferred her to read only the Bible. She and her brother, in con-spiracy with others such as Ben Newton, had been forced to smuggle more modern reading matter into the house, to hide it in various places, usually under the piano cover or in a bush by the door. Longfellow's *Kavanagh*, she said, was one of the books read in this way, and when her father came upon it accidentally he was mightily displeased. All in all, it must have appeared to Higginson that the wistful creature sitting across from him had won her way to literature only by fierce determination and over the stern objections of a narrow-minded, unfeeling parent. When he learned after Emily's death—in talks with Austin and by reading her early letters—that the Dickinson house had always overflowed with books, he asked Mabel Todd in deep puzzle-ment, "How is it possible to reconcile her accounts of early book-reading . . . with the yarns (O irreverence!) she told me?" The three Dickinson children, from their earliest days, he found, had read whatever and wherever they pleased and were not overly troubled by their father's occasional harrumphing.

A more serious and more truthful moment occurred in the conversation when she mentioned the eye trouble. Her first awful fright, she explained, was over the possibility that she would be cut off from literature, but she had managed to console herself with the thought that "there were so few real books that I could easily find some one to read me all of them." That remark was recorded by Higginson in the letter he mailed his wife on the night of the meeting. The next day on the train, while making further memoranda, something else she had said about the eye trouble recurred to him and if it belongs in the context of the above remark, as it very probably does, then it may hold an unsuspected echo of those afternoons with Judge Lord in Cambridge. "After long disuse of her eyes," Higginson noted her as saying, "she read Shakespeare and thought why is any other book needed."

The most surprising element in the lengthy string of notes concerns Emily's poetry: mention of it is entirely absent. They do not appear to have dwelt much on her own work at all, beyond an inquiry as to her preferences. How had she formed her tastes, Higginson probably asked, what was poetry to her? It was entirely emotional, Emily in effect replied. If something made her go cold past the ability of fire to warm, she knew that was poetry; and if she felt "as if the top of my head were taken off" she knew that was poetry. Gazing at her Preceptor through the cool dimness of the parlor she begged, "Is there any other way?" Higginson supplies no answer from himself to that question and it was the closest either of them came to bringing up the topic of poetic technique. Just possibly, Emily was here making a timid effort to broach the subject. Why judge a poem only on the correctness of its form, she seems to be asking, only on its adherence to accepted grammar and vocabulary? If the emotion pulses through, what can be added by a prosaic verb or a tinkling chime? If there was power in her verses, as he in his letters had admitted, would a different form make them more powerful? Did he ever consider that a glancing rhyme might add a delicate nuance of sound and therefore of mood? A discussion along these lines would have added much to the value of the visit, but unfortunately the opportunity died away in the silence while Higginson perhaps sat in contemplation of Emily with the top of her head coming loose. She may have made it finally clear, however, that she no longer looked forward to becoming a published poet, and in that case, Higginson's lax attitude, now and in succeeding years, is further excused.

Still, they must have spent a few minutes talking about her verses, and an offhand remark in a later letter of Emily's shows that he probably repeated his former high estimate of her artistic potential. "Thank you for Greatness," she wrote. "I will have deserved it in a longer time!" Was she actually thinking, even tentatively, of renewing her pursuit of fame, as that implies? If so, she was doing very little about it.

The day of despair, six years before, had brought a very sharp drop in the quantity of her poems, and for a year or two she had probably ceased writing altogether. In seclusion she had begun again, but fitfully, and she was never to recapture her former feverish abandon. Poetry now received only a small fraction of her time, an odd moment here and there while she waited for a cake to rise or a pudding to bubble, perhaps a quiet Sunday evening by the fire in her room when the rest of the family was out. Two or three poems a month became the average, most of them very brief, seldom running to more than eight lines. As often as not she became impatient with a poem in progress or lost interest and it was never completed; nearly two hundred of these discarded drafts still exist. She was no longer binding finished poems into those neatly threaded manuscript packets and at one point she said openly that composition was now a matter of relaxation, her "only Playmate." Nor was it a case of trying for greater originality, since she can still be seen in a dozen instances drawing on other writers.

In the area of nature, it is true, she did catch a freshening wind, achieving a lyric charm and force not present before. In place of bashful flowers and blushing birds, butterflies and bees, she is now attracted to mushrooms, lightning and frogs. Her winds are either terrifyingly destructive or else they dutifully "clarify scenery," and even rats and bats come in for a good word. Much of this is interesting, and she is still able to throw off a compelling phrase when dealing in human affairs, yet it is sadly apparent that the old visionary word magic is gone. Only once did she seem about to break into her former stunning strain when she began a poem with the evocative lines,

> Great streets of silence led away
> To neighborhoods of pause . . .

but the remainder of the poem's two quatrains trail off flat and unfocused. Its theme—an attempt to depict the blurring of the sense of time—is perhaps the reason for the poem's failure. It was of herself she was writing, the disintegrating time her own.

To Higginson's questions about her restricted home life, she replied quite readily that she had enough to keep her busy, especially in the kitchen. The making of all the bread, she said, was in her charge, her father insisting her baking was best, and "people must have puddings." This last, Higginson told his wife, was delivered in a very dreamy manner, as if the puddings were comets. He couldn't have known that the making of puddings was not the other-worldly affair Emily pretended, and that she actually took great pride in her abilities with the pan, particularly when it came to fancy desserts. ("She was rather *précieuse* about it," her niece said later, remembering the many hours she had spent watching and helping in Emily's kitchen, "using silver to stir with and glass to measure by. Her utensils were private . . . Her technique was as precise as that of a musician playing scales.")

But even if she was able to keep busy, Higginson returned, didn't she feel excessively shut off by never going out and seldom having visitors? Her reply to that, while it certainly answered the question, was more than a little overextended. "I never thought of conceiving," she protested, "that I could ever have the slightest approach to such a want in all future time." Then, almost as if she had been waiting for the question, after a pause she added inimitably, "I feel that I have not expressed myself strongly enough." Admittedly, Emily was one of those favored souls who are able to live happily without embroilment, possessing in good measure what she called "the appetite for silence." But were all her days really so ecstatic and undulled? In her bureau drawer upstairs there lay two poems, both written about this time, which identify her as more human than she liked to admit. In the first she assures herself that "Time does go on," though it often appears to stand still. The second is aimed even more tellingly and might have been written as she stared from her window at the lethargic horse-drawn traffic on Main Street:

> This slow day moved along,
> I heard its axles go
> As if they could not hoist themselves,
> They hated motion so;
>
> I told my soul to come,
> It was no use to wait;
> We went and played and came again,
> And it was out of sight.

She was not totally isolated, Higginson would have realized, since she had her mother, father and sister, as well as her brother's family next door, which now included the two children Ned and Martha. He mentioned something along that line and must have been nonplussed, to say the least, at what was elicited. A pattern emerges from his notes which shows that Emily deliberately imposed on his sympathies with grotesque pictures of both her parents. Ignoring the fact that her father was a very busy lawyer, often working late into the night at the office and at home, she dismissed him as the uninspiring sort of person who "only reads on Sunday—he reads lonely and rigorous books." (There was no mention of the set of Shakespeare he had bought or of the large and varied library he had built up.) But surely it must be a comfort to have her mother in good health and nearby, someone in whom to confide? "I never had a mother," she answered without preliminaries. "I suppose a mother is one to whom you hurry when you are troubled." (Did Higginson squirm a little when he heard that answer? And where was Mrs. Dickinson while he was in the parlor? Where was Vinnie? He saw no sign of either and the curious may be pardoned for thinking that Emily had arranged to have the premises to herself for the performance.)

One other stray sentence in the notes seems to fit in here and it may have provided the signal to conclude the interview; after all, enough was enough. "Could you tell me," she asked, "what home is?" Later, Higginson was to say that he would have been glad to reach a level of simple truth with Emily but she had proved an enigma; during almost the entire hour he had been able to do little but sit, look and listen. Going down the stone steps, he was acutely aware of the "abnormal life" into which he had intruded.

Before leaving town the next morning, since he went by the Dickinson house on his way to the station, he decided to stop for a final leave-taking. It was shortly after eight when he walked through the door and came face to face with Mr. Dickinson, who was departing for his office. There was a brief, polite exchange, fully confirming in Higginson's mind the sour portrait sketched by Emily: to his wife he reported that the father was "thin, dry and speechless—I saw what her life has been like." His parting with the daughter was also brief, though there was time enough for her to murmur at the door, "Gratitude is the only secret that cannot reveal itself," while she presented him with a portrait of none other than Mrs. Browning. The real reasons for her gratitude, she had evidently decided, would remain mute. Higginson was never to learn just how he had saved his pupil's life.

• •

At suppertime on June 16, 1874, Mrs. Dickinson and her two daughters sat down together, all of them aware of the empty place at the head of the table. Mr. Dickinson had returned to Boston the day before, where he was again serving in the legislature after a long absence from politics. It was a post he did not desire, his public ambitions having evaporated with age, but he had dutifully responded to the call, and the absence of his staunch figure left the women of the house feeling vaguely discomfited. As they ate, a downcast Austin hurried in carrying a piece of paper. The women looked up apprehensively, Emily especially feeling from the look on her brother's face that "we were all lost though I didn't know how." A telegram had come from Boston with the news that Mr. Dickinson had been taken ill in his quarters at the Tremont House. His condition was critical and the doctor advised that his family should come up. Writing of that moment later, Emily recalled Austin saying that he and Vinnie would go; there seems to have been no thought that she might accompany them. She was hardly posing now, and if one instant is to be picked as marking her final surrender to the shadows, this will serve as well as any—even a dying father could not draw her out. As it happened, there was no need for anyone to go. With Austin and Vinnie speeding their preparations, a second wire arrived announcing the father's death.

The shock sent Emily into a state of quiet hysteria lasting for a week or more. In her mind glowed the memory of her father as she had last seen him at home two days before. It had been a serene Sunday afternoon, the two of them alone in the parlor, Emily at the piano playing his favorite hymns. Mr. Dickinson, deeply enjoying the companionship of the daughter who had caused him so much silent worry and who most often kept to herself, sighed a wish that the day would never end. "His pleasure almost embarrassed me," Emily remembered later, "and my brother coming—I suggested they walk. The next morning I woke him for the train and saw him no more." Now, in a daze, she wandered about the house repeatedly inquiring, of Austin's children as well as of her own family, "Where is he? Emily will find him!" Martha, then eight, never lost the memory of her aunt's tear-filled eyes and the way her lips quivered as she charged, "You must remember your grandfather. You must—you must *never* forget him!"

The funeral was held on the nineteenth, bringing a crowd of mourners that overflowed the house so that chairs and settees had to be placed on the lawn outside. Services were simple—a hymn, a prayer, the reading of scripture, but, at the request of the family, no eulogy—and through it all Emily remained upstairs with her door opened just a crack. The only mark of her connection with the ceremonies was a small wreath of white daisies that lay in solitary simplicity on the otherwise unadorned coffin.

Her lacerated spirit did not heal quickly, burdened as it probably was with some vague sense of guilt. Weeks afterward she admitted "my mind never comes home," and nearly a year later she was still referring to her father's death in great anguish, calling it "the first mystery of the house." Even conceding the special circumstances of her relationship to her father, this lengthy sorrowing seems excessive, and it is probable that a more fundamental sensitivity was at work underneath. Her father's death powerfully thrust back on her the one real and continuing hobgoblin of her life, fears about the reality of the soul's survival. Writing to Higginson in July she admits the concept of an afterlife is comforting, "but would have tested it myself before entrusting him." This dark turmoil probably provides the answer to a minor mystery that turned up among her papers, a hurried, undated note from the Rev. Charles Wadsworth, in which her name is misspelled:

My Dear Miss Dickenson

I am distressed beyond measure at your note, received this moment, —I can only imagine the affliction which has befallen, or is now befalling you. Believe me, be what it may, you have all my sympathy, and my constant, earnest prayers. I am very, very anxious to learn more definitely of your trial—and though I have no right to intrude upon your sorrow yet I beg you to write me, though it be but a word. In great haste

Sincerely and most
Affectionately *Yours*—

It is a wooden intellect which sees in that solicitous pastoral note a reply to Emily's Master letters, but such has more than once been innocently suggested. Considering that Wadsworth here claims to know nothing about Emily or her affairs, and recalling the intimate tone of the Master letters, that suggestion would make her a woefully troubled woman, indeed, not to say a shameless one. Unfortunately, there are no other documents relating to this exchange between Wadsworth and the bereaved Emily. In all likelihood, however, this note dates the start of her affection for the minister, an affection based on his ability to calm, if not convince, her heart about the terrors of death.

Concern over her mother's worsening health at last terminated her private grieving. Mrs. Dickinson had been even worse afflicted than her daughter, and it was in care for her that Emily found she could carry on, though it still depressed her to pass her father's door at night, "where I used to think was safety." And there was need for care. While a semblance of normalcy had returned to the house by the start of the new year, Mrs. Dickinson's brooding decline resulted at last in a massive stroke. A year to the day after the death of her husband she collapsed into paralysis and delirium. With unaccustomed strength and tenderness, Emily remained by her bed through many days and frequently far into the nights because "She asks for my father, constantly, and thinks it rude that he does not come, begging me not to retire at night, lest no one receive him." She offered the sick woman soothing lies about her condition and was careful to call little Martha from the room whenever she saw the child in fright at some sign of sudden distress in the ailing woman. Mrs. Dickinson eventually got back on her feet, but she was more or less permanently enfeebled.

These were the years, with her father dead and her mother bedridden, that saw the final molding of the myth, even to the point where Emily became a figure of superstition to many of the village children. One little girl, who lived diagonally across from the red brick house, long remembered how at night she would peer from her window at the glowing blind on the second floor, and if she was lucky would now and then glimpse with a shiver "Miss Emily's shadow!" Other children, especially at dusk, would hurry along the sidewalk by the high hedges in order to get clear as quickly as possible of the house where the white witch hovered. If by chance one of them caught sight of her luminous figure moving among the fruit trees in the garden, as occasionally happened, the incident was bravely recounted to the less favored.

Not all the children entertained such gross imaginings about the house on Main Street, since some were privileged to have a closer contact with it—though none regarded it as in any way ordinary. One neighbor's boy, a minister's son whose parents were good friends of Austin, now and then was allowed to confront the recluse in the kitchen or hallway, and was often among those favored with cakes and candy from the upper floor: "On a window ledge," he recalled, "would appear a basket. It would be slowly lowered. I can see it now, jerking its way down from what seemed to us then an incredible height. We saw two delicate hands playing out a much knotted cord, and framed in the window above a slender figure in white and a pair of laughing eyes."* As the children devoured the warm gingerbread or the long oval buns with their light brown crust and sweet yellow insides, none of them questioned why their benefactor had taken the trouble to go from the kitchen to her upstairs room with the

* Jenkins, *Neighbor,* 40.

cakes, instead of handing them out the back door. That was just the way Miss Emily did.

Infrequently other less well acquainted children would find themselves unexpectedly close to the apparition. A boy and two sisters, after the trio sang the Twenty-third Psalm in church one Sunday, were invited by Vinnie to repeat the performance in the Dickinson parlor. They did so, to an empty room, and were rewarded when "a light clapping of hands, like a flutter of wings, floated down the staircase." While the children knew that Emily and her mother had been listening from above, they never expected to catch sight of either, and at the close of the performance were thrilled to hear Vinnie say her sister would see them in the library. They crossed the hall to the unlit room, illuminated only by the faint rays of evening, and stood still as "a tiny figure in white darted to greet us, grasped our hands and told us of her pleasure."* In the gloom the children were chiefly aware of a pair of large, dark eyes set in a small, pale face, and of the quick breathless voice, so like a child's.

Otis Lord, meanwhile, had not dropped out of Emily's life; their renunciation did not by any means entail losing sight of each other. During the decade that followed the Boston interlude it is known that Lord was at the Dickinson house some half dozen times, and since only one of these visits occurred while he was holding court nearby, the true total is probably double that number—his presence, of course, needing no explanation. That his appearances were occasions both of pleasure and pain to Emily is amply shown by several poems which fit themselves, neatly and without struggle, into the puzzle.

The conferring of an honorary Doctor of Laws degree brought Lord to town for the commencement of 1869, and he was back again two years later to attend the fiftieth anniversary of the college's founding. At the usual Dickinson reception this year, with Fanny Norcross beside her, Emily seems to have been uncommonly busy and helpful, not her usual wraithlike self. A day or

* *Bookman*, November 1924.

two afterwards, in a letter to Loo, she observes pensively that "No part of mind is permanent. This startles the happy but assists the sad . . . No lodging can be had for the delights that come to earth to stay." That plaintive remark has little to do with the context in which it occurs, even granting Emily's veering habits, and what other comments may have surrounded it in the original manuscript, now destroyed, it would be interesting to see. More positive evidence turns up in a short poem written about this time, a poem which begins with the unusual line "The voice that stands for floods to me." Only ordinary acquaintance with the New Testament is needed to detect in that phrase St. John's "I heard a voice from Heaven like the sound of many waters," with all its too clear implications. After another visit in October 1873, Lord wrote Emily a letter which is now missing, but from which the envelope has survived. Its interior surface contains the following frank sentiment pencilled in Emily's hand:

> Through what transports of patience
> I reached the stolid bliss
> To breathe my blank without thee
> Attest me this and this . . .

It is not beside the point to note in passing that the continued existence of that envelope may be laid to the accident of its having spent fifty years in Mrs. Todd's camphorwood chest, beyond the reach of destroying hands.

Of course there is no way of telling how much of their relationship was suspected by others, her own family or Mrs. Lord. If the wife did detect a hint of unwonted tenderness between the two, what might have been her reaction? Remembering that Mrs. Lord's given name was Elizabeth, that the Lords lived in Essex County, and that Emily often referred to people by the names of their places of residence, the following lines, written about 1874, may hold more meaning than the surface reference to England's Queen:

> Elizabeth told Essex
> That she could not forgive;
> The clemency of Deity,
> However, might survive.
>
> That secondary succor
> We trust that she partook
> When suing, like her Essex,
> For a reprieving look.

Early in 1875 Lord's health declined, necessitating a long stay in the mountains. While he was away Mrs. Dickinson suffered her stroke, and almost immediately on his return home in September he went to Amherst to stay with the Dickinsons for a week. While there he helped the three women to make their wills, an action prompted by the fact that Mr. Dickinson had died intestate, leaving a tangle that took years to straighten and led to settled ill feeling between Vinnie and Sue. (This visit, supposedly, is a good example of Lord's natural and commendable solicitude toward the family of his dead friend, and perhaps that is so—perhaps he thought that Austin, then nearing fifty, a successful lawyer and the head of the family, was not to be trusted.) Every day for an entire week, Emily was thus able to look on the beloved countenance to which she so often referred in her poetry. What difference in its vigor had ten years made? None, she decided in a poem written at this time, or only so much as to enhance the character:

> An antiquated grace
> Becomes that cherished face
> As well as prime;
> Enjoining us to part,
> We and our plotting heart,
> Good friends with time.

This intimate week was the longest she had shared Lord's company since those afternoons in Cambridge. Moved to record her delight, she did so by assigning her friend the role of traveling bee and herself that of a patient rose:

> . . . .
> The rose received his visit
> With frank tranquility,
> Withholding not a crescent
> To his cupidity;
> Their moment consummated,
> Remained for him to flee;
> Remained for her, of rapture
> But the humility.

Conceding that no absolute proof links any of these verses with Lord, there comes a point at which coincidence fails as an explanation. With Lord, it is asserted in good conscience, that point was overtaken some pages back.

It is somewhat of a disappointment, to normal curiosity if nothing else, that no contemporary account of Lord as a guest in the Dickinson home has been preserved. There were times, however, when he joined distinguished company at Austin's table next door, Emily remaining behind, and one such occasion has been described by Sue, in a manuscript memoir written for her children. In her recollection, significantly, the Judge is seen as an unmellow relic of earlier times, unable to mix easily with the other diners:

. . . he was an anxious element to his hostess in a group of progressive and mellow although staunch men and women. At an informal dinner with us once we saw him at his best. Your father was ill and he kindly took the head of the table, your Aunt Vinnie sat at his right, the other guests I do not seem to remember. As it was Sunday we naturally got upon the subject of hymnology in New England. The Judge remarking that he was brought up on "Watts and Select" unabridged, asked if any of us were familiar with the hymn beginning, "My thoughts on awful subjects roll, damnation and the dead." In astonishment we answered no! whereupon he layed down his

fork, made himself a little more stiff and erect behind his old-fashioned silk stock than usual, if that were possible, and recited with an
energy worthy himself and the subject, the whole hymn. There was
really a horrible grandeur about it, although our nervous laughter
might have misled one in the next room as to our real emotions.

Despite this stark portrait, Lord's presence at the dinner was not
stifling. His performance, Sue makes clear, was followed by one
from Vinnie in which she humorously imitated a choir singing
another somber hymn, taking on different voices and bringing
great applause from the guests. His personality, in fact, was an
equal mixture of the tragic and the trivial, so to speak, and perhaps it is Emily's own remark, coinciding with everything else
that is known of him, that best sums it up: "Calvary and May
wrestled in his nature," she observed after his death.

For a decade Lord's judicial duties provided a handy mech-
anism for meetings with Emily. Then, in December 1875, a
change came over the situation when he was elevated to the
bench of the Massachusetts Supreme Court, bringing to an end
his annual trips to the western part of the state. His Amherst so-
journs were not ended, though, only curtailed, for he was back
again in October 1876, at which time Emily is found jotting
further relevant lines on the inside of another slit open envelope:

> Long years apart can make no
> Breach a second cannot fill;
> The absence of the witch does not
> Invalidate the spell . . .

This particular absent witch, appropriately, lived in Salem.

That there was steady correspondence between Lord and the
Dickinson house throughout this period is known, though with
the exception of one letter from Lord to Vinnie, it has all disappeared. Written about this time, perhaps early 1877, the one surviving letter reveals little of his attitude beyond his concern for
the health of the two girls, as well as the fact that his own wife

was ailing. For whatever it is worth, it also shows that he and his
wife were on good terms:

There has not been a day since receipt of your letter written in January, (I am ashamed to say) that I have not had it in my mind to
write you; but I have been either in court all day or in consultation
with my associates or writing opinions and in the evening I have
felt jaded with aching eyes and the listlessness and ennui of soli-
taire with one or more packs of cards has been the summit of my
capacity; and still I have thought of you and of Emily, whose last
note gave me a good deal of uneasiness, for knowing how entirely
unselfish she is, and how unwilling to disclose any ailment, I fear
that she has been more ill, than she has told me. I hope you will
tell me particularly about her . . . Elizabeth has had a great deal
of rheumatism or neuralgia or of both and a great part of the time
is quite lame; but she is as uncomplaining and as thoughtful of
everybody's comfort except her own as she has ever been, and is the
only 'crown of glory' I have ever, thus far, had . . . Elizabeth joins
me in love to you, and to all. I wish you would give me a *full* account
of the health of *each* of you . . .*

Lord's own health, which had been slow in mending, was now
stable again, and there is no sign that Emily was suffering any incapacity. The waning of the year, though, brought around her,
among family and friends, an onslaught of sickness and death
that reduced her to a continued state of worry and depression,
making her feel, as she said, "like a troubled top, that spun without reprieve." Her nephew Ned revealed the first signs of an
epilepsy that was to handicap him for years and shorten his life.
Both Austin and Vinnie came down with worrisome illnesses,
Vinnie's particularly so because of its undiagnosable nature and
unyielding grip. Mrs. Dickinson was still very weak, spending
most of her time in bed, unable to go out when she did rise, and
suffering very much from her enforced seclusion. Sam Bowles,
now loved and revered by Emily as an elder brother, succumbed

* Ms. at Houghton Library.

to exhaustion, and his condition fast declined. Higginson's wife sickened and died and also the wife of a well-liked neighbor. And in the first days of December there came from Salem the news of another impending death that made the top spin even more wildly. Mrs. Lord was in the final stages of a crisis, a condition in which she lingered for about three weeks. On the evening of December 10 she died. It was Emily's birthday.

More than ten years before, on her return from Boston, one of the first of Shakespeare's plays to captivate Emily was *Antony and Cleopatra,* perhaps in time her favorite. Something in the third act of that play, something never specified, especially intrigued her. About the time of Mrs. Lord's death, as is shown by a reference in a letter, it was again in her mind. Did she, when she heard the news from Salem, with trembling hand take down her Shakespeare and look again into that third act, the thirteenth scene? Speaking to Antony, Cleopatra exclaims:

> It is my birthday.
> I had thought t'have held it poor, but since my Lord
> Is Antony again, I will be Cleopatra. . . .

And Antony responds with gusto:

> Come on, my Queen,
> There's sap in't yet! The next time I do fight,
> I'll make Death love me; for I will contend
> Even with his pestilent scythe. . . .

Contend with time the elderly Lord now did, and admirably. Wasting little effort in mourning, this supposedly gloomy and rigid sexagenarian was soon exchanging heated sexual confidences with his white-robed virgin, Emily responding joyfully and learning a colorful vocabulary. "When it is right I will lift the bars," she whispers, "and lay you in the Moss. You showed me the word." With true Shakespearean rightness, the childish Emily now vanishes and in her place stands a woman newly aflame with hope and desire.

· 8 ·

BASKING IN BETHLEHEM

ONE OF EMILY's lifelong possessions was a small Bible, her name stamped in gold on the leather cover, given to her by her father. Today that volume rests among the Dickinson papers at Harvard and one overlooked circumstance connected with it speaks eloquently of concerns more human than divine. A phrase in *Revelations,* Chapter twenty-one, has been carefully scissored out, the tiny slip of paper no longer extant. Assuming that Emily's own hands wielded the scissors, the extracted words provide the key to a timely three-way link between the Master, the widower Lord and the rejuvenated recluse.

In the second Master letter Emily had expressed her deep conviction that she and her loved one would eventually be together. "Each Sabbath on the sea," she wrote, "makes me count the Sabbaths till we meet on shore." This is familiar symbolism in her poems and letters, the sea standing for life and the shore being a vague kind of afterlife—in some moods Heaven. In the early months of 1878 these same symbols are found occupying her thoughts again, only in an indirect manner. While describing her mother's feeble health in a letter, she says it reminds her "of Hawthorne's blameless ship—that forgot the port." Now the ship she had in mind here had nothing directly to do with either her mother or Hawthorne, but concerns a famous legend of Salem. The waters adjacent to that coastal town, ran the old tale, were haunted by a phantom ship which was unable for some ghostly reason to enter the harbor; thus mysteriously interdicted, it perpetually rode the seas nearby. The perfect fitness of that story to Emily's situation is undeniable even if her reference to it is oblique. With the undreamed demise of Mrs. Lord, however, her lengthy vigil on the sea was done, the way into Salem clear. And that is exactly what the slip of paper cut from her Bible proclaims: "And the sea is no more, and I saw the Holy City, New Jerusalem." The Heavenly meeting envisioned in the Master letter has been altered by fate to an earthly reunion in Salem, Lord's home town appropriately serving as the Holy City.

Marriage, judging from the surviving correspondence, was to have been a definite part of this New Jerusalem. What has never been explained is why the step did not take place, a denouement that would have drastically altered Emily's history, perhaps even to the point where, with Lord's encouragement, she would have begun to publish. More than five years remained to them before the question was to be decided by Lord's death, sufficient time, it would seem, for a trip to the altar. But for once there is no real mystery, only a piling up of circumstance, family opposition, and the predictable psychic burden resulting from Emily's self-imprisonment. There were, nevertheless, a few moments when it all seemed about to come true, and perhaps one particular instant when Lord, grown mightily impatient, almost forced a culmination.

After losing his wife, Lord's first known visit to Amherst took place in the summer of 1880. During the two-and-a-half-year stretch between those two events, not the barest mention places him in the vicinity, an unlikely development certainly, and if he wasn't there more than once then he had an enviable facility for arousing sexual desire by mail. A few of Emily's poems, written about now, record some ecstatic face-to-face encounters that are patently factual; four of them, when taken together, frame the touching scenario of the first meeting the two enjoyed as unhampered lovers, probably in mid-1878.

It is spring, perhaps early April. From her bedroom window Emily peers toward the tracks of the Amherst-Belchertown railroad, anxiously listening for the whistle that will announce Lord's arrival, and feeling "the train would never come." Silently, she rehearses her welcoming words, "taught my heart a hundred times precisely what to say." When the train at last pulls in, she can hardly restrain her eagerness to reach the Holy land, to be "basking in Bethlehem," but when they meet, all her rehearsing goes for nothing as her "treatise" is forgotten. Lord, too, becomes tongue-tied as the fifteen empty years drop away in a moment:

> Pausing in front of our palsied faces,
> Time compassion took;
> Arks of reprieve he offered us,
> Ararats we took.

As it turned out, they did not quite surmount Ararat, but those frank lines reinforce the claim that the affair was not of recent vintage. When they did find their voices—his "decrepit with joy," while her words "tottered"—neither could cope with the tumbling thoughts. Not smiling, not outwardly radiant, brimming only in the sanctuary of their hearts, they clung in awed acceptance of their resurrection.

After that first meeting letters flowed between them steadily, unafraid outpourings of physical and emotional delight. "Also my Naughty one," she scolds when he has forgotten to write, "too seraphic naughty, who can sentence you—certainly not my enamoured heart." Relating a conversation she had with her nephew about Lord's reputation as a judge, she tells of some high compliments repeated by the lad from his father and admits, "I wanted to fondle the boy for the fervent words, but made the distinction . . . Oh my beloved, save me from the idolatry which would crush us both—'and very sea-mark of my utmost sail.'" If that last phrase seems strange, it was not so to Lord; after consulting his Shakespeare concordance he would have come up with the following teasing message:

> Do you go back dismayed? 'Tis a lost fear;
> Man but a rush against Othello's breast,
> And he retires.

Perhaps on his next visit Lord tried acting on that cute invitation. If he did man a rush against Emily's breast he found her unwilling to yield and himself putty in the frail hands. "Don't you know you are happiest while I withhold and not confer?" she soothed. "Don't you know that 'no' is the wildest word we consign to language?" Even after a dozen sheltered years Emily needed no lessons.

If this unabashed coquetry is any sign, marriage plans were in the air very early. While a decent interval would have been required, in this case the period could rightly have been curtailed, and perhaps the subject had arisen by the summer of 1878. But it was just here that there occurred the first of the frustrations that were to keep the two apart. Mrs. Dickinson, a little recovered, while wandering about the house fell and broke her hip. She was put back to bed in worse condition than she had been in for two or three years, the delirium at times also returning. Thereafter, both Emily and her sister were in constant attendance, particularly Emily, whose company seems to have been preferred. "Her poor patience loses its way," she sighed to Mrs. Holland, "and we lead it back . . . to read to her, to fan her, to tell her 'health will come tomorrow' and make the counterfeit look real . . . I hardly have said 'Good Morning, Mother' when I hear myself saying 'Mother, Good Night.'"

With ample time to reflect, she seems also to have become apprehensive about the major upheaval that an emergence from the shadows would entail—a new life in a strange city, her role as wife to one of the state's high officials and best-known figures. Nearing her fiftieth year, she possessed enough wisdom even in the midst of her euphoria to question warily whether bliss coming so late and after such a life as hers could be unalloyed. She needed Lord's constant assurance that love was enough, that "the pile of years," as she poetically phrased it, was not too high.

Despite his eagerness, Lord himself was having his difficulties. The running of his house had been taken over at his invitation by his widowed sister-in-law, Mary Farley, and her thirty-one-year old daughter, Abbey. These two, with another niece, provided the smooth organization needed by an old-time Supreme Court Justice, and the women on their part were happy to have a place in life, with Lord's sizable estate perhaps forming no negligible factor in the women's thinking—he was eventually to settle his property and about thirty-five thousand dollars on them. His marriage could put all this in jeopardy, and Abbey Farley at least was not backward about voicing her disgust over her uncle's new friendship. Long after Emily's death, Abbey was still spitefully calling her a "little hussy . . . crazy about men," who had tried "to get Judge Lord," and branding her eccentricities as "insanity."[*]

To this, some further complications were added by the fact that Abbey was a close friend of Sue whose role in the affair is equivocal at best. It was Sue who chiefly manufactured the Wadsworth-as-lover thesis, an action that betrays a wish to cloud the real truth, perhaps involving some action or word of her own that contributed to obstructing the marriage. She may have found Lord distasteful, the thought of Emily's marriage to him grotesque; she may have been unduly influenced by loyalty to the Farleys—at this juncture no one will ever know. Behind all, finally, there broods the figure of Vinnie, now grown abrasive in personality, her disappointed youth far behind her, Emily the

[*] Bingham, *Revelation*, 23.

only one in the world to whom she can turn. The skein of con-
flicting alliances tangling around the heads of the two at the
center, it can be seen, becomes hard to straighten with any assurance, especially where guilty hands have been busy. Only
Austin's attitude appears above suspicion: it was he who gave
the Lord letters to Mabel when he could easily have destroyed
them, wiping out forever all record of the episode.

Despite the aggravation of delay, emotional rebirth in the
meantime had wrought some changes in the recluse. The severely
banded hair-do noted by Higginson gave way once again to a
softer arrangement of curls, and in her eyes a new light shone.
She did not entirely desert the shadows, but neither did she always run to concealment from an intruder. Once when a student
from the college arrived with a message for Vinnie, he was rewarded by the unusual pleasure of a chat with Emily on the back
porch. He carried away with him the memory of a warm smile
and a pleasant voice, a tasselled snood that enclosed the reddish
curls, and a white dress long enough to cover her shoes and brush
the floor. It was also about this time, the summer of 1880, that
she answered a knock at the kitchen door to find an Indian woman offering baskets for sale, beside her a ragged little girl of
four or five. For Emily to open a door herself was rare enough,
and the interest she took in the strangers was even more out of
character. Leading the child by the hand into the garden, she
watched in delight as the "dazzling baby" with much laughter
chased birds and tumbled in the grass. Another untypical incident involved an auction at the First Church on behalf of local
orphans; with scant hope, a request was made of Emily that she
donate some manuscript poems for the sale. Against all expectation she gladly sent three. The outside world was becoming real
again.*

Whether at this stage her long-suffering wooer may have
taken direct action is a question, but there is just enough basis of

* For the incidents in this paragraph, see Leyda II, 328, and ED
letters 653, 654.

fact to make such a theory plausible. By all accounts, impetuosity was a leading trait of Lord's character and, as often happens, this had its good and bad sides. In the role of politician or as a pleader before the bar, his forcefulness brought him attention and success; when he became a judge, the tendency to override formal procedure was frequently a handicap. As his colleagues more than once publicly charged, his was not the judicial temperament required by a position on the bench. That explosive nature, just possibly, may have boiled over when, in the fall of 1880, Mrs. Dickinson's doctor offered the depressing diagnosis that she would never walk again. Something, at any rate, brought him to Amherst twice in the space of a month at this time, and Emily shortly afterward is heard referring to him as "Papa" and to herself as "Mama." Meager enough facts, it is true, and the urge to build a dramatic scene on them, showing Lord in hot protestation before Emily and her family, is hereby abjured. Such a confrontation, however, could be the kernel of truth in the story later told by Martha—the coming of "that man" with his demands that Emily go away with him, the dash next door by Vinnie to enlist Sue's help, the tearful refusal of the confused and shaken recluse. If it did happen, it led only to further reluctant waiting for Lord and to nervous prostration for Emily. As her letters show, she was taken suddenly ill after Lord's second visit, and was in bed for almost a month.

For more than a year the situation remained static. Then in the spring of 1882 Emily is suddenly found talking much like any other bride-to-be. "Momentousness is ripening," she writes to Lord, "I hope all is firm. Could we yield each other to the impregnable chances till we had met once more?" Evidently, marriage was fairly imminent, perhaps a matter of weeks—it is at this time that she refers to herself by the pet name Lord had bestowed on her: "Emily Jumbo! Sweetest name, but I know a sweeter—Emily Jumbo Lord. Have I your approval?" But she was wiser than she knew in her playful reference to the wheel of chance. A few days afterward, while she was happily writing again to Lord,

Vinnie entered the room to inquire if she had seen anything in the papers that morning concerning them. On answering that she hadn't, Emily listened in a daze to the news, reported in the *Republican*, that Otis Lord had suffered a stroke. "My sight slipped and I thought I was freezing." As she stood immobile, Tom Kelley, the Irish handyman and intermediary for her letters to Lord, entered the room. "I thought first of you," he said. Sobbing, Emily threw herself on his chest. A week was to pass before Lord was out of danger.

Dejected, with marriage once again far away, she slipped back into the shadows, refusing to see a number of people who called. One, a friend of her youth, fully expected to be received, and when she was informed that Emily could not come down, went away in some resentment. Later the friend composed a sonnet on the incident, concluding that her old friend's exclusivity was based on a lofty aversion to things of the world, which makes this visitor one of the first to draw mistaken cosmic notions from very ordinary human hurt.

Another caller, in September, could not be entirely ignored, since she entered the house as a good friend of both Austin and Vinnie. As the vivacious Mabel Todd was playing the piano in the brightly lighted parlor, Emily came quietly down the stairs to sit in the darkened hall and listen. When the music stopped, she slipped into the kitchen, poured some wine, placed one of her poems—probably written for the ailing Lord originally—on the silver tray and had Maggie take it in. It is clear that she liked Mabel and was ready to accept her, yet her admiration may have had in it something of personal regret, some wan touch of envy. This charming, talented, socially accomplished neighbor was Emily herself at the same age, ambitious as she was, with the same artistic instincts. How different, how sadly different it had all turned out; how unutterably far she had drifted from the exuberant young girl who had so confidently planned to become distinguished. A month later her mother was dead and the transformation from childhood was complete.

Mrs. Dickinson's death left Emily feeling numb, consoled only by the knowledge that the two had somehow found each other during those last weary bedside hours. The mother had worsened in the winter cold, developing neuralgia on top of her other ills. On the night of November 13 Emily fed her, laughing delightedly at the ravenous appetite that seemed to herald a recovery. The next morning the woman was lifted from the bed to a chair as usual. After bundling her up, Vinnie was turning from the room when she heard a weak "Don't leave me." While her two daughters clung tearfully, Mrs. Dickinson, in Emily's phrase, "soared from us unexpectedly as a summoned bird."

•　　•

It was in January 1883 that Sue Dickinson first made an open issue of her husband's interest in Mabel Todd. This incident, always shrugged off as a mere tangent that had little effect on Emily personally, calls urgently, if not trumpet-tongued, for a more sustained look.

After that first interview between Mabel and Sue, a second meeting took place a few days later, resulting in permanent bitterness on both sides. This led to a temporary but complete break as Sue made it clear that she would not have the younger woman in her house, and for eight months Mabel was exiled. Only in September and at Austin's insistence did Sue relent—"partially" as Mabel recorded—and reluctantly permit a renewal of visiting. So much is undisputed fact, but where in all this did Emily stand? During the eight months of Mabel's banishment, it develops, unable to believe her brother culpable, she found herself taking Mabel's side, as did Vinnie. Making an effort to smooth things over, she sent Mrs. Todd a veiled plea that Sue not be judged harshly, couching her request in terms of the classic jealousy tale. "Why should we censure Othello," she asked, "when the Criterion Lover says, 'Thou shalt have no other Gods before me'?" That would have been perfectly clear to Mabel even if it has escaped later readers, and it was enigmatic enough to find a place in the volume of Emily's letters that Mabel edited, though to obscure its real significance she dated it three years later.

Toward Sue, Emily's feelings were mixed, her unbroken forty-five-year loyalty and love severely strained. Again with hidden meaning that was readily grasped by the recipient, she sent a note across to her sister-in-law expressing her disapproval: "Dear Sue—with the exception of Shakespeare, you have told me of more knowledge than anyone living—To say that sincerely is strange praise." This note has always before been read in isolation, separated from all immediate frame of reference, the cold words taken as proof of long estrangement between the two women. Yet of the hundred-and-fifty surviving letters and notes from Emily to Sue, that is the only one whose tone approaches open censure. Its true import, lost with the passing of time, in light of the other note to Mabel is almost transparent: Emily is bracketing Sue's jealousy with that of Othello, knowing Sue would quickly identify the "exception" in Shakespeare.

When at last a makeshift accommodation was reached between the two warring women in September, Emily's old affection toward Sue was resumed. The chasm for the moment had been bridged, but Mabel, without being aware of it, had put the seal to her hopes of meeting the recluse. With the storm calmed, the pressure off her brother, Emily had no intention of causing another squall by taking up with Mabel.

That reading of the evidence will hold before any disinterested court in the world, yet that is not the way the passage at arms between Sue and Mabel is presently viewed. Throughout the whole of Dickinson biography and criticism, in a unanimous chorus of assent, Sue is condemned as a shallow, worldly, selfish woman who began the slow destruction of her own marriage shortly after pronouncing her wedding vows. Mabel Todd, it is said, blundered innocently into an already hopeless situation. And, astonishingly, the sole source for that idea was the Todds themselves, mother and daughter.

Except for the claims of those two there exists no hint that Sue and Austin were anything but congenial up to the arrival in Amherst of the Todds. One or two scant phrases in Emily's letter, which in reality allow and even demand the most innocuous of interpretations, are all that can be cited.* The Dickinson neighbors, on the other hand, had their own ideas about what was going on at the time. John Erskine, well-known scholar and author, who resided and taught in Amherst while Sue was still living, has preserved a faint echo of the talk that went round: "Popular report went on to say that Austin had a brilliant wife, Susan, whose disposition was in every way cordial until Austin contracted or developed the habit of spending his spare time in Mabel's company." Erskine further recalled the prevalent rumor that it was in order to get closer to Emily that "Mabel vamped Austin, leaving to posterity in excuse some poisonous hints that his wife didn't deserve him."†

The hints became broader when Millicent Todd, after her mother's death, gave up a professional career in order to plunge into Dickinson affairs. In various publications she stated, in effect, that for over twenty years before her mother's arrival Sue and Austin had grown steadily apart, and were separated in mind and heart long before Mabel entered their house. Offering no proof, but implicitly believing her mother's assertions to that effect, she succeeded in imposing that view on all who followed. Thus it was accepted that during much of Emily's life, weighing down even the years of her intensest literary effort, she suffered deep sorrow over the failing marriage in which her brother and her best friend were trapped. If the blatant falsehood of that picture cannot be absolutely demonstrated, neither can the truth of it any longer be accepted without serious reservation. For the time being, perhaps the last word may be permitted to Emily's nephew Ned. A young man of twenty when he first met Mabel, and then among her most fervent admirers, he ended by stigma-

* See, for example, letter no. 715 and the editor's unjustified note to it.
† John Erskine, *The Memory of Certain Persons*, Lippincott. 128 ff.

tizing her as "a woman who has brought nothing but a sword into the family."

These later developments, of course, did not affect the living Emily. When some tolerance was gained between Sue and Mabel, she quietly withdrew, turning her thoughts once again to marriage. The New Jerusalem so imminent five years before, and so repeatedly blocked, now for a brief while seemed about to descend to earth. Lord, making preparations for the few years he had left, resigned from the Supreme Court, then proceeded to arrange a settlement on the Farley women in his will. Emily's spirit, too, expanded, even to the point where she thought once more of publication. A Boston publisher, alerted by Helen Hunt Jackson, made inquiries about her poetry, and she hesitantly submitted half a dozen examples. All were concerned with nature and probably had been written from original observation (she did include "Further in summer," which owed all its substance to Hawthorne, but the craftsmanship in that is so fine she could legitimately have claimed it for her own). The publisher, however, knowing that verse by an unknown would be a risky business, decided that Emily's interesting vignettes, while charming, were too ephemeral to command attention. His reply consisted of faint praise followed by silence. The curtain had dropped, once and for all, on the poet; three months later with terrible swiftness it rang down on the woman, when the loved eight-year-old Gilbert was taken away by typhoid fever.

With this devastating loss, Emily ceased caring about poetry or marriage or anything else. She became gravely ill and was confined to bed soon after the boy's funeral, arising from it in April 1884 in the knowledge that she had Bright's disease. Just when she began weakly roaming around the house, the final doom sounded: word came that Otis Lord, who had suffered a number of relapses, was dead. With that she let go. Three times in the following weeks the doctor was called for her, once to attend aching eyes. Then in the middle of June, as she helped Maggie with a cake, "a great darkness" blotted out the familiar kitchen and she collapsed.

Two years remained, years largely of invalidism and a fine indifference to everything but immediate small cares. More than half the time she either lay in bed or sat in a chair in her room. Reading little, poetry almost forgotten, her recreation consisted of an exchange of letters with friends, and the delicate messages sent with fruit or flowers to her neighbors. She saw no outsider except once, when she welcomed back the same woman whose visit twenty years before had been relegated to the other side of a half-open door, the woman she called "the angel of childhood," and who in these aimless days brought misty memories of the house on Pleasant Street. Occasionally she was well enough to be up, but another collapse in which she lay for two hours on the parlor rug warned her family that her illness needed close watching.

She seems to have guessed, as the winter of 1885 drew on, that the end was near. To the consternation of family and physician, she refused any further medical examination—a startling reflection of Emily Brontë's famous last days—agreeing only that the doctor might have a glimpse of her as she walked by an open door. Making bundles of the masses of old correspondence that crowded her bureau drawer, she labeled them to be burned unopened, and interestingly, confided a portion of that task to the faithful Maggie. Her last poem to Lord, the touching "So give me back to death," was composed about now, a short verse in which she confesses her distaste for existence—life itself, she says, is only a grave in which she continues to breathe. Somehow she had come—perhaps through the counseling of Wadsworth, perhaps through the intensity of her long, hopeless love—to a calm assurance of the soul's survival. Frequently, toward the end, she would read aloud to Vinnie the jubilant lines in which Emily Brontë had declared a passionate belief in a personal Heaven:[*]

[*] Leyda, II, 475.

No coward soul is mine,
No trembler in the world's storm-troubled sphere:
I see Heaven's glories shine,
And faith shines equal, arming me from fear. . . .

With the first week of May her premonitions enlarged, prompting a last flourish. Feeling that death was only a matter of days, she borrowed the two-word title of a book she had just read, a widely popular thriller, and to the Norcross girls wrote simply, "Little Cousins, Called Back, Emily."

Waking on the morning of May 13, she complained to her sister of distress then quickly sank to unconsciousness, her respiration rapidly becoming labored. For nearly sixty hours the coma and the "terrible breathing" continued as the family gathered round and neighbor women dropped by to console the stricken Vinnie. Death came quietly on the evening of the fifteenth a few minutes before Amherst's factory whistles, as Austin noted ruefully, sounded quitting time.

At Vinnie's request a burial robe of soft white flannel was made by a neighbor, Mrs. Powell; on the nineteenth with Sue's help the same woman dressed the body. As the mourners gathered in the long parlor, the small white coffin was brought down and secluded in the library. Mrs. Jameson, a neighbor of whose children Emily had been fond, was called in by Vinnie to view the open casket. Gazing down at the woman she had known for years but never seen, she was mildly surprised to note a resemblance to Austin rather than Vinnie, but impressed by the "wealth of auburn hair and a very spirituelle face." When Thomas Higginson arrived, he was afforded the same privilege and he marvelled at Emily's youthful appearance; "not a gray hair or wrinkle and perfect peace on the beautiful brow." While he stood beside the casket Vinnie placed two heliotropes in her sister's hand, whispering tenderly that they were for her to take to Judge Lord.

After the service the coffin was carried out back and raised to the flowered bier on the shoulders of the six workmen, the mourners forming behind. Slowly the winding procession passed the barn, passed the garden where Emily's beloved blossoms frolicked in the bright sun, passed the fields of grain along Triangle Road, and paused beside the mounds that held her mother and father. Since then it is nearly a century, yet for Emily each of those years must have felt infinitely shorter than the day she first somberly questioned what lay beyond the grave.

Notes and Sources

MOST OF WHAT I have to say about Emily Dickinson will have found its proper place in the narrative. Here, especially for more concerned readers, perhaps I should explain the position I have taken on two of the most vexing technical questions in Dickinson scholarship: the dating by handwriting of her manuscripts, and the degree of acceptance to be afforded to her somewhat, shall we say, individual punctuation.

As to the handwriting scale, I reject the precision assumed by the editors of the Harvard *Letters* and *Poems*. Firstly, the dating of fair copies has no necessary relation to the time of composition, a point insufficiently noticed; in a number of cases an extremely wide divergence is demonstrable; and in many others is probable. Secondly, the handwriting changes themselves—I conclude from my own careful study of the lengthy analysis set down in the first volume of *Poems*—cannot place an undated manuscript, poem or letter, any more exactly than within a flexible five-year period, about two years, say, on either side of the suggested date. The desire to achieve greater exactitude is understandable and even commendable, but does anyone really believe that Emily's handwriting changed, with traceable regularity, every year for thirty-six years? Or every two years? Or three? That is not only untenable in theory, but untrue in fact, as patient study of the crucial years 1858–1868 makes clear.

The punctuation and use of capitals in the poetry has become a minor branch of study in itself, into which I will not be drawn. In my opinion there is nothing to study. After reading through all that has been written on this topic, weighing arguments while peering at the actual manuscripts, I conclude that Emily was at best regardless, at worst illiterate, when it came to punctuation. It was as if she used a leaky pen that dripped commas, dashes, and capitals indiscriminately. The claim that she had some ingenious system, some new slant on these things, belongs with such other literary anomalies as the quarrel over the shape of Shelley's nose. Let me give one little example, out of the hundreds that have struck me, of the nonsensical aspect in all this. In letter 736, as printed, there is a comma after the word "rather," which not one in a thousand persons would have used at that point. Turning to the manuscript of that note we find that the comma is really an elongated dot over an *i* in the line below. Similarly, letters 241 and 243 do not fit the description provided for 1861, yet the ascription to that year is correct on internal evidence.

If Emily had published, I am convinced she would have been more than happy to have someone tidy up for her. Consequently, believing that most readers, even most scholars, are as tired of the slap-dash punctuation as I am, I have regularized it. That this may produce delicate alterations in nuance I concede as possible if unlikely; on the other hand, I submit that the possible loss is not nearly so great as the certain gain. In quoting from her letters I have for the most part allowed her mutinous style to stand, though I shouldn't wonder if I have overlooked a dash here and there; the supply in any case is plentiful.

BIBLIOGRAPHY

Main Sources

Bianchi, M., *Life and Letters of ED*. Boston, Houghton Mifflin, 1924.

Bianchi, M., *ED Face to Face*. Boston, Houghton Mifflin, 1932.

Bingham, M. T., *Ancestors' Brocades*. New York, Harper & Brothers, 1945.

Bingham, M. T., *ED's Home*. New York, Harper, 1955.

Bingham, M. T., *ED: A Revelation*. New York, Harper, 1954.

Capps, J. L., *ED's Reading, 1836–1886*. Cambridge, Harvard University Press, 1966.

Clendenning, S., *ED, A Bibliography*. Kent, Ohio, Kent State University, 1968.

Dickinson, Emily, *Poems.* T. H. Johnson, ed., 3 vols. Cambridge, Harvard University Press, 1955.

Dickinson, Emily, *Letters.* Johnson and Ward, eds., 3 vols. Cambridge, Harvard University Press, 1958.

England, M. W., "ED and Isaac Watts," in *Hymns Unbidden.* New York, The New York Public Library, 1966.

Franklin, R., *The Editing of ED.* Madison, Wisc., University of Wisconsin Press, 1967.

Jenkins, M., *ED, Friend and Neighbor.* Boston, Little, Brown and Co., 1930.

Leyda, J., *The Years and Hours of ED.* New Haven, Yale University Press, 1960.

McLean, S., "ED at Mt. Holyoke." *New England Quar.,* VII, Norwood, Mass., 1934.

Rosenbaum, S. P., *A Concordance to the Poems of ED.* Ithaca, N.Y., Cornell University Press, 1964.

Sewall, R. B., *The Lyman Letters.* Amherst, Mass., University of Massachusetts, 1965.

Todd, M., "ED's Literary Debut." *Harper's,* CLX, 1930.

Whicher, G. F., "ED's Earliest Friend. *Amer. Lit.,* VI, 1934.

The following, while I disagree with much that they say, have provided stimulating discussions, especially where they treat the primary facts of ED's life and art:

Anderson, C., *ED's Poetry: Stairway of Surprise.* New York, Holt, Rinehart and Winston, 1960.

Blake, C. R., and Wells, C. F. (eds.), *The Recognition of ED.* Ann Arbor, Mich., University of Michigan Press, 1968.

Chase, R., *Emily Dickinson.* New York, W. Sloane Associates, 1951.

Gelpi, A. J., *ED: The Mind of the Poet.* Cambridge, Harvard University Press, 1965.

Griffith, C., *The Long Shadow.* Princeton, Princeton University Press, 1964.

Higgins, D., *Portrait of ED.* New Brunswick, Rutgers University Press, 1967.

Johnson, T. H., *Emily Dickinson.* Cambridge, Harvard University Press, 1955.

Lindberg-Seyersted, B., *The Voice of the Poet.* Cambridge, Harvard University Press, 1968.

Notes and Sources

Miller, R., *The Poetry of ED*. Middletown, Conn., Wesleyan University Press, 1968.

Pollitt, J., *ED: The Human Background*. New York, Harper & Brothers, 1930.

Sewall, R. B. (ed.), *ED: A Collection of Critical Essays*. Englewood Cliffs, N.J., Prentice-Hall, 1963.

Sherwood, W., *Circumference and Circumstance*. New York, Columbia University Press, 1968.

Taggard, G., *The Life and Mind of ED*. New York, A. A. Knopf, 1930.

Whicher, G., *This Was A Poet*. New York, Charles Scribner's Sons, 1938. (Reprinted: University of Michigan Press, 1965.)

NOTES

Prologue: EMILY'S HOUSE

When the Dickinson house was occupied by two families there must have been a second kitchen; no trace of this remains.

The bed in Emily's room may not be hers; Vinnie had one just like it and both were stored for many years in Austin's attic.

The poem describing the view from her window is "The angle of a landscape."

Emily calls herself "Jumbo" in letter 780 to Otis Lord.

The merciless probing and the continued fascination with her personality may most succinctly be demonstrated by some bare totals: since her death there have appeared nearly sixty books of criticism and biography, over a hundred other books in which she is treated more or less at length, and about 650 articles, not to mention thirty or forty doctoral dissertations, as well as two plays and a couple of novels.

Chapter One
A LADY WHOM THE PEOPLE CALL THE MYTH

Extracts from Mabel Todd's journals and diaries are in Leyda, vol. 2; other sources on her were *Ancestors' Brocades*; M. L. Todd's *Contributions to the Town of Amherst* (1935), a privately printed brochure by her daughter; and Franklin, *The Editing of ED*. It was Franklin who discovered, in a neat bit of detective work, the deliberate mutilation of the manuscript of "One sister have I in our

250

house," though he did not assign a reason, a time, or a specific perpetrator for the act.

During my visit to Emily's house one thing I was most curious about was her habit of conversing with guests from the cover of darkness. What exactly had the setting been like, I wondered, for these legendary interludes? With the help of my young guide, I turned off the hall lights and dimmed the lamps in the parlor. When only two widely separated 60-watt bulbs remained lit, the objects in the hall—chairs, a chest, paintings—could still be discerned rather clearly. Spotting a small fixture on the parlor wall, appropriately in the shape of a candle and containing a single 40-watt bulb, I turned it on, snapping off all the other lights. Even this comparatively weak source cast a stronger glow into the hallway than might have been expected, though the resultant murky illumination could well be described as dusky or in shadow. The trouble was that Emily's guests had usually been seated in a parlor which was well, even "brilliantly" lighted, implying something more than a single 40-watt source even for the standards of a hundred years ago.

I needed an Emily out there to complete the experiment, I decided, and my guide kindly agreed to wrap herself in a sheet and talk with me between the rooms. I first positioned her on a chair against the far wall of the hallway and placed myself some distance within the parlor. In the half-darkness the girl's presence still showed clearly, the white sheet concentrating the available light; even her face was dimly discernible. I doubted that Emily would have exposed herself like this; evidently she had kept herself well out of the line of sight. Conversing in normal tones, I moved the girl to various positions behind the intervening parlor wall, but to be comfortable and avoid the necessity of straining to hear, I had to pull a chair somewhat near to the doorway.

The staircase itself seemed a likely possibility. It was roomy, carpeted in Emily's time as now, and its lower portion was in line with the rear parlor door, while anyone sitting there would be effectively screened by the balustrade. It was also handy to the narrow passageway leading off to other parts of the house that Emily regularly used as an escape route whenever she was surprised by sudden arrivals. We tried it and found that it answered nicely: the girl's hushed voice was easily heard and I could see no more than dim bits of the sheet draped around her. Still, it was clear that if the lights in the parlor were in any way brilliant, Emily would not have chanced the staircase. She and her privileged guests, I concluded, must have spent a good deal of time talking around corners and saying "Excuse me?" or "What?" or "I'm sorry, I didn't hear you."

The most useful result of the little experiment, for me, was an increased sense of the unreal atmosphere that must have attended these sessions. It is one thing to read about such goings-on, their downright peculiarity softened in the afterglow of Emily's present fame. It is quite another to sit in her silent parlor and attempt normal conversation, the voice from the hall assuming a spectral quality because of the distance between the speakers, the spaciousness of the rooms and the high ceilings. With this habit added to her life of seclusion, it is no wonder that Emily became the village myth. It is only surprising that her good neighbors—despite their easy acceptance of traditional New England eccentricity—did not consider her altogether round the bend.

The lawsuit was reported in *The Springfield Republican* for March 1, 2, 4, 1898; decision for the plaintiff was reported on April 16 with the comment that the outcome had been "foretold several weeks ago." Mrs. Bingham, while claiming to be impartial (*An. Broc.*, 349–67) in her lengthy presentation of the facts, has no mention of her parents' countersuit against Vinnie. Alfred Stearns (*An Amherst Boyhood*, 1946) was twenty-six at the time of the lawsuit; he recalled that the scandal split the town so that hostesses had to be careful whom they invited to parties. There was much talk, he remembered, about Sue Dickinson's part in the suit—how she had managed to influence Vinnie: "town gossip played with the topic, suggesting such devious devices as hypnotism, threats, blackmail and deceit." For another reference to threats, see Bingham, *An. Broc.*, 372.

Mabel Todd's singular brand of egotism is displayed in a 1901 diary entry. She had just lectured at the Twentieth Century Club in Pittsburgh: "Talked on Singkep with real genius. Everybody quivered under it and my whole self thrilled with it. It nearly used me up but it was the best I ever did. The jungle talked to them— and enveloped them—the eclipse clasped them—I was the only medium. Everybody was in breathless tears. I was received after—they nearly devoured me—with such praises as even I have rarely listened to" (*Contributions*, etc.). Letter 736 is listed by Mabel Todd as the first she received from Emily; I see it as the last.

The manuscript poems Vinnie hid just before her death were discovered in June 1927 by Martha Dickinson Bianchi in an old security box crammed with mortgages and deeds (*Republican,* March 31, 1929). They were published in 1929 as *Further Poems,* with the false statement that they had been withheld by Vinnie; it was, of course, Vinnie's death that had halted publication. According to the *Republican,* neither Dickinson family ever destroyed any papers except after a death, and then only on specific instructions; the attics of both houses harbored many barrels filled with old documents. Martha told the *Republican* that "When Emily died two great barrels of letters were burned," and at Vinnie's death, "eight bushels of her personal papers met the same fate." And whose hand was it that emptied those eight baskets of Vinnie's papers into the fire? After Vinnie's death, Sue Dickinson, who lived until 1913, remained in sole possession of both houses and everything in them.

Mrs. Todd's action in taking possession of Emily's manuscripts and other papers did not go permanently unchallenged, though nothing was done until years after her death, when the material had passed to her daughter. In 1950 Harvard University acquired the Dickinson-Bianchi papers from Alfred Hampson, the heir of Mrs. Bianchi, and promptly announced a claim to sole ownership in all the papers in the hands of Mrs. Bingham, including copyright of the poems she had published in *Bolts of Melody* (1945). Mrs. Bingham rejected this claim, and the legal disagreement, while it never reached court, halted the imminent publication of her book, *Emily Dickinson's Home,* for four years. Eventually Harvard's claim to copyright was accepted by Mrs. Bingham but she steadfastly refused to give up the manuscripts themselves. In time she donated them to Amherst College, where they repose today under the joint control of Harvard and Amherst. This cumbersome arrangement was the result of an uneasy compromise induced by Mrs. Bingham's realization that she could not produce documentary evidence to show that the papers had come to her mother as a gift from Austin.

Chapter Two
NOBODY KNOWS THIS LITTLE ROSE

Regarding Mr. Dickinson's character, his long-time rival in the law and politics, I. F. Conkey, said at his death: "Sometimes it has been said of him, even by his townsmen, that he was austere, aristocratic, perhaps cold-hearted, but little did those who said this of him know him; it was *not* true of him—behind this natural dignity and commanding reserve lay a kind and warm heart." (*Hampshire Express,* June 24, 1874.)

The Amherst Sewing Society is mentioned in a letter of Austin's to Joseph Lyman (*Lyman Letters*, 11–13); undated, it can only refer to 1848.

Benjamin Newton's role in Emily's life has pretty obviously been overstated, perhaps because of its sentimental appeal and the dearth of solid information on this period. The two were certainly friends and he certainly encouraged her, their correspondence (none of which has been found) continuing until his death early in 1853. But he was of no more real inspiration to her than Humphrey or Emmons; that much is made clear in my Chapter Three, where the real source of her inspiration is detailed. For what it is worth, I cannot overcome the feeling that Newton was romantically interested in Emily, and left Amherst because she preferred the company of James Kimball—it was this that gave him a sentimental niche in her memory. Sue, I am satisfied, was far more important to Emily's early endeavors than any young man.

My choice for Emily's earliest surviving poem is "A train went through a burial gate," which describes a funeral entering a cemetery to the accompaniment of bird song. No manuscript now exists but even a manuscript in a late hand would not affect the point since it might have been recopied, and the two quatrains are certainly the work of an imitative teen-ager. The Dickinson house on Pleasant Street stood near the entrance to West Cemetery, about a hundred feet south of it. In a letter of March 1846 Emily writes: "Yesterday as I sat by the north window the funeral train entered the open gate of the churchyard. . . ." The cemetery's entrance now is on Triangle Street; the two stone pillars of the old, disused gateway on Pleasant Street still stand, hidden by a gas station.

That Emily studied formally with Humphrey is reflected in letter 39: "The hour of evening is sad—it was once my study hour—my Master has gone to rest, and the open leaf of the book, and the scholar at school alone, make the tears come." This is among her remarks on Humphrey's death.

The name of Emily's dog, Carlo, could not have come from Marvel's *Reveries*, as has been suggested. The name existed by January 1850, at the latest (letter 34), and according to a little diary kept by Vinnie the girls were not reading Marvel until a year later.

George Gould is not specified as the caller who urged Emily to go riding (letter 36), but he is the most likely one since he seems to have filled the interregnum between Kimball and Emmons.

The poem, "Sexton! my master's sleeping here," is presently assigned by fair-copy handwriting to about 1859; since its connection with Humphrey is patent, this serves as a warning against too-innocent use of the handwriting scale. Poem 47, "Heart! We will forget him," is Emily's comment, I believe, on the broken affair with Emmons.

My claim that sixty or so of the packet-poems can be identified as the work of 1850–56 is based on the facts laid out in Chapter Three; certainly Emily could not have written these banal effusions after the conversion experienced with *Aurora Leigh*. Most of the verses in packets 80 and 82, as well as some in 1, 2, 7, 14, 15, and 83 are plainly early. No guessing is needed about "On this wondrous sea," which was written in 1853 but is included in packet 82 in a fair-copy handwriting of 1858. Similarly, "I never told the buried gold," fair-copied in 1858, was apparently composed in 1853; several of its phrases are anticipated or reflected in letters 91, 102 and 120.

Chapter Three
AND SHATTER ME WITH DAWN

That Vinnie received the news of Joseph Lyman's defection in May 1856 is evident, though not stated precisely, in *Lyman Letters*, 33–35. More than anyone has suspected, this disappointment of Vinnie's probably had an effect on later village tales about Emily, the result of a not unusual transference. And it pushed Vinnie later in life to defensive distortions that compounded the confusion. In 1893 she went out of her way to impress the credulous Mabel Todd with the fact that her single life was not her own doing but her parents': "Some of Vinnie's stories were appalling—of the way they were watched and guarded for fear some young man might wish to marry them" (*An. Broc.*, 231). That the girls were not guarded all that closely is only too clear from Emily's letters, which portray a house overrun with young men, as well as from Vinnie's 1851 diary, in which she recorded declining an offer of marriage, and which shows her mixing freely and happily with Amherst youth. After riding alone with a Mr. Chapin on January 15, she disdainfully recorded, "I reverence him no longer," indicating perhaps that Puritan repression did not always repress.

Among the poems in which Emily recorded her joyous reaction to *Aurora Leigh* are: "One blessing had I," "Struck was I," and "As if I asked a common alms." The poem "Her sweet weight on my heart" is another elegy on Mrs. Browning. The comparison between herself and St. Paul is in "The farthest thunder"; the connection of these lines with the Apostle's conversion was first pointed out by Anderson (*Stairway*, 212) but he made no biographical link. Anderson, whose exhaustive exegesis of Emily's work stands as a milestone in Dickinson scholarship, is a prime example of the ease with which her extremely subtle borrowing can be missed. In his opinion, "she escaped any serious influence from Elizabeth Barrett," and he concludes generally that "the search for influences yields little in the case of such a burry original. A native intensity of mind and heart gave her all the power she could manage." Burry she was, but as the evidence in this chapter affirms, not often original.

The exact day of *Aurora Leigh's* publication in this country is hard to pin down; it was reviewed at some length in the *New York Times,* December 9, 1856. Emily's imitation of Mrs. Browning's hair style is in "The Likeness of ED," by Louise Graves (daughter of Emily's cousin John) *Harvard Library Bulletin,* Spring, 1947, and an article by Helen Bullard (Emily's niece) in *Boston Cooking School Magazine,* June-July 1906, where the memories refer to a time prior to 1864.

A previous investigation of *Aurora Leigh* was carried out by Rebecca Patterson ("Elizabeth Browning and ED," *Educational Leader,* July 1956), in an article which attempts to assess the total influence of Mrs. Browning. Her conclusion that the Englishwoman was a major influence, with *Aurora Leigh* in the foreground, goes far beyond the evidence she presents. Turning up only isolated images, she never suspected the extensive foraging I have detailed. Like everyone else who has dealt in Dickinson influences, she asserts that "Emily was nowhere a simple copyist," which in a great many cases she certainly was. Before Patterson, Taggard (1930) briefly treated *Aurora Leigh,* noting that it was the source of some Dickinson imagery and attempting to use it as a connection between Emily and George Gould.

Patterson is also the author of *The Riddle of ED* (1951) which tries to identify a friend of Sue's, Kate Scott Anthon, as the object of Emily's affection. Written before the appearance of the Master letters, based wholly on innuendo drawn from the poems, blithely misinterpreting individual verses and changing pronouns at will, the thesis warrants no regard. Kate Scott, twice-widowed, was an old schoolmate of Sue's; during a number of visits to Amherst in the 1860's she became friendly with the entire Dickinson circle, including Sam Bowles who found her particularly attractive. Emily reacted warmly to her airy spirit and literary bent, a feeling no doubt enhanced by Kate's worship of Mrs. Browning.

Following is a complete list of Emily's borrowings from *Aurora Leigh* as I have so far been able to identify them. In my original reading I used an 1857 copy of the poem but since the only readily available edition now with numbered lines is *The Complete Works of Elizabeth Barrett Browning*, in the Cambridge series published by Houghton Mifflin, I have conformed my identifications to that. The occasional slight differences in phrasing and punctuation between early and later editions of *Aurora Leigh* do not affect the present study. Emily's poems are given by first lines.

	AURORA LEIGH (*lines*)	ED POEM (*P–partial*)
Bk. I	8–12	Exultation is the going
	40–45	A loss of something ever felt I
	118–120	I measure every grief I meet
	187–190	Strong draughts of their refreshing minds
	210–211	The soul's distinct connection
	215–219	'Twas like a maelstrom
	299–303	Peril as a possession
	326–330	That after horror, that 'twas us
	470–471	More life went out when he went—P
	477–480 1026–1029 1057–1062	The outer from the inner
	558–565	Just lost when I was saved
	647–651	I watched the moon around the house—P

689–690	My cocoon tightens	
733–751	Through lane it lay, through bramble	
769–771	Success is counted sweetest—P	
815–820 (& Bk. VII, 147–149)	We grow accustomed to the dark *See also:* I think I was enchanted Ourselves were wed one summer; *also some seventy other poems linked to "dark" and "midnight" symbolism*	
858–867	This was a poet	
934–938	I'm saying every day	
1003–1012, 1061	Not all die early *See also:* There are two ripenings Except the smaller size	
1022–1026	We play at paste	
Bk. II 5–7	Bring me the sunset in a cup—P	
55–56	Unto my books so good to turn —P; *See also those poems in which bells symbolize thought*	
66–71, 324–328	I started early, took my dog	
77–78	I think I was enchanted—P	
101–103 (& Bk. V, 258–261)	Publication is the auction	
104–106	Is bliss then such abyss	
287–291	A death blow is a life blow	
356–359	I rose because he sank	

Bk. III	151–153	Split the lark and you'll find the music
	170–173	Further in summer than the birds—P
	260	I can wade grief—P
	279–283	I cried at pity, not at pain
	326–340	Deprived of other banquet
	344–358	What soft cherubic creatures
Bk. IV	421–425	The rose did caper on her cheek
	488–492	Unit, like death, for whom—P
	714–717	We talked with each other—P *See also:* The winters are so short
	1213–1219 (& Bk. V, 145)	A solemn thing it was, I said
Bk. V	200–203, 213–215	Volcanoes be in Sicily—P
	423–426	You've seen balloons set
	979–981	It dropped so low in my regard
	1173–1178	The nearest dream recedes unrealized
Bk. VI	478–484, 500–502	I stepped from plank to plank
	922–977	My worthiness is all my doubt
	1084–1087	I heard a fly buzz when I died *See also:* I had not minded walls
	1194–1197	Because I could not stop for death—P

Bk. VII	395–409 (& Bk. VIII, 461–464)	I felt a funeral in my brain—P
	429–437	I like to see it lap the miles
	705–714	Victory comes late
	873–876	A word made flesh is seldom—P
	986–1001	Safe in their alabaster chambers
	1040–1052 (& Bk. VIII, 77–79)	'Twas the old road thru pain
	1149–1151	If pain for peace prepares
	1192–1216	To hang our head ostensibly
Bk. VIII	667–689	Going to her! Happy letter—P
Bk. IX	274–286	If he dissolve, then there is nothing more
	702, 740–742	He put the belt around my life —P

The following (with reference to the poem "In winter in my room," as a wish-fulfillment dream) are the occurrences of worms, snakes and the Lamia in *Aurora Leigh*:

Worms: I, 551–552, 556; III, 869, 1181; IV, 388; VII, 1019; VIII, 399–401; IX, 602–603.

Snakes: I, 157–159; II, 723–726; IV, 565–569; VII, 1078; VIII, 978; IX, 175.

Lamia: I, 161–163; VII, 147, 152, 170–171.

Aurora Leigh as a *mouse* is in I, 833–840; II, 798–800.

So much has been made of Emily's use of the word "circumference" that I feel I should spotlight an especially interesting passage in *Aurora Leigh*:

> . . . bats, that seem to follow in the air
> Some grand circumference of a shadowy dome

To which we are blind . . . (VII, 1068–1070)

Among the seventeen poems in which Emily employed this word, five (354, 533, 798, 1084, 1343) precisely echo Mrs. Browning's usage.

There survive two 1857 copies of *Aurora Leigh* from the Dickinson circle. The one now at Amherst College belonged to Emily and contains her signature (in a late hand, of about 1880). Many passages are pencil-marked but only very occasionally do these markings coincide with the borrowings. The second copy, now in the Houghton Library, belonged to Sue; her name is written in twice. In this also many passages are marked, with heavier lines and less precision. My guess is that the marks in both volumes have nothing to do with Emily's borrowing, but represent the girls' exchange of opinion on the poem's superior moments. I have gone only a short way into Emily's possible use of Mrs. Browning's other poems, but it promises to be a fertile field. For instance, compare poems 756, 799 and 1243 with Mrs. Browning's sonnet, *Grief*. It will be seen that Emily's much-praised line, "contented as despair," can no longer be wholly credited to her. See also, "Elizabeth and Emily," by Betty Miller, *Twentieth Century*, CLIX (1956) for further but superficial examination of the "grief" theme.

The lengths to which clever but badly-aimed analysis can reach are evident in Clark Griffith's comments (*Long Shadow,* 177–183) on that worm in Emily's room. Viewing the poem as a deliberate composition and not a dream, he says the *string* with which the worm is tied is one of Emily's most fascinating images. It represents both the "flimsy defense" of woman against the male aggressor, as well as Emily's eager attempt to claim masculinity for herself, and, finally, is a means of "retaliation" against dominating maleness—the string-collar gradually chokes and binds as the worm expands into the erect phallus-snake. It must now be admitted, I believe, that the verse really does describe an actual dream connected with *Aurora Leigh,* and in that case Griffith's all-purpose string loses much of its sexual cast. The change from worm to snake is plainly symbolic of Emily's intensive use of Mrs. Browning's material, and the poem even mirrors the subconscious at work: the worm is discovered, tethered and left alone, the change taking place only after an interim. Interestingly, the movement of the oncoming serpent is described in terms that also serve as a capsule comment on Emily's metrical technique: ". . . a rhythm slim / secreted in his form." In

Notes and Sources

this context, the string, if its dream meaning is at all recoverable, most likely relates to the strings of the conventional poet's lyre.

In quoting from the 3-volume *Poems,* in this and the chapters that follow, I have occasionally, for greater relevance, used one or another of the variant words and phrases listed.

Chapter Four
GET GABRIEL TO TELL IT

Emerson's visit to Sue's house, called the Evergreens, is in a manuscript memoir by Sue, *Annals of the Evergreens,* now at Harvard. For discussions of ED and Emerson see in particular Capps, Anderson, Whicher and Gelpi. For Emily's use of imagery from Emerson's "Shakespeare," compare poem 475 with the conclusion of paragraph 15, and poem 709, third stanza, with the conclusion of paragraph 7.

Following are Emily's borrowings from *Jane Eyre* and *Letters from New York.*

JANE EYRE (Chap.-par.)	ED POEM (P-partial)
4–22	On a columnar self
7–10 (& 5–penult.)	They shut me up in prose
7–21	The soul selects her own society—P
14–101, 27–123	I never hear the word escape
15–26	I make his crescent fill or lack *See also:* She laid her docile crescent down
15–78	A night there lay the days between *See also:* I many times thought peace had come It tossed and tossed
17–24	A light exists in spring *See also:* The maddest noise

262

24–last	You constituted time
	See also:
	I cannot live with you
25–56	My river runs to thee
26–last 3	I got so I could hear his name—P
30–12	He fumbles at your soul
35–85, 88	He put the belt around my life—P
	See also:
	Our journey had advanced
	If I'm lost now

LETTERS FROM NEW YORK	ED POEM
(*Letter-par.*)	(*P-partial*)
2–1	Much madness is divinest sense
2–10 (& 17–11)	To fight aloud is very brave
25–*passim*	The manner of its death
27–2	As if the sea should part
27–20	Her smile was shaped like other smiles
29–22	Will there really be a morning?
30–5	Upon the gallows hung a wretch

Emily's writing of a poem a day can most obviously be seen in poem 843. The arrangement by which Mr. Dickinson allowed his daughter to sleep late is my interpretation of poem 13, and its accompanying note. The Norcross girls' jealous hoarding and eventual destruction of Emily's letters to them is in Bingham, *An. Broc.*, 247.

Richard Chase made the identification of the word "anthracite" as coming from Marvel's *Reveries*; he was not aware that the entire poem was thus inspired. Emily's second poem in the *Republican* (March 1, 1862), was "The Sleeping" ("Safe in their alabaster chambers"), the verse discussed with Sue the previous summer.

Regarding Tennyson, who was much read by Emily but whose

works have so far yielded only one possible borrowing (see *Poems*, I, 190), a rather obvious and undeniable link exists between his "Tears, Idle Tears," third stanza, and Emily's "I heard a fly buzz when I died." Interestingly, the fly she substituted for Tennyson's "half-awaken'd birds," have been taken from life: see letter 206 where Emily talks about a buzzing fly that kept her company while Vinnie was away. It is more than instructive to realize that this poem of Emily's is another of those about which critical commentary has come up with differing meanings. She was, of course, only expanding in a personal projection on Tennyson's simple but poignant image; again, the seeming depth of the verse arises from her mastery of language and phrasing.

The Burnside expedition was lengthily reported in the *Republican;* on February 15 the paper referred to "the difficulties with which it has been embarrassed and delayed," and in the same issue with Emily's poem there was a report headed "Burnside Moving Again." An acquaintance of Emily's, Frazar Stearns, son of the Amherst College president, was an officer with the Burnside forces. On March 14 he was shot to death in the successful assault on New Bern, the first Amherst man to lose his life in combat. A few weeks earlier Emily had mentioned him in a letter to Loo Norcross, saying "I hope that ruddy face won't be brought home frozen." Her comment on the public funeral held in Amherst is pertinent in its studied phrasing to her distant attitude about the whole war: ". . . His big heart shot away by a 'minie ball.' I had read of those—but didn't think Frazer would carry one to Eden with him. Just as he fell, in his soldier's cap, with his sword at his side, Frazer rode through Amherst, classmates to the right of him, and classmates to the left of him, to guard his narrow face. . . . The bed in which he came was enclosed in a large casket shut entirely, and covered from head to foot with the sweetest flowers. He went to sleep from the village church. Crowds came to tell him goodnight, choirs sang to him, pastors told how brave he was—early soldier-heart. And the family bowed their heads as the reeds the wind shakes" (Letter 255).

Poem 570, "I could die to know," shows Emily wishing she could look in on someone who lived where brick houses "hunch" together, which suits well with Worcester, where Higginson was then living.

Johnson (*Poems*, III, 1201) assigns nearly a thousand poems to the years 1858–1864 on the basis of fair-copy handwriting. He places fully 366 of the total in 1862, but says elsewhere (p. 1203) that about 250 of these appear to have been copied "in a relatively brief span of time," an important observation but one which has been overlooked. To me it is clear that most of these thousand poems were *composed* during 1857–1861, with peak production in the latter year. The large amount of fair-copying early in 1862 was evidently done in preparation for the approach to Higginson.

Chapter Five
MY VERSE, DOES IT BREATHE?

For Higginson's careers in literature and the military see Anna Wells, *Dear Preceptor* (1963), and H. N. Meyer, *Colonel of the Black Regiment* (1967).

My claim that Emily did not hear from Higginson between the early fall of 1862 and the summer of 1864, by which time it no longer mattered, is based on a close study of all the correspondence and circumstances; no smallest detail obviates or modifies it. Sue's knowledge of Higginson's advice about not publishing is reflected in a letter in *An. Broc.*, 86. Austin's opinion of his sister's letters to Higginson was recorded in Mabel Todd's diary on October 18, 1891: "As to the 'innocent and confiding' nature of them, Austin smiles. He says Emily definitely posed in those letters. . . . He thought they put Emily in a false position" (*An. Broc.*, 167).

Curiously, Emily herself seems to have suspected the connection between her final despair and the eye trouble. In two poems written about this time (410 and 761) she hints at a causal relationship between loss of hope and loss of sight. "The first day's night" refers to some terrible event (Higginson's initial letter?) that had stifled all song in her soul, and from which she was just recovering when

> . . . a day as huge
> As yesterdays in pairs
> Unrolled its horror in my face,
> Until it blocked my eyes . . .

"From blank to blank" shows her wandering helplessly in a labyrinth (not named as such, though the description, especially in the phrase "a threadless way," is unmistakable) until at last

> I shut my eyes and groped as well;
> 'Twas lighter to be blind.

Ruth Miller (*The Poetry of ED*, 227) also cites the poem "I was

a Phebe" as a sort of admission that much of Emily's work after 1862
was commentary and variation on her reading. But the thesis by
which she reached that conclusion belongs among the more aberrant
curiosities in literary biography. At first, says Miller, Emily wrote
poetry in the ordinary way, poetry of genius; then after Sam Bowles
rejected both her love and her verse—practically thrown at him, as
Miller sees it—she withdrew from the race and spent the rest of her
life in a fine glow of anger rewriting the work of others to prove her
superiority. After that, it is not surprising that many of the borrowings cited by Miller are unconvincing. She also attempts to show that
there is a pattern in the packets, based on Quarles' *Emblems*. Aside
from her consistently wrongheaded reading of individual verses, she
overlooks the probability that occasional accidental groupings would
result from crowding nearly fifteen hundred highly repetitive poems
into the limited space of less than fifty slim booklets. But to refute all
the distortions in Miller's volume would require another book, and
would not always be worth the effort. She tries to show, for instance,
that the poet changed the spelling of her name from *Emilie* to *Emily*
because of a joshing article in the *Republican* by Bowles, in which he
chided the fashion among young women for the more exotic spelling.
The article appeared in July 1860, and it is true that thereafter
Emilie, except for one instance, disappears (a conclusion that could
conceivably be altered if *all* of Emily's letters had been preserved).
Yet here is a more pertinent fact: for 1858–59 the number of surviving
manuscript letters to which the poet's surname is appended totals fifteen; of these, ten are *Emilie* and five are *Emily*. Furthermore, in the
period 1848–56 both spellings were used interchangeably with *ie*
only slightly predominating. A final example: Miller quotes (p. 119)
a Bowles note in which Emily is referred to as someone "who never
forgets my spiritual longings." This, says Miller, relates to the religious concerns that were "inextricably interwoven" with Emily's love
for Bowles. The note is quoted from Leyda (I, 366) but if she had
checked Leyda's source (Bianchi, *Face*, 149) she would have found
the phrase reading: "who never forgets my *spiritual* longings," accompanied by an explanation that this meant the glass of sherry with
which Emily usually welcomed Bowles' visits.

The date of composition for "Further in summer" is in doubt. I
think this poem caused her more than ordinary effort, beginning in
1861 and progressing through three or four versions to its completion in late 1865 (see *Poems*, II, 752–55, and Anderson, *Stairway*,
169–73).

Chapter Six
THUNDER IN THE ROOM

The Gould-as-lover thesis is by Genevieve Taggard; there are many intrinsic deficiencies in the theory, not least the fact that it started with Vinnie. Hunt-as-lover was put forth in the same year by Josephine Pollitt; a prime example of the pitfalls of one-eyed analysis, it begins and seems to end with Higginson's notation of Emily's remark that Hunt was "the most interesting man she ever saw."

George Whicher's *This Was a Poet* brought the first breath of order, as well as literary style, to Dickinson studies; considering what was available to him at the time, he did a remarkable job of sorting out the tangle, and he had little choice but to accept Wadsworth as the lover. His book, out of date in many respects, is still of some value, as well as engagingly readable.

Besides Ruth Miller, mentioned above, the Bowles hypothesis has most recently been championed by David Higgins. Nothing new is developed and the same avoidance of obstructing facts is in evidence, the same tendency to convenient exaggeration. Trying to elicit significance from Bowles' departure for Europe, he quotes (p. 128) a letter Emily sent to *Mrs.* Bowles, a letter calm and warm in its offer of friendship, and labels it as "almost speechless, almost hysterical." Again, trying to tie Bowles to the poem, "If it had no pencil," he states flatly that it was sent to Bowles, giving as "direct proof" of this a *transcript* of the poem made by Mabel Todd and headed by her with Bowles' name. Emily's manuscript of that verse contains no such heading, and its true import, I believe, is demonstrated in the text of this chapter. In reality, as I see it, Bowles was both puzzled and intrigued by Emily, their relationship a game on both sides. Much of the cryptic quality in her letters to him, especially the reference to the "east" (letter 220) can be explained by the fondness of both parties for *Aurora Leigh* (See II, 818–820 and VII, 1001–1003). I suspect him, in addition, of being the intermediary for the first letters between Emily and Otis Lord; some such service is implied by their correspondence in 1862.

The original Master letters are now at Amherst College; they are printed, corrections and all, in *Letters*, and dated respectively about 1858, 1861 and early 1862, on the basis of handwriting. All are referred to as drafts. I affirm that, against the very scale set up by the editors, these documents cannot be certainly dated by handwriting more exactly than 1859–1865. The errors fostered by an attempt at thinner slicing are evident; one example is the reliance on the lower-case *e*. According to the official scale this was uniform as a narrow loop until 1859, when two new forms appeared. Now both of these new forms are present in the first Master letter, yet it is dated to spring 1858. My feeling is that the editors have placed the Master letters so as to accord chronologically with their sincere belief that Wadsworth was the man.

Another poem much referred to as connected with Emily's secret love is "To pile like thunder," which is taken as proof that Emily's writing career and her broken heart had a simultaneous origin in time. The poem, however, almost certainly was suggested by the Introduction to a book in Emily's possession, *The Loves of the Poets* (1857) by Mrs. Jameson.

The Lord letters first appeared in *ED: A Revelation*, by Mrs. Bingham. Neither there nor at their printing in *Letters* was an adequate description of them supplied. Studying them at Amherst College, I found they consisted of perhaps a half-dozen much-mutilated, single letters, all fair copies, along with many scissored fragments, most of them also from fair copies. One (561) has been cut and restored in such a way as to make it appear continuous, a fact that goes un-noticed except for the shape of the fragments. Very puzzling to me is the fact that, despite all this careful scissoring, so much of the blatantly sexual matter was allowed to remain. What could have been taken out? Did the deleted portions serve to place the beginning of the friendship too far in the past, that is, within Mrs. Lord's life-time?

The mystery of how the Lord letters were saved from the flames in the first place also continues to haunt. After long pondering, I have concluded they were not in Emily's hands at her death, but reached Austin later from an outside source. That source, I suggest, was a blackmailer named Gardner Fuller. In *Ancestors' Brocades* the other-wise unknown Fuller makes a brief, unexplained appearance, through some correspondence printed but not understood by Mrs. Bingham. All the marks of an extortion attempt are on this incident, primarily involving love letters written by Emily to someone in Boston. Fuller surfaced a month after the publication in the October 1891 *Atlantic* of Higginson's article on "Emily Dickinson's Letters." He claimed to be in possession of some twenty letters "giving a clear insight into that beautiful and secluded life . . . with just a tinge of rosy-romance running all through, making them intensely interesting."

His further description of the letters as marvelous essays on everything from politics to art to religion to literary criticism was only a cover; her family well knew that she did not concern herself in correspondence with such propounding. Austin was away at the time and Vinnie—not quite grasping the import of that phrase "tinge of rosy-romance"—had a friend contact Fuller, who replied that the letters had been written to him "during the war when I was engaged in the publishing business in Boston." One of the letters, he said, contained a lock of hair. "If you wish to make an offer *of your own originating* it will be considered." When Austin returned, he asked a friend in Fuller's home town, Taunton, for information on the man's background, and the answer came back that Fuller "has *no* business, *no* reputation, *no* position in society . . . a reputation for *everything that is bad* . . . I hear he is notoriously bad *every way*." At this point the subject vanishes from *Ancestors' Brocades,* with no indication as to its resolution. Fuller, obviously, was not bluffing, and it is likely that Austin did meet with him and probably bought whatever he had to offer. Aside from the likelihood that this purchase included many of the hundreds of letters from Emily to Lord, there is also a possibility that Fuller had gotten hold of the Master letters, the documents whose provenance is most perplexing of all.

A phrase in the second Master letter, "the love of the Plantagenet," may be clarified by Mrs. Gaskell's reference to "old Plantagenet times" in Yorkshire (*Life of Charlotte Brontë,* Chap. 6, par. 3). Perhaps Emily used the word as a term of endearment for the aristocratic, old-fashioned Otis Lord, who was eighteen years her senior. Also with regard to the second Master letter, as it is printed in *Letters* (II, 374) the crucial phrase *confessed and denied not* appears without quotation marks, but such marks are plainly to be seen in the original manuscript.

The records of Lord's judicial whereabouts in fall 1864–65 are in the Old Courthouse, Boston; I am grateful to several members of the Superior Court Clerk's office for help in locating them.

Emily's poem, "When I see not I better see," adapts Shakespeare's sonnet 43. Another verse, "The admirations and contempts of time," is unmistakably indebted to the same source, but I have not been able to place it.

That the Lords had at least one child who died is clear from a phrase in an 1852 Amherst graduate's brochure: "No children living."

My reading of the context of letter 188 is that it was sent to Lord;

the editors of *Letters* make a guess at Emily's aunt, Elizabeth Currier. It was published, in part, by Mabel Todd in the first volume of letters, though she placed it among the correspondence of 1885, some twenty years off the mark—the same sort of obfuscation she indulged in with a portion of the second Master letter.

The owl card at Harvard (Dickinson papers, box 8) bears no further identification and no outright proof that it was sent to Emily, though doubts are hardly justified. The reverse of the card, which could have been bought at any stationery store, pictures two cats and is labeled in the same unknown hand: "Bull run and Elise." The names may refer to Vinnie's pets.

The most important poem of the many that deal with the lover's "countenance" is "The face I carry with me last," which links itself to both Master and Lord letters. The manuscript of this turned up as the last entry in packet 80, and was so printed in *Poems*, though with a later date. Franklin (p. 72) first suggested that it did not belong to the packet, and pointed out that its reverse once bore the name of an addressee which had been erased. My own inspection confirms Franklin; the erasure has been so thorough as to remove the paper's heavy gloss and almost penetrate the sheet.

If Emily was little moved by the horrors of the Civil War, it seems that Lincoln's assassination did affect her. I suggest that she wrote four poems on the tragedy: 999, 1006, 1044, and 1083. The third, especially, "A sickness of this world," is striking in its similarity to the well-remembered waves of sick shock that followed the death of President Kennedy. No. 1006, "The first we knew of him," was probably written after Emily read Dr. Holland's *Life of Abraham Lincoln* (1865).

Chapter Seven
GREAT STREETS OF SILENCE

The newspaper clipping about the seamstress, Miss Marian, is owned by an Amherst resident; it was printed in Leyda, II, 479. Sylvia Weinberg is given as author, along with a July 10 date, but no year. Leyda thinks it may be from a Hartford or New Haven paper.

By 1878 Emily's mythical status in the village, as well as the fame of the white dresses, was confirmed in a curious way. Two years before, Helen Hunt Jackson had published *Mercy Philbrick's Choice*, anonymously. There was much guessing as to the author's identity, with Amherst residents quick to note that the scene of the story was

their own town. Rumor soon settled on Emily, and in July 1878 the
Republican carried a lengthy analysis of the novel, concluding with a
flourish that the author was an Amherst recluse "robed in white." A
few days later the *Springfield Union* mentioned "the honored name
of Dickinson," and the *Amherst Record* focused on "the daughter of
the late Hon. Edward Dickinson, a lady of superior culture and
education, and who has for many years secluded herself from society
for the purpose of indulging in literary tastes and pursuits." The
Republican brought the matter to a close by asserting it knew for a
fact that "no person by the name of Dickinson" was involved (Leyda,
II, 296). No doubt this was all vastly annoying to Emily, who was
then, as my next chapter shows, endeavoring to throw off the effects
of her twelve-year retirement.

From about 1880 comes this recollection of Emily's spell on the
town's youth: "In my boyhood days and in common with my friends
I had heard stories of a mysterious woman who with her less gifted
but equally peculiar sister lived in the house next to that occupied by
Austin Dickinson. . . . We youngsters dubbed them both crazy and
let it go at that, though we did cast stealthy glances in the direction
of that house behind the hedges when we passed that way" (Alfred
Stearns, *An Amherst Boyhood*, 146).

The fullest discussion of Emily's poetic use of symbolic white is in
"ED's White Robes," by J. Wheatcroft, *Criticism*, V, 1963. He does
not notice that the symbolism terminated about 1867. Statistically,
before that year the symbol ("white" and "snow") occurs some
seventy-five times, while afterwards there are less than a dozen instances, none symbolic.

Higginson's notes on his visit to Emily are in *Letters*, II, 473–6; he
also refers to it in *Atlantic*, Oct. 1891. He saw her again in 1873 but
the novelty was gone and he left no record. The poem "The spider
as an artist" appears to be Emily's comment on an article in the *Republican*, Oct. 24, 1868, in which debasement of the word "artist" is
decried.

In reporting Mrs. Lord's death, the *Boston Globe* (Dec. 12, 1877)
said she had been sick "for two or three weeks." I take it that Emily
would have known this.

Chapter Eight
BASKING IN BETHLEHEM

The legend of the Salem ghost ship was pointed out by Johnson
(*Letters*, III, 605) but he attempted no biographical connection. The

four poems that supplied my picture of the first meeting between Emily and Lord are 1237, 1449, 1473, 1476. Her fears about the possible difficulties inherent in a late marriage are in "The pile of years is not so high."

I have drawn on Bingham, *ED: A Revelation,* for information about the Farley family.

The notes Emily sent (as I conceive it) to Mabel Todd and Sue during the jealousy blow-up are 1016, dated by Mabel to Sept. 1885 (which Johnson accepts on her word) and 757, dated "about 1882." The message to Sue contrasts sharply with the nearly forty surviving notes Emily sent across the lawn in her last four years; they are all warm expressions of affection and dependence.

I am not urging scriptural authority for John Erskine's opinion, only a judicious consideration. Pertinent are some of his other remarks. He called Mrs. Bingham's attacks on Sue a disgrace to American biography. "Austin's wife" he said, "had a mind much above the ordinary. Those who knew her agreed that in her prime she was a proper mate for Austin, his equal in culture and his superior in social grace. . . . In gifts of mind and rather obviously in gifts of heart she was superior to her detractors."

As one example of Millicent Todd Bingham's disdain of Sue, here is a passage from *ED: A Revelation:* "It was Emily's way to form extravagant attachments. . . . In particular she squandered her affection on Sue Gilbert, whose wit, cool composure and tart remarks about the peculiarities of their mutual acquaintances fascinated her. She endowed Sue with characteristics Sue did not possess. Her capacity for warm generous affection proved to be limited. After her marriage to Emily's brother, Emily looked for a tenderness deeper than Sue was capable of feeling. Emily withered in the atmosphere of disharmony which was not slow to develop in the house next door. The slow realization that in things that mattered her beloved Sue cared more about appearance than reality left a permanent scar. Emily's disillusionment, reflecting that of her brother, should not be overlooked as a positive if secondary element in her withdrawal." The proof of all this? None—neither offered nor, according to those who have followed the official line, required.

David Higgins (*Portrait of ED,* 111), who acknowledges Mrs. Bingham's help, asserts that "Austin's disappointment in his marriage" was a constant source of tension between Sue and Emily. He specifies Sue's failings to be social climbing, extravagance, and a refusal to have children. The first of these charges is not new, but the other two are; still no documentation is provided. It was five years after her marriage that Sue bore the first of her three children. About seven months before that event, in December 1860, Austin told a neighbor "that if he had three children he believed it would cause him to start for Europe and stay as long as he could." When the neighbor remonstrated that he was incapable of fatherly feelings, "he intimated that he considered himself fortunate in being so" (Leyda, II, 19). This, of course, is no real proof of Austin's true feelings, since he might have been joking, but it is more to the point than unsubstantiated tales about Sue's unmaternal instincts.

Mrs. Bingham died December 1, 1968, aged 88. In a letter to me earlier that year, with greater significance than she knew, she admitted that her mother was "the crux of the whole Dickinson saga."

Ned Dickinson's remark about Mabel Todd is in a letter to Vinnie of August 27, 1896 (Houghton Library, Dickinson Papers, box 8).

Emily's hesitant try for publication in spring 1883 is clear from the correspondence with Thomas Niles, head of Roberts Brothers.

Helen Hunt Jackson, who had urged Emily's merits on Niles, became aware of the poetry through T. W. Higginson, and thereafter was fascinated by both the verse and the eccentric. Once she told Emily she was a great poet and more than once begged her to publish. Twice she drew on her knowledge of the recluse for literary material, first for a short story ("Esther Wynne's Love Letters," *Scribner's*, Dec. 1871) and later for the novel *Mercy Philbrick's Choice*. The plots of both are completely imaginary, without relation to Emily's life except, as I am inclined to think, that the novel may have suggested to Sue a framework for her fabrications about Wadsworth as the lover. Mrs. Jackson was also responsible for publication of Emily's "Success is counted sweetest," in a volume of anonymous poetry issued in 1878, announced as containing work by the foremost poets. Why Emily initially declined the use of this poem to her friend is evident in the sequel: it is clearly derived from Emerson (with help from *Aurora Leigh*) and reviewers unerringly attributed it to the sage, perhaps confirming Emily's long-standing fears.

Adams Drug Store in Amherst still preserves the prescription book for 1882–85, containing forty prescriptions for all the Dickinsons; at least a dozen of these, perhaps as many as twenty, were for Emily. (Leyda also consulted this, but printed only two examples.) The limitations of nineteenth century pharmacology are sadly evident, with various mild stimulants and innocuous syrups prevailing; the most powerful specifics seem to have been digitalis and belladonna. On August 17, 1885, though there is no record of a more than usual indisposition, Dr. Fish prescribed the following concoction for Emily: "Quinine Sulp. gr. 32, strychnine Sulph. gr. ½, acid phos dil oz ½, syr calcis lactophosph, syrup simplicis oz 1, aynor purae ad oz 4, one teaspoon in water after meals." A month later he reduced this to quinine sulphate and Newton's Bitters.

Emily's last outside visitor of record was Mrs. Samuel Mack, who called in the autumn of 1884. She was wife to the son of David Mack who with his family had occupied the red brick house while the Dickinsons were at Pleasant Street. Dr. O. F. Bigelow was the physician whose examination of Emily was confined to a peek through an open door; "Now what besides mumps," he asked helplessly, "could be diagnosed that way!" (Leyda, I, XXIX).

The fact that Maggie Maher was given some letters to burn by Emily, most probably those from Lord, is in Bianchi, *Face to Face*, 60. Mrs. Powell's part in the funeral is in the same source (p. 61) though Sue claimed (*Riddle of ED*, 214) that it was she who dressed the body. Probably both women were employed in the task.

The six workmen who, at Emily's request, bore the coffin to the grave, may have been suggested by *Wuthering Heights* (last chap.), where Heathcliff arranges a like burial for himself. As a matter of coincidental interest, I should mention that, despite a very careful reading, Emily Brontë's stark narrative has yielded up no certain sources of Dickinson poems. Some seeming echoes, vague murmurs, occur in the second half but they have resisted capture. So far as is known, Emily Dickinson did not become really interested in the work of the English girl until later in life, and the spark of that interest, assuredly, lay in the hopeless love between Cathy and Heathcliff, which mirrored her own feelings about Otis Lord. Not to be overlooked is the fact of Heathcliff's having *willed* his own death. It was Bright's disease that took Emily, but she was evidently quite ready and willing to succumb.

The Dickinson drama is even yet not played out. Amherst officials are presently wrestling with a clause in the will of Martha Dickinson Bianchi (died 1943) which specifies that her parents' house, The Evergreens, after occupancy by certain heirs, must be destroyed. "The house must be taken down to the cellar," she directed, in forbidding sale or removal.

Notes and Sources

Acknowledgments

For various sorts of timely assistance I extend my gratitude to Mr.
J. R. Phillips of Frost Library, Amherst College; Mrs. W. D. Sayer of
Jones Library, Amherst; Houghton Library, Harvard University; Mrs.
Jean Mudge and Miss Isis Daxelhoffer; the staff of the Dixon Home-
stead Library, Dumont.

Index

Amber Gods, The (Spofford),
    162–63
American Civil War, 132–33,
    138, 194, 270
    end of, 196–97
    Higginson's role in, 139, 148–
    150
Amherst, Mass., 23–26, 64–65,
    72–75, 203–5
    Dickinson family position in,
    55
    Austin Dickinson settles in,
    87
    Emerson in, 110–14
    Higginson in, 212–20
    Lord in vicinity of, 125, 189,
    193–95, 197, 224, 226–28,
    232–33, 237
    property suits in, 49–50
    religious revival in, 70
    rumors circulated in, 171, 204,
    207, 241
    seamstresses in, 207

snobbery in, 122
Rev. Wadsworth in, 124–25
See also Emily Dickinson
    house
Amherst Academy, 57–58, 70
Amherst Cattle Show, 78, 88–89
Amherst College, 18–19, 23–24,
    55, 76, 224
    commencement speakers at,
    194
    Lord at, 184–85, 190
Amherst Sewing Society, 63–64,
    69, 73, 254
Anthony, Kate, 256
Antony and Cleopatra (Shake-
    speare), 230
Atlantic (magazine), 112, 127,
    128, 130, 138, 162
Aurora Leigh (Browning), 92–
    109, 112–13, 122, 128–29,
    131, 134–35, 145, 150–51,
    255–61

Aurora Leigh (*Cont.*)
  appropriation of its images, 98,
    102–3, 200–1
  "Because I could not stop for
    Death" and, 164–65
  love lyric allied to, 178
  poems indebted to Hawthorne
    and, 159–61
  white dresses related to, 210

Barrett, Elizabeth, *see* Browning,
  Elizabeth Barrett
Bianchi, Martha, *see* Dickinson,
  Martha
Bible, 88, 196, 214
  clipping from, 231, 232
  New Testament, 225
  Revelations, 141, 210, 231
  Song of Solomon, 117
Bingham, Millicent Todd, 37,
  38, 52–53, 272–73
  poems and documents re-
    covered by, 175, 179, 185–
    186
  supports her mother's story,
    240–41
Blackmur, R. P., 155
Boston, 59, 97, 190, 203, 220,
  242
  Dickinson's Boston cousins,
    124
  See also Cambridge
Boston Alumnae Club, 47
Bowdoin, Elbridge, 176
Bowles, Mary, 123, 176
Bowles, Samuel, 133, 136–38,
  142, 144

Dickinson's refusals to see,
  136, 148–49
fruit of Dickinson's friendship
  with, 121–23
illness of, 229–30
as romantic interest, 29–30,
  176, 266–67
Brahma (Emerson), 112
Brontë, Charlotte, *see Jane Eyre*
Brontë, Emily, 38, 117, 243–44,
  274
Browning, Elizabeth Barrett,
  90–109, 122
  death of, 90, 135
  Dickinson's style contrasted
    to, 98
  influence of, 90–92, 94, 96–
    109, 112, 132, 141, 213
  poem connected with, 134–35
  portraits of, 147, 219
  See also Aurora Leigh;
    Dickinson-Browning
    parallels
Browning, Robert, 122, 135, 141
  Dickinson's debt to, 163–65
Burgess, John, 205

Cambridge, Mass., 152, 167–69
  romantic clues involving,
    189–91, 195–97
Child, Lydia Maria, 65, 117–20,
  128
Christian Union, The (newspaper), 42–43
Colt, John, 120
Congress, U.S., 55, 79, 83,
  193, 194

De Quincey, Thomas, 130
Dickinson, Austin (brother),
    35–36, 48–49, 73, 76, 79,
    121–23, 131, 174, 179, 229
  as Browning admirer, 94
  church building and, 205
  death of, 49
  on Dickinson's death, 244
  on Dickinson's romance, 78
  Emerson as guest of, 110, 111
  his father's death and, 220
  his sister's seclusion and, 149
  Lord and, 226–27, 236
  marriage of, 87
  publication of Dickinson and,
    48, 121, 123
  reaction to his sister's talent,
    40, 42
  reading habits of, 214
  relationship with his father, 56
  on Sewing Society, 63
  Mabel Todd and, 25, 27–29,
    31–33, 35, 236, 239–41
Dickinson, Edward (father), 18,
    55–57, 65, 70, 73, 78, 82,
    103, 119, 141, 169, 185,
    193–94, 217–23, 231
  annual receptions given by,
    205
  character description of, 55–
    56, 253
  death of, 186, 220–23, 226
  as Dickinson's shield, 113–14
  Higginson's impression of, 197,
    214, 218–19
  Main St. house reacquired
    by, 84
  on Marvel, 128

  opposes his daughter's mar-
    riage, 29, 173
  political career of, 55, 79, 220
Dickinson, Mrs. Edward
    (mother), 61, 71, 79, 141,
    169, 218–20, 224–26, 231–
    232
  character description of, 56–57
  death of, 31, 238–39
  as invalid, 25–26, 57, 87, 223,
    226, 229, 234, 237
Dickinson, Emily
  DEATH OF, 37–39, 244–45, 274
  EARLY LIFE OF, 54–86
  birth, 57
  birth of literary ambition,
    69–70
  education, 57–58, 60–62, 70
  family life, 55–57
  fledgling works, 54, 84–86, 128
  literary influences, 65–70, 74
  social life, 63–65, 75, 255
  travels, 82–84
  AS LITERARY PUZZLE, 253
  abrupt literary development,
    86, 89–94, 109
  handwriting, chronological
    scale, 94, 247, 264–65, 267–
    268
  hidden manuscripts and
    documents, 51–52, 175,
    185–86, 200, 225
  poems discovered posthu-
    mously, 39, 43
  possible clues in correspon-
    dence, 39
  LITERARY STYLE OF, 135–36,
    215–17

Dickinson, Emily (*Cont.*)
Mrs. Browning's vs., 98
choice of symbols, 104
critical confusion over, 153–
156, 162
critique of early works, 85–86,
254, 255
her friend's evaluation, 130–31
her late works, 216–17
interpretation of symbols, 95–
97, 231–32
rhyme, grammar, and punctuation, 41, 44, 136, 140, 145,
247–48
sources of her ideas, 114–21,
126–32, 147, 154–67, 177–
178, 191; *see also* Dickinson-
Browning parallels
MUTILATION OF MANUSCRIPT
OF, 46, 250–51
PERSONAL CHARACTERISTICS OF
change in appearance, 236
child-pose, 83
eccentricities, 26, 38, 47, 203,
211, 235, 251–52
health, 21, 34, 36–37, 141,
237, 242–44, 273–74
her use of white dresses, 18,
20, 22, 26, 205–8, 210–11,
271
homely appearance, 54, 55,
62–63, 67, 212–13
involuted personality, 35
physical size, 20–21
religious pose, 58–62
self-dramatization tendency,
54–55, 58–61, 210, 211
shyness, 113, 146

POEMS HEREIN QUOTED OR
MENTIONED (identified by
initial phrases)
A bee his burnished, 227
A death blow is a life, 100
A loss of something, 99
A precious mouldering, 127
A sickness of this world, 270
A train went through, 254
An antiquated grace, 226
As if I asked a common, 97
As imperceptibly as grief, 161
Because I could not stop, 161
Elizabeth told Essex, 226
Elysium is as far, 28
Exultation is the going, 99
From blank to blank, 265
Further in summer, 160, 242,
266
Get Gabriel to tell, 134
Going to her!, 134
Good Morning, Midnight, 152
Great streets of silence, 217
Have you got a brook, 85
He fumbles at your soul, 116
He put the belt around, 177
Heart! We will forget, 255
Her sweet weight on my, 255
His voice decrepit was, 233
I could die to know, 264
I felt a funeral in my, 158
I got so I could hear his, 201
I heard a fly buzz when, 264
I know some lonely houses,
117
I learned, at least, what, 195
I measure every grief, 101
I never told the buried, 255

I reckon when I count, 92
I started early, took, 106, 260
I stepped from plank, 104
I taste a liquor never, 133
I tend my flowers for thee, 199
I think I was enchanted, 89
I thought the train would, 233
I was a Phebe, 155, 265–66
I went to thank her, but, 135
If it had no pencil, 201, 267
If pain for peace prepares, 104
I'm ceded, I've stopped, 134
I'm saying every day, 134
In winter in my room, 95, 260, 261
It dropped so low in my, 102
Just lost, when I was, 100
Long years apart can make, 228
More life went out when he, 129, 263
Much madness is divinest, 118
My heart ran so to thee, 233
Nobody knows this little, 85
On a columnar self, 115
On this wondrous sea, 255
One blessing had I than, 97
Ourselves were wed, 91, 177
Safe in their alabaster, 131
Sexton! my master's, 72, 254
Split the lark and you'll, 151
Struck was I nor yet, 97
Success is counted, 273
Summer has two beginnings, 92
Superfluous were the sun, 270
The admirations and, 269

The face I carry with me, 270
The farthest thunder, 97, 256
The first day's night, 265
The first we knew of him, 270
The Judge is like the owl, 198
The outer from the inner, 106
The pile of years is not, 272
The rose did caper on her, 102
The soul selects her own, 167
The spider as an artist, 271
The sun and moon must make, 198
There are two Mays, 36
There came a day at, 146
This slow day moved, 218
Through what transports, 225
Title divine is mine!, 144
To fight aloud is very, 119
To pile like thunder, 268
'Twas here my summer, 209
Upon the gallows hung, 119
We learn in the retreating, 270
We talked with each other, 233
What if I say I shall not, 127
When I hoped, I recollect, 151
When I see not I better see, 269
When night is almost done, 138
You constituted time, 115
You love the Lord, 200
See also listings on pp. 257–260 and 262–63
PROLIFIC PERIOD OF, 87–169, 264–65

Dickinson, Emily (*Cont.*)
autobiographical poem, 150–
    151
center of her existence, 121
first professional criticism,
    137–48, 194, 264
impairment of her eyesight,
    136–37, 143, 152, 167, 169,
    189–91, 197, 215, 265
loss of her ambition, 166–69
number of works, 135, 138
PUBLICATION OF, 137–38, 242
first serious poems, 121,
    133–34
her decision not to publish,
    166–67
her valentines, 69, 75
love verses, 171
posthumous, 40–49, 52, 132,
    200
AS RECLUSE, 26–39, 203–44,
    270–71
beginning of seclusion, 203
exploiting her seclusion, 43–
    45
final surrender to seclusion,
    220
frustrated marital plans, 234–
    38, 242
her reasons for withdrawing,
    208–11
last outsider to see her, 168–
    169, 274
last venture outside the
    grounds, 204–5
neighbor's attempts to pene-
    trate her isolation, 26–31,
    33–39, 238, 240

precursors of withdrawal, 78–
    81, 111–14, 136, 146, 148–
    149
reception of her visitors,
    203–4, 212–20, 243
resumption of her writing,
    216
ROMANTIC DISAPPOINTMENTS
    OF, 29–30, 54, 76–81, 169–
    202, 208–10, 225–38, 242,
    243
December romance, 126, 186,
    230–38
her love for a married man,
    53, 83, 169, 176, 189, 225
"Master" love letters, 175–76,
    178–84, 187–89, 195–202,
    210, 222, 231, 267–68, 269
poems reflecting, 195–202
WORK HABITS OF, 19–21,
    112–13
nocturnal schedule, 113, 263
writing table, 19
Dickinson, Gilbert (nephew),
    27, 34, 242
Dickinson, Lavinia (Vinnie)
    (sister), 28–29, 33–35, 38–
    53, 77–79, 167, 169, 196,
    207, 218–20, 224, 226–29,
    234–39, 243–44
death of, 52
death of her sister, 38–39,
    244
Dickinson's love life and, 172–
    174, 235–38
early life of, 57, 70, 71, 73
family relations of, 33–34, 40,
    44–46, 52–53, 226, 235–36

her sister's seclusion and, 149
as literary executor, 39–48,
    252–53
as Marvel admirer, 128
in property dispute, 49–51
as spinster, 78, 87–88, 255
Mabel Todd first meets, 25–26
travels of, 79, 82–84
Dickinson, Martha (niece), 19,
    27, 52, 125, 218, 223, 274
on Dickinson's arrogance,
    210–11
on Dickinson's cooking, 217
on Dickinson's love life, 171–
    175, 185, 237
on her grandfather's death,
    221
Dickinson, Ned (nephew), 27,
    34, 218, 229
on Mabel Todd, 241–42, 273
Dickinson, Susan Gilbert (sis-
    ter-in-law), 31–35, 51–53,
    121–22, 127–32, 163, 211,
    226–28, 244, 272–73
alleged cruelty of, 52–53
as Browning admirer, 90, 94
Dickinson's collaboration with,
    130–32, 137–38, 143
Dickinson's friendship with,
    42, 53, 72–77, 79–81
Dickinson's love life and,
    172–74, 235, 237
as Emerson admirer, 110–12,
    114
on Lord, 227–28
marriage of, 87, 91, 177
publication of Dickinson and,
    42–43, 45–46, 132, 167

seamstress of, 207
Mabel Todd and, 25–27, 29,
    31–33, 35, 51, 239–42
transcript made by, 95, 96
Dickinson-Browning parallels,
    99–109, 218–29, 134–35,
    151–52
in "Because I could not stop
    for Death," 164–65
on childhood, 99–100
in Dickinson letter, 200–1
on grief, 101
Hawthorne's influence and,
    159–61
in love lyric, 178
in 60 Dickinson poems, 108,
    257–61
Dudley, Rev. John, 177

Elsie Venner (Holmes), 218
Emerson, Ralph Waldo, 64, 65,
    69, 110–14, 133, 137, 262
justification supplied by, 166
materials culled from, 114,
    166
Emily Dickinson Face to Face
    (Bianchi), 174
Emily Dickinson house (Am-
    herst), 57, 84, 224, 250
as museum, 17–22
Emmons, Henry, 75–81, 176, 255
Erskine, John, 241, 272

Farley, Abbey, 235
First Church (Amherst), 236

Gilbert, Susan, *see* Dickinson, Susan Gilbert
Gould, George, 71, 173, 177, 254, 267
Graves, John (cousin), 76, 79–81, 176

Hamlet (Shakespeare), 192
Hampshire Express (newspaper), 126–27
Harper's (magazine), 40, 41, 130
Harvard University, 56, 94, 193
 Dickinson collection of, 199, 231
Hawthorne, Nathaniel, 157–61, 231–32, 242
Henry VI (Shakespeare), 190
Higginson, Thomas Wentworth, 38, 137–51, 166–69, 177, 192, 194–95, 265
 Dickinson's correspondence with, 139–51, 166–68, 197, 203, 221
 at Dickinson's funeral, 244
 Dickinson's impression on, 212–20
 as editor of Dickinson, 43–45, 58
 politics of, 137, 139
Hills, Dwight, 50
Holland, Dr. J. G., 29–30, 83, 142, 146
Holland, Mrs. J. G., 88–89, 142–43, 146, 204, 234
Holland, Annie, 204
Holland, Sophia, 58

"Hollow of the Three Hills, The" (Hawthorne), 157–160
House of the Seven Gables, The (Hawthorne), 157
Humphrey, Jane, 66
Humphrey, Leonard, 69–72, 80, 254–55
Hunt, Lt., 126, 173, 177, 267
Hunt, Helen, 126, 168, 242

Ipswich, Mass., 193

Jackson, Helen Hunt, 126, 168, 242, 273
Jane Eyre (Brontë), 66–70, 93, 114–17, 178, 262–63

Kavanagh (Longfellow), 74, 214
Kelley, Tom, 238
Kimball, James, 64, 67, 70, 254
King Lear (Shakespeare), 192

"Last Ride Together, The" (Browning), 163–65
"Letter to a Young Contributor" (Higginson), 138
Letters (Dickinson), 48, 69n, 73n, 74n, 209n
 first publication of, 171
 1894 edition of, 185
 Mabel Todd's additions to, 173–74, 179

Letters from New York (Child), 117–20, 128, 263

"Life in the Iron Mills" (short story), 127–28

Life of Charlotte Brontë (Gaskell), 114, 117

Lincoln, Abraham, 132, 196, 270

Longfellow, Henry Wadsworth, 65, 74, 214

Loomis, Mabel, *see* Todd, Mabel Loomis

Lord, Elizabeth, 193–94, 225, 228–29
  death of, 126, 186–87, 230, 232

Lord, Otis, 125–26, 146, 210, 224–38, 242–43, 268–69, 272
  as candidate for secret love, 184–202, 225–38, 242
  character descriptions of, 227–228, 237
  death of, 199, 232, 242
  political career of, 193, 194, 237

Lyman, Joseph, 78, 87–88, 176–177

Lyon, Mary, 60–61

Maher, Margaret (Maggie), 28, 34, 169, 207, 212, 238, 242–43, 274

Marian, Miss, 207–8, 270

Marvel, Ik, 128–29

Massachusetts legislature, 55, 193

Massachusetts Superior Court, 125, 189, 191, 193, 196–97

Massachusetts Supreme Court, 51, 228, 242

Meeting Hall (Amherst), 110–111

Men and Women (Browning), 163–64

Mill on the Floss, The (Eliot), 147

Montague, Zebina (Bina) (cousin), 147

Mosses from an Old Manse (Hawthorne), 160–61

Mount Holyoke Seminary for Young Ladies (South Hadley, Mass.), 60–63

Mount Vernon (Va.), 82–83

Mudge, Jean, 17–19, 21–22

Newton, Benjamin F., 65, 69, 80, 112, 214, 254

No Coward Soul Is Mine (Brontë), 38, 243–44

Norcross, Frances (Fanny) (cousin), 152, 167, 224, 244
  in Amherst, 124

Norcross, Louise (Loo) (cousin), 136–37, 142, 146, 152, 167, 190, 225, 244
  in Amherst, 124

Northampton, Mass., 125, 193–194

Ode to a Nightingale (Keats), 108

Othello (Shakespeare), 234, 239–40

Phelps, Susan, 79, 81
Philadelphia, 82–84, 125, 174
Powell, Mrs. (neighbor), 244, 274

Rainy Day, The (Longfellow), 65
Reveries of a Bachelor (Marvel), 128–29, 263
Root, Abiah, 58–59, 61, 66, 71–72
    invitation from, 80–81
Round Table, The (newspaper), 167

Salem, Mass., 125, 193, 230
    famous legend of, 232, 271
Shakespeare, William, 35, 64, 75, 219, 239–40
    Dickinson's interest in, 132, 190–93, 215, 230
    lovers' code based on, 190, 234
    sources employed, 120, 269
Springfield Daily Republican, The (newspaper), 75, 121, 122, 132–34, 142, 252, 253, 263, 264, 266, 271
    Dickinson published in, 133–134, 138, 167
    on Higginson's activities, 149, 150
    on Lord's health, 238
    obituary in, 132
Springfield Women's Club, 47
Stearns, Frazar, 264

Taney, Roger, 82
Tennyson, Alfred (Lord), 65, 263–64
Todd, David Peck, 23–25, 31, 48–50
    writings of, 41, 48
Todd, Mabel Loomis, 23–41, 46–52, 124, 173–75, 205, 214, 236, 238–42, 250, 252–253, 265, 267, 272, 273
    family quarrel instigated by, 240–42
    journal of, 28–29, 31–32, 34–36
    letters edited by, 173–74, 179, 240
    in property dispute, 49–51, 252
    publication of Dickinson and, 40–41, 43–44, 46–49
Todd, Millicent, *see* Bingham, Millicent Todd

Wadsworth, Rev. Charles, 124–125, 172–76, 184, 235, 243, 267
    ministerial post of, 83–84
    note from, 221–22
Washington, D.C., 27, 79
    Dickinson's visit to, 82–83
    glamor of, 23, 24
Whitman, Walt, 140
Willard's Hotel (Washington, D.C.), 82
Worcester, Mass., 139, 143, 148
Wuthering Heights (Brontë), 274

JOHN EVANGELIST WALSH *is the author of* Poe the Detective, *named the best fact-crime book of 1968 by the Mystery Writers of America. He has also written* The Shroud, *a study of the controversial burial cloth of Christ;* Strange Harp, Strange Symphony, *the definitive life of poet Francis Thompson (whose* Letters *he also edited); and several books for younger readers. By profession an editor, Mr. Walsh is currently involved in a number of writing projects, including a new, full-length biography of Poe. He lives with his wife and four children in Dumont, New Jersey.*